Christopher Marshall, William Duane

Extracts from Diary

Kept in Philadelphia and Lancaster During the American Revolution, 1774-1781

Christopher Marshall, William Duane

Extracts from Diary
Kept in Philadelphia and Lancaster During the American Revolution, 1774-1781

ISBN/EAN: 9783337006617

Printed in Europe, USA, Canada, Australia, Japan

Cover: Foto ©ninafisch / pixelio.de

More available books at **www.hansebooks.com**

EXTRACTS

FROM THE

DIARY OF CHRISTOPHER MARSHALL,

KEPT IN

PHILADELPHIA AND LANCASTER,

DURING THE

AMERICAN REVOLUTION,

1774—1781.

EDITED BY

WILLIAM DUANE,

Corresponding Member of the Historical Society of New York, and Honorary Member of the Historical Societies of Vermont, Delaware and New Jersey.

ALBANY:
JOEL MUNSELL.
1877.

PREFACE.

Christopher Marshall, from whose Diary, called by him a "Remembrancer," the following extracts have been made, was by birthright a member of the Society of Friends, being of one of the oldest families of English origin in the Province of Pennsylvania. His sympathy with the cause of American liberty caused his exclusion from the religious denomination to which he had belonged. This expulsion will explain and perhaps excuse the severity of his views respecting the political conduct of some of his fellow citizens. His associates were among the most prominent Whigs of the country, by whom, it is evident, that he was held in high esteem. I have been unable to ascertain the exact date of his death, but as his will was dated in 1796, and proved on the 3d of May in 1797, I think that his decease probably occurred in the early part of the latter year.

The portions of his diary omitted in the following pages relate mainly to private matters, the state of the weather, &c., and possess no interest at this day. It is believed that no important entry has been omitted in the following pages.

The early portion of these extracts was published in the year 1839, and extracts from another year appeared in 1849.

WILLIAM DUANE.

PHILADELPHIA, *December* 1876.

MARSHALL'S DIARY.

1774.

JANUARY 9. Very little news has transpired this week, except an observation on the conduct of the Bostonians. See *Pennsylvania Journal*, No. 1623.

18. Sundry resolves were passed by our Assembly respecting the riots in the county of Northumberland; also, some resolutions were laid before the House from Maryland.

20. This day was published a scheme for a Society of Innoculating for the Small Pox.

MARCH 23. Account of [the] destruction of tea in Boston reached London about [the] 20th of January, and our tea ship sent back arrived at Dover the 25th same month.

APRIL 25. Received by ship Concord, Captain Volans, from Bristol, eighty-four pamphlets from my friend, George Stonehouse. Great debates in the House of Commons. See *Pennsylvania Journal*, No. 1641.

MAY 21. This day part of [the] Standing Committee met to consider the resolve of the town of Boston, sent here by express, but as they were uncertain what the Provinces of Maryland, Virginia, and Carolina would do, they appointed a suitable answer to be wrote back to New York and Boston, and at [the] same time wrote to other Provinces to know their minds on this alarming occasion, which was sent by express, and [they] wait till its return. The same day arrived the ship Prosperity, Captain M'Culloch, from Belfast in twenty-eight days, with four hundred and fifty passengers.

30. A number of the inhabitants, composed of

most of the different Societies in this city, met and agreed that it would be proper to express their sympathy for their brethren at Boston, by suspending all business on that day, viz. the first of June.

JUNE 1. This being the day when the cruel act for blocking up the harbor of Boston took effect, many of the inhabitants of this city, to express their sympathy and show their concern for their suffering brethren in the common cause of liberty, had their shops shut up, their houses kept close from hurry and business; also the ring of bells at Christ Church were muffled, and rung a solemn peal at intervals, from morning till night; the colors of the vessels in the harbor were hoisted half-mast high; the several houses of different worship were crowded, where divine service was performed, and particular discourses, suitable to the occasion, were preached by F. Allison, Duffield, Sprout, and Blair. Sorrow, mixed with indignation, seemed pictured in the countenances of the inhabitants, and indeed the whole city wore the aspect of deep distress, being a melancholy occasion.

4. This being the birth-day of King George III, scarcely, if any, notice was taken of it in this city, by way of rejoicing: not one of our bells suffered to ring, and but very few colors were shown by the shipping in the harbor; no, nor not one bonfire kindled.

8. This day a petition was presented to John Penn, our governor (signed by near nine hundred respectable freeholders in and near this city), requesting him to call the Assembly, in order to consider the proceedings of the British Parliament towards America in their proceedings against the town of Boston, &c., &c., to which his Honor was pleased to return the following answer: "Gentlemen, upon occasions when the peace, order, and tranquility of the Province require it, I shall be ready to convene the Assembly; but as that does not appear to be the case at present, I cannot think such a step would be expedient or consistent with my duty."

9. A great number of mechanics met at the State House about six o'clock in the evening, in order to consider an answer to send to the tradesmen of New York, who had written to this city respecting what was necessary to be done. At this meeting, John Ross, Esq., opened the reasons for calling them together, read their letter, &c.; upon which a committee amongst the tradesmen was appointed, who are to answer the said letter, and communicate and keep up a correspondence with the committee at New York.

10. There was a meeting held at the Philosophical Hall, and also the day after, consisting of the committee and a number of other inhabitants, called in from all Societies in town, to advise, consult and deliberate upon the propositions that were to be laid before the general meeting of the inhabitants on the eighteenth instant, near the State House, at three o'clock in the afternoon.

18. A very large and respectable meeting of the freeholders and freemen of this city and county met in the State House yard, where Thomas Willing and John Dickinson were chairmen, when they entered into six spirited resolves, and chose forty-three persons as committeemen to transact their affairs.

22. This day twenty-nine of the committee met at the Carpenters' Hall, in Chesnut street, Thomas Willing in the chair, agreed and appointed three of their members, viz. Joseph Reed, John Nixon, and Thomas Wharton to wait upon the Speaker of the Assembly, requesting him to call upon the Assembly, and to give them a positive answer whether he would or not, before they made their report to the General Committee that is to meet on Monday, the 27th inst. They also, at this meeting, appointed a number of their members to go to different parts of the city and suburbs to crave collections for poor Boston.

JULY 11. This day arrived at New Castle, the ship Minerva, Captain Lindsey, from Newry, with four hundred and fifty passengers.

15. This day, about four o'clock P.M., met at the Carpenters' Hall, in this city, the representatives appointed to attend from the several committees of the different counties in this Province, viz. Bucks, Chester, Lancaster, York, Cumberland, Berks, Northampton, and Northumberland, to confer with the committee chosen by this city and county, and also to consult and consider what may be proper to propose to our General Assembly that is called by our Governor to meet the 18th instant, respecting the critical situation of all the American Colonies. There appeared in this meeting great unanimity, and a set of resolves [was adopted] in general, declaratory of the sense of this Province on the present state of British America, and the peculiar sufferings of our brethren in Boston, in order to lay before our Assembly, the 18th.

Arrived this day at New Castle, the ship Peace and Plenty, Captain McKinzey, with four hundred passengers, from Belfast.

21. The delegates from the several counties of this Province have sat every day (First Day excepted) since the 15th inst., preparing a set of general resolves declaratory of the sense of this Province on the present state of British America, and the peculiar sufferings of our brethren in Boston, and as our Assembly have resolved themselves into a grand committee, and appointed this day at ten o'clock for the consideration of the sundry letters from the committees of our sister colonies, they have given leave for our Provincial Committee to attend and hear their debates.

22. The Assembly of this Province, taking into consideration the difficulties that had subsisted between Great Britain and her colonies, came into the measure proposed, that a Congress of Deputies from the several Colonies be held, as soon as may be convenient, [and] have appointed the following, viz., Joseph Galloway, *Speaker*, Samuel Rhoads, Thomas Mifflin, Charles Humphreys, John Morton, George Ross, and Edward Biddle.

25. Accounts from New Castle of the arrival of the Snow Charlotte, Captain Gafney, from Waterford, with one hundred and ten passengers, and the ship Hope, Captain McClanahan, from Newry, with two hundred and twenty passengers.

August 6. The ship Renown, Captain Keith, arrived at New Castle, from Newry, with three hundred and fifty passengers; as is also the ship Needham, Captain Chevers, at New York, with three hundred passengers.

9. In the Charleston packet, Captain Wright, came passengers, the Hon. Henry Middleton and Edward Rutledge, Esq's., two of the gentlemen who are nominated to attend the Congress from the Colony of South Carolina.

10. Also arrived, the ship Hannah, Captain Mitchell, from Londonderry, with four hundred passengers, and Captain Jones, from London, with one hundred passengers, mostly tradesmen.

22. Arrived, brig Sea Nymph, Captain Moore, from Charleston, South Carolina, with whom [came] passengers Thomas Lynch and Christopher Gadsden, two of the delegates from that Province. The latter end of this week came to town, Col. Nathaniel Fulson and Major John Sullivan, delegates from New Hampshire.

29. Came to town, Hon. Thomas Cushing, Samuel Adams, Robert Treat Paine, and John Adams, delegates from the Province of Massachusetts Bay, with whom came in company, from New York, John Rutledge, delegate from South Carolina, who took his passage to New York.

30. Arrived, the ship Alexander, Captain Hunter, with about six hundred passengers, from Londonderry.

31. Also, this week, arrived the delegates from New York, New Hampshire, Connecticut, [and] Maryland, with sundry members from the lower counties[1], and some from this Province.

---

[1] The three counties now forming the State of Delaware.

SEPTEMBER 5. The gentlemen that arrived in town as delegates, about fifty-three in number, met at the Carpenters' Hall, when Hon. Peyton Randolph was chosen chairman, and Charles Thomson, secretary.

12. The delegates from North Carolina viz., Joseph Hewes and William Hooper, Esq's., arrived this day, and Richard Caswell, Esq., the other delegate, is hourly expected. This same day and yesterday, the eight companies of the Royal Regiment of Ireland marched from hence, in two divisions, for Amboy and Elizabethtown, to be shipped for Boston.

24. This same day began the Quakers' Yearly Meeting, and continued from day to day, until the first of October, from which meeting, they sent forth an epistle that has given great offence to the friends of freedom and liberty in America.

OCTOBER 1. Election this day, when G. Gray, Henry Pawling, John Dickenson, Joseph Parker, Israel Jacobs, Jonathan Roberts, Michael Hillegas, and Samuel Rhoads, were chosen Representatives for this county.

3. This day Thomas Mifflin and Charles Thomson were elected Burgesses for this county.

4. Samuel Rhoads was chosen mayor of this city.

20. This day the Assembly of this Province gave a grand entertainment unto all the delegates from the different Provinces at this time in the city, at what is called the New Tavern, in Second street.[1]

NOVEMBER 7. Notice being given this morning of a meeting, to be held this afternoon at the State House, a number met, at which it was concluded that a new committee, to the number of sixty, should be chosen, to manage public affairs for this City, the Southern and Northern Liberties, to be chosen by ballot, the 12th inst., and to continue in that station till the meeting and

---

[1] The building above Walnut street, afterwards known as the Merchants' Coffee House. It was pulled down not many years ago.

sitting of the next Congress, and two weeks after the said Congress breaks up, and no longer.

14. This day the Freeholders meet pursuant to agreement, at the State House, and chose, by ballot, sixty inhabitants for committee men, as was before agreed upon; but as the Southern District complained that it was not fully represented, they therefore requested that four of their District might be added to the sixty that were chosen, the which was granted them, and also three were afterwards added on the Northern Liberty account. Within the week past, some vessels are arrived from Ireland, and one from Holland, with a number of passengers.

DECEMBER 4. Arrived, the ship Jamaica, R. Graham, from London, with a great quantity of goods, upon which, the committee was called; also arrived, the ship ———, from ———, with salt and coals. As these arrived after the time specified by the General Congress, they come under the regulation of Article the 10th of the Association.

5. The ship Friendship, Captain Jann, from Cork, is arrived at New Castle, with two hundred passengers.

6. Arrived, the ship Pennsylvania Packet, Captain Osborne, from Liverpool, in seven weeks, said to be full of goods; upon which there was a meeting of the merchants to consider what was necessary, and to wait on the committee with an application in order to hear their resolutions, the which were published in handbills, the next day, for their government.

8. In the handbills published yesterday, the committee recommended to all importers of goods, a perusal of, and attention to, the 11th Article of the General Congress, viz., "That a committee be chosen in every county, city, and town, by those who are qualified to vote for Representatives in the Legislature, whose business it shall be, attentively to observe the conduct of all persons touching this Association, and when it shall be made to

appear, to the satisfaction of a majority of any such committee, that any person within the limits of their appointment has violated this Association, that such majority do forwith cause the truth of the case to be published in the *Gazette*, to the end that all such foes to the rights of British America may be publicly known and universally contemned as the enemies of American liberty, and thenceforth, we respectively will break off all dealings with him or her.

30. Debates in the Quaker Monthly Meeting this day which held by and with adjournment till ten at night, and then adjourned to the second day of next month.

1775.

JANUARY 2. Which meeting held from six until near ten o'clock. The debates ran high respecting their conduct in these troublesome times that are expected. In regard thereto, their members were enjoined not to concern themselves in the public disputes, nor to interrupt any of the king's officers in the discharge of their duty, but to pay all humble and dutiful obedience unto the king or his ministers' mandates, from time to time; not to join, nor to be in any of the city, county, provincial, or general committees, if so, whoever offends is to be dealt with as walking contrary to their discipline.

6. A remarkable circumstance: — This day, about three P.M., a girl brought up by my wife, named Polly ———, about twelve years old, went out to slide or play, dressed as usual, without cap or bonnet, and did not return till about nine o'clock next morning. Al this space of time, she says that she was in no house, nor near any fire, but sat between two logs all that night, in an open lot, in Spruce street (as she says) yet received nor took no cold, although it was one of the coldest freezing nights this winter.

18. This evening the city and suburbs committee

met. Some of them waited on the Carpenters' Company for the use of their Hall for the Provincial Committee to meet in, and were answered that they might have [it] for paying ten shillings per diem.[1] Spokesman, Joseph Fox.

23. The committee from all the counties in this Province met (except from Bucks), to the amount of near one hundred, at the State House; broke up the twenty-eighth, having finished all their business amicably.

24. Meetings daily amongst the Quakers, in order, if possible, to defeat the pacific proceedings of the Continental Congress, calling upon their members not to meet the county committees, but entirely to withdraw from them, under the penalty of excommunication. ...... This day was also a paper published, called a Testimony of the People called Quakers, in which is contained such gross abuse against all persons that oppose their fallacious schemes, and stuffed with such false contradictions, that it will be a lasting memento of the truth of what Robert Walker, one of their public preachers, now here, often told them, and warned them to take care, because, says he, the Lord is departed from you, as he did from Saul, and has given you over to your own devices.

27. This day John Dickinson attended the Provincial Congress in order to show and contradict the notorious lies promulgated in Rivington's paper, No. 91.

At Dr. Chovet's Lecture.[2]

FEBRUARY 11. This day was published, in J. Humphrey's *Ledger*, No. 3, a scandalous letter, said to come from Kent County, Delaware.[3]

13. Some time last week arrived, from London, the ship Polly and Peggy, but brought no kind of merchant

---

[1] Pennsylvania Currency — seven shillings and sixpence of which were equal to a dollar.
[2] See Appendix (B.)
[3] See entry of April 29th.

goods: in that time also arrived a brig from Madeira, having a few pipes of wine. The owner advised the committee, and declared his intentions to send away the said vessel and wines, agreeably to the direction of the Congress.

28. This day a petition was presented by the Quakers' interest, requesting the suspending of our fairs in this city : also, a petition from our committee respecting no negroes to be any more imported here.

MARCH 1. Early this morning, departed these parts, universally lamented by the friends of slavery, but to the joy and satisfaction of the lovers of freedom, that baneful and detested weed, East India TEA, whose return is never desired or wished for by the true sons of American liberty.

9th. Yesterday evening, arrived, ship Chalkley, Captain Spain, from Bristol, who brought account that his Majesty had received the petition of our American Congress, and promised to lay it before the Parliament, who were to meet, by adjournment, the nineteenth of January. In the interim, petitions are preparing by the body of merchants in London, Bristol, and all over England. This news causes our Tories to be quite jaw-fallen and sullen.

17. Yesterday an election was held at the Carpenters' Hall, for choosing officers for the new manufactory, set on foot for making woollens, linen, and cotton, when Joseph Stiles was chosen Treasurer, James Cannon, Secretary, and twelve managers, viz., Christopher Marshall, Jacob Winey, Isaac Gray, Samuel Wetherill, Jr., Christopher Ludwick, Frederick Kuhl, Robert Strettle Jones, Richard Wells, Thomas Tilbury, James Popham, and Isaac Howell, for one year.

21. Last night, nine of the managers met at Captain Stiles's school room, sent for William Smith, who came, of whom we took his house in Market Street, for three years, for forty pounds per annum.

22. The *Pennsylvania Journal*, No. 1685, gives a succinct account of the proceedings of [the] New York and Elizabeth Town Committees respecting the state of the case of Messrs. Robert and John Murray, merchants of New York, who had landed goods out of the ship Beulah, from Londonderry, contrary to the resolve of Congress.

23. Account from New York yesterday, that Messrs. Murrays' house and store [were] shut up, and a seal put upon the latter. Thus may be seen the manly behavioi of the committee of New York, notwithstanding the opposition they met with, both in their Assembly House and public proceedings, by the enemies of our country. The committee of the county of Cumberland, New Jersey, have also published the behavior of Silas Newcomb, Esq., respecting persisting in drinking East [India] Tea, since the first of March, agreeably to the eleventh Article of the American Congress. See *Pennsylvania Gazette*, No. 2413.

APRIL 13. This morning was published the Address of the Lords and Commons to his Majesty, on the ninth of last February, wherein they declare Massachusetts Bay in a state of rebellion, and countenanced and encouraged by unlawful combinations in several of the other Colonies, and also, that all the Bostonians who signed, as they call it, a league and covenant, are declared by the crown lawyers, to have committed an overt act of high treason. Thereupon were ordered for Boston, to chastise them, three regiments of foot, one of dragoons, seven companies of marines, a large train of artillery. Notwithstanding all this, some of our staunch friends in England beheld with horror the ministerial proceedings, and as proof thereof, and to their lasting fame be it recorded, that the Constitutional Society stepped forth, and showed their dislike of those cruel proceedings by their resolving unanimously, that one hundred pounds sterling be sent by that Society to Dr. Franklin, requesting him to transmit the same for the relief of the town of Boston.

20. News brought by post this day, of the arrival of the Snow, Sir William Johnson, Captain Dean, at New York, the 19th, in thirty-one days from London. It is said his papers are to [the] 5th [of] March, and [he] says that " Sixteen men-of-war and ninety-five transports are certainly coming out to America, to bring over eleven regiments and two troops of horse, he thinks, to New York," and that "a nobleman is ordered out to New York, in order to bring about a pacification," (I hope) and that " the city of London have subscribed thirty thousand pounds sterling for the poor of Boston."

21. Went to the Manufactory before ten, stayed till eleven, in company and back with Frederick Kuhl, my attending partner each day for one week; morning at ten, afternoon at three. ...... James Cannon came, brought the first and second *Crisis*, read them, and stayed to supper.

22. Under the London head, Feb. 7th, it is said, " The regiment of light-horse, destined for America, are all equipping with new accoutrements. On their caps is the following motto, 'Death or Glory,' and a death's head likewise embroidered ;" and it is farther said that " It is intended to put the refractory Colonies under military government, and to grant special charters and privileges to those of them who are obedient. This day, March the 7th, at noon, the two sheriffs and the hangman attended at the Royal Exchange, in order to burn a periodical paper, called *The Crisis*, No. 3, and the pamphlet entitled *The Present Crisis with respect to America*. As soon as the fire was lighted before the Exchange, it was immediately put out, and dead dogs and cats thrown at the officers. A fire was then made in Cornhill, and the pelting still continued." It is farther said, " there are at this time, between London Bridge and Lime House, more than three hundred vessels, with brooms at their mast-heads, as a token that they are for sale." Feb. 10—it is said " An eminent Quaker, at

the meeting of the merchants declared, however lightly and contemptuously their petitions were treated, he was fully satisfied that the Americans would, to a man, die, if the act in his hand, which he held up, was not repealed:" to which add, in a paragraph of [a] letter from York, Feb. 13, it is said, " A certain celebrated lady amongst the body of Quakers, waited on the king to address him on the times, and after promising her an audience, he abruptly withdrew." ...... March 10th, It is said from London, that " Deputations are sent from hence to Boston, to try several persons in America," and that "the twelve sail of frigates destined for Boston, have stores, and are completely victualled for twelve months. The Generals, MacKay, Howe, and Clinton, were to embark with the troops, the 12th of March.

24. About five this afternoon, arrived an express, for the particulars of which see the printed piece annexed.[1]

25. Went to the manufactory with my partner. At four, he and I went to the State House, there being a meeting pursuant to public notice, which, by computation, amounted to eight thousand, in order to consider the measures to be pursued in the present critical affairs of America.

26. A second express came this afternoon, which see in printed piece annexed.[2]

27. Another account, being several extracts of letters per post, from Boston, of the 19th and 20th, giving further account of the behavior of the troops, and of their precipitate retreat unto Charleston. See postscripts to *Pennsylvania Journal and Gazette* (No. 1690, and No. 2418).

---

[1] The leaf marked A., an exact copy of the original slip.
[2] The leaf marked B., an exact copy of the original slip. The statement that Lord Percy was killed is erroneous. He afterwards became Duke of Northumberland.

[A]

PHILADELPHIA, APRIL 24, 1775.

An express arrived at Five o'clock this evening, by which we have the following advices:

Watertown, Wednesday Morning, near 10 of the clock.

To all friends of American Liberty, be it known, that this morning before break of day, a brigade consisting of about 1000 or 1200 men landed at Phipp's Farm, at Cambridge and marched to Lexington, where they found a Company of our Colony Militia in arms, upon whom they fired without any provocation, and killed six men and wounded four others. By an express from Boston, we find another brigade are now upon their march from Boston, supposed to be about 1000. The bearer, Trail Bissel, is charged to alarm the country quite to Connecticut; and all persons are desired to furnish him with fresh horses, as they may be needed. I have spoken with several, who have seen the dead and wounded. Pray let the Delegates from this Colony to Connecticut see this, they know Col. Forster, one of the Delegates.

J. PALMER, one of the Committee.

A true Copy from the original, per order of the Committee of Correspondence of Worcester, April, 1775.

Attested and forwarded by the Committees of Brookline, Norwich, New London, Lyme, Saybrook, Killingsworth, E. Guilford, Guilford, Brandford, New Haven.

Fairfield, Saturday, April 22, 8 o'clock.

SINCE the above was written we have received the following by a second express.

Thursday, 3 o'clock, afternoon, A. M.

Sir,

I am this moment informed by an express from Woodstock, taken from the mouth of the Express, then two of the clock, afternoon — That the contest between the first Brigade that marched to Concord was still continuing this morning at the town of Lexington, to which said Brigade had retreated, that another Brigade had, said to be the second mentioned in the letter of this morning, landed with a quantity of Artillery, at the place where the first did. The Provincials were determined to prevent the two Brigades from joining their strength if possible, and remain in great need of succor.

N. B. The Regulars, when in Concord, burnt the Court House, took two pieces of cannon which they rendered useless; and began to take up Concord bridge on which Capt. ——— (who with many on both sides were soon killed) made an attack upon the king's troops, on which they retreated to Lexington.

I am,   Eb. Williams.

To Col. Obadiah Johnson, Canterbury.

P. S. Mr. McFarlan of Plainfield, Merchant, has just returned from Boston, by way of Providence, who conversed with an express from Lexington, who further informs, that 4000 of our troops had surrounded the first brigade above mentioned, who were on a hill in Lexington, that the action continued, and there were about 50 of our men killed, and 150 of the regulars, as near as they could determine, when the express came away: it willing will be expedient for every man to go who is fit and.

The above is a true copy as received per express from New Haven, and attested by the Committee of Correspondence, from town to town. Attest

> Jonathan Sturgis
> Andrew Rowland
> Thaddius Burr
> Job Bartram
> } Committee.

The above was received yesterday at 4 o'clock, by the Committee of New York, and forwarded to Philadelphia, by Isaac Low, Chairman of the Committee of New York.

Printed by W. and T. Bradford.

[B]

PHILADELPHIA, *April* 26, 1775.
Wednesday, 12 *o'clock.*
By an Express just arrived, we have the following.

Wallingford, Monday morning, April 24, 1775.

Dear Sir

COL. Woodworth was over in this place yesterday and has ordered 20 men from each company in his regiment, some of which have already set off, and others go this morning. He brings accounts which came to him authenticated as late as Thursday afternoon. The king's troops being reinforced a second time and joined as I suppose from what I can learn by the party who were intercepted by Col. Gardiner, were then encamped on Winterhill, and were surrounded by 20,000 of our men who were entrenching.

Colonel Gardiner's ambush proved fatal to Lord Percy, and one other General Officer, who were killed on the spot the first fire. ... To counterbalance this good news, the story is, that our first man in command (who he is I know not) is also killed. ... It seems they have lost many men on both sides. ... Col. Woodsworth had the account in a letter from Hartford. ...

The country beyond here are all gone off, and we expect it will be impossible to procure horses for our waggons, as they have or will in every place employ their horses themselves. In this place they send an horse for every sixth man and are pressing them for that purpose. I know of no way but you must send immediately a couple of able horses, who may overtake us at Hartford possibly, where we must return Mr. Noy's and Meloy's, if they hold out so far. Remember the horses must be had at any rate. I am in great haste

Your entire friend and humble servant

JAMES LOCKWOOD.

P. S. Col. Gardiner took 9 prisoners, and 12 clubbed their firelocks and came over to our party. ... Colonel Gardiner's party consisted of 700, and the regulars of 1800 instead of 1200, as we heard before. ... They have sent a vessel up the Mystic river as far as Temple's Farm, which is about half a mile from Winterhill. ... These accounts being true, all the King's troops, except 4 or 500, must be encamped on Winterhill. At the instance of the gentlemen of Fairfield just departed this copy is taken verbatim from the original, to be forwarded to that town. ISAAC BEARS

The above is copied and authenticated by the several Committees through Connecticut, New York, and New Jersey.

⁎ *Winter Hill is about two miles from Boston. Wallingford is fourteen miles from New Haven.*

Printed by W. and T. BRADFORD.

29. Went and drank coffee at James Cannon's. He was not there, being gone to [the] State House Yard to help consult and regulate the forming of the militia. After coffee, I went back to [the] Factory by an appointment of some of the managers, who had appointed to meet ——— Gardiner, a committee man of New York, with whom we spent the evening. This day, about noon, Jabez F...... came by persuasion to the Coffee House, and there declared, in the presence of a great concourse of people, that it was Robert Holliday, of DuckCreek, that wrote and sent that letter to him, which he had caused to be published in the *Pennsylvania Ledger*, No. 3, and no other person, upon which the people, with some reluctancy, let him go; but the overseers of the poor interfered, by obliging him there to give security for the maintenance of his two bastard children. J...... and D...... had bonded a vessel for Newfoundland, and

intended to slip away with her, but a number hearing waited on them. At first, they equivocated, but the people being resolute, they delivered up the ship's papers, and hindered her proceeding. That also prevented Samuel S...... from loading a vessel to the same place.

MAY 1. This day a number of the associators to the militia met in each of the wards of this city, to form themselves into suitable companies, and to choose their respective officers.

2d. Viewed some companies learning the use of firearms. ...... This day, about noon, Thomas Loosly, shoemaker, was brought to the Coffee House, and there being exalted as a spectacle to a great number of reputable citizens, he there very humbly and submissively asked and entreated their pardon and forgiveness for his illiberally and wickedly villifying the measures of Congress, the Committee, and the people of New England, sincerely promising that his future conduct should be just, true, and equitable, as should recommend him to the particular notices of all those whom he had so unjustly, falsely, and wickedly villified. On those assurances and promises, the company discharged him.

3. There was a company of young men, Quakers, who this day asked leave of the managers to learn the military exercise in the Factory yard, which was granted, and they began this evening.

4. This day account came that Mr. Hancock and Mr. Adams are arrived at New York, on their way to this city, to attend the Continental Congress. The Quaker company, Humphries, captain, about thirty, exercised in the factory yard, and such is the spirit and alacrity of them, that few, if any, of the companies will sooner learn the military art and discipline, and make a handsomer appearance, nor be more ready to assert, at the risk of their lives, the freedom of America on Constitutional principles.

5. Visited two families that have left Boston govern-

ment through the violent oppressive measures exercised over them. ...... This afternoon arrived [the ship Pennsylvania Packet,] Captain Osborne, from London, in which came passenger, Dr. Benjamin Franklin, to the satisfaction of his friends and the lovers of liberty.

6. After dinner, went to the State House Yard, from thence to the commons, seeing the various companies exercise. While standing there, Major John Sullivan and John Langdon, Esq., two of the delegates from New Hampshire, with my son Benjamin, came, who, the delegates, spoke to me very kindly.

7. It's admirable to see the alteration of the Tory class in this place, since the account of the engagement in New England. Their language is quite softened, and many of them have so far renounced their former sentiments as that they have taken up arms, and are joined in the association; nay, even many of the stiff Quakers, and some of those who drew up the Testimony, are ashamed of their proceedings. It is said that J ..... P ......, who signed that paper, and had called the people rebels, now declares in favor of the opposition made to king and parliament. The Friends held a meeting last Fifth day afternoon, in order to consider how to send a supply to the Bostonians, it being a matter that before they had treated with contempt and ridicule. A petition has been presented to the House, praying them to grant a sum, not less than Fifty Thousand Pounds, for the use of the Province at this critical time, and another petition praying them to consider the situation of our City, and requesting them to grant leave to stop our navigation, by sinking some vessels at Red Bank. Both these petitions were signed by great numbers, of all the different ranks and sects of this city. This was done last week. This day, arrived Captain Robinson, in [the] ship [Sukey,] from London, in six weeks, who brought account that the marines were embarked, and the vessels sailed for Ireland to take the soldiers on

board. He brought also a copy of the petition of the Quakers to his Majesty, and that the printers of the piece called the *Crisis*, were had before the Ministry on account of finding out the author, who being interrogated and pressed hard, declared that one of the writers was the Duke of Gloucester. They immediately discharged them without any farther confession.

8. Account from New York is that a general association was set on foot on the 29th ultimo, and signed by above one thousand of the principal inhabitants of the City, and it is to be transmitted to all the counties in the Province, when they make no doubt but it will be signed by all ranks of people. The purport is, that they will abide by and put into execution, whatever measures may be recommended by the Continental Congress, or resolved upon by their Provincial Convention. This they engage to perform under all the sacred ties of religion, honor, and love to their country. (See *General Advertiser*, No. 185.) We hear also from Williamsburgh,[1] of Governor Dunmore's delivering to Captain Collins's party of men, in the night, out of the Magazine, twenty barrels of gunpowder, which they carried on board the schooner Magdalen. This was highly resented by the people, who addressed him on the occasion, and requested him to return it; but instead of his complying, the locks were taken off the magazine, and the schooner put under the protection of the Fowey, man-of-war, in York river, and that the Governor had fortified himself in the palace, &c.

9. This morning, arrived four of the delegates from South Carolina, in the brig Charleston Packet, Captain Barton, in four days passage, viz., Henry Middleton, Christopher Gadsden, John Rutledge, and Edward Rutledge, Esq's. Christopher Gadsden came to see me, and dined with me. In conversation, he expressed the

---

[1] Then the capital of Virginia.

great satisfaction he had received in reading some of the books he had from me, when he went last home to Carolina from this City, particularly Paul Sigevolk's book, entitled *The Everlasting Gospel*, and those two books, entitled *The World Unmasked, or the Philosopher the Greatest Cheat*, requesting, that if it should please God that he and I should live to see peace and harmony once more restored among us in these parts, I would promote a correction of the *Everlasting Gospel*, and have it, with the two other volumes of the *World Unmasked*, fairly and neatly printed, unto which he would subscribe largely, and, upon completing them, I might draw on him to the amount of Sixty Guineas, which he would immediately pay. This conversation gave me great pleasure. ...... N. B. This day, arrived these sundry delegates, viz., Peyton Randolph, George Washington, Patrick Henry, Richard Henry Lee, Edmund Pendleton, Benjamin Harrison, and Richard Bland, Esq's., from Virginia; Richard Caswell, and Joseph Hewes, Esq's., from North Carolina; Samuel Chase, Thomas Johnson, and John Hall, Esq's., from Maryland; Cæsar Rodney and George Read, Esq's., from the counties of New Castle, Kent, and Sussex, on the Delaware. It is said they were met, about six miles from town, by the officers of all the companies in the city, and by many other gentlemen, on horseback, to the amount of five hundred. Within two miles of the city, the company of riflemen and infantry, with a band of music, met them, and conducted them through the City with great applause.

10. This day about one o'clock, came into town these following delegates, namely: John Hancock, Thomas Cushing, Samuel Adams, John Adams, and Robert Treat Paine, Esq's., from Massachusetts Bay; Eliphalet Dyer, Roger Sherman, and Silas Deane, Esq's., for the Colony of Connecticut; (and Thomas Lynch, South Carolina, arrived in the evening.) Delegates from New

York, James Duane, Francis Lewis, John Jay, Lewis Morris, Philip Livingston, [and] John Alsop. Delegates from the Jerseys, [   ]

11. This afternoon, the delegates opened the Congress at the State House: began with prayer, in which officiated Jacob Duché.[1] There were also added to them by our Assembly, now sitting, Dr. Benjamin Franklin, Thomas Willing, and James Wilson, Esq's. The Congress this day elected Peyton Randolph, Esq., President, and Charles Thomson, Secretary.

13. The Congress are daily sitting, but scarcely any thing transpires from them, saving the depositions taken relating to the beginning of the engagement at Lexington and Concord.

14. This morning, set off from this city, for Burlington, the Captains, Bradford, Pryor, and Melchor, with a number of others, on the report of a deserter from General Gage's being confined in prison there, for desertion, the which, upon their arrival at Burlington, they found to be true. They immediately went to the prison, took him out, and brought him to Philadelphia.

15. This day, arrived the Hon. Samuel Ward, Esq., one of the delegates from the Colony of Rhode Island. Within these two weeks past, sundry families have arrived in this city from the territories of Boston, whose relations of their sufferings and distress there, are very melancholy and afflicting to hear, and at present no prospect of any relief from under the hand of unmerited cruelty. A vessel this day arrived, which left Cork the 4th day of April, says the troops were not sailed, but were taking their horses aboard, &c.

17. In *P. Journal*, No. 1693, is [a] copy of Robert Holliday's recantation and acknowledgment of his misconduct, the which was accepted by their committee in Kent county. In the *Evening Post*, No. 49,

---

[1] Rector of St. Paul's Church, Philadelphia — author of the Letters of T. Caspipina.

is [an] account of Governor Dunmore's Proclamation, and an account of his paying for the gunpowder he had suffered to be taken away, to the amount of three hundred and twenty pounds sterling, also the resolves of the committee of King William's county on that occasion, with the New York General Committee's Circular Letter to the other Colonies.

18. Account brought of the taking of Fort Ticonderoga. See *Evening Post*, No. 50, for particulars.

20. The Congress sitting every day this week constantly, and the militia, light infantry, horse, and company of artillery, exercising every day, and some of them twice a day.

22. This day was published, in the *Pennsylvania Packet*, No. 187, the Congress's advice in answer to the New York request, how they should behave in regard to the troops expected there. In said paper is the Address of the General Committee of Association for the city and county of New York, to Governor Colden.

24. In the last *Evening Post*, No. 52, is, it is said, General Gage's circumstantial account of the attack on his Majesty's troops by a number of people of the Massachusetts Bay, April 19th. In said paper is [an] account, via Liverpool, 30th [of] March, that the whole regiment of light dragoons had, to a man, refused to come over to fight against this country. ...... From there to son Christopher's; stayed and supped with eight of the delegates. About nine, an alarm was spread by beat of drum, that our prison was beset by a number of men, in order to rescue two prisoners who were under sentence of death; but by the interposition of Captain Bradford's company, they were prevented, and some of the offenders, it's said, secured. However, this company, with the assistance of ———, watched the prison all night.

25. Yesterday morning, Peyton Randolph, President of the Congress, set off for Virginia, as his presence was necessary in their General Assembly, that

is called by their governor to meet on the first of next June, at Williamsburgh, of which he is speaker, and the Hon. John Hancock was elected President. For the etymology of the word Yankee (alias Yankee Doodle) see *Evening Post*, No. 53.[1] ...... Part of two companies mounting guard at the prison, as I came home, in order to keep watch all night.

27. After dinner went to the place ;[2] drank Balm Tea; from thence to a walk on the commons, near [the] Bettering House,[3] seeing sundry companies of militia exercising, till past seven.

28. This day, it is said, Mary Harris, a Quaker preacher from Wilmington, visited the three Quaker Meeting Houses in this city, in a very odd manner, viz., by walking through each of the preacher's galleries, then down, passed amongst the people backwards and forwards, seemingly in great affliction and distress, uttering, it's said, words to this effect — "See to your standing, for that thus the Lord was about to search and examine his camp," &c. &c., and then said, "I shall have peace in having thus discharged and done my Lord's errand. So farewell."

31. For several particulars of public remarkable occurrences, see this day's *Pennsylvania Journal*, No. 1695.

JUNE 1. Guards at [the] prison, as has been every night since the 24th of last month, kept by the militia.

2. Account came that while Parson Stringer was at prayers with Andrew Steward, in the dungeon of our prison, the said Steward took that opportunity to walk up stairs, go out at the several prison doors into the street, and without any ceremony, walked off with himself, without bidding Robinson, the prison keeper, fare-

---

[1] See Appendix (C.)

[2] Mr. Marshall's country place was in Moyamensing, between Broad Street and Irish Tract Lane. Balm Tea was probably substituted for the interdicted article.

[3] The Bettering House was the Philadelphia Alms House. It was on the south side of Spruce Street, between Tenth and Eleventh Streets.

well, although he was sitting at the front door on the step, when he passed him.

7. In the evening, arrived ship Prosperity, Captain McCulloch, with, it is said, about four hundred passengers, from Belfast: from London, ship Sally, in which came passenger, Major Skene, as Governor of Ticonderoga and Crown Point. ...... Came home near eleven; fine clear moonlight weather: a sentry at [the] New Tavern, over the above governor.

8. Cloudy weather, and so continued all day. I rose before five, breakfasted, and went on the commons past seven. Came back past nine; then by ten went again and staid till past two, viewing the parade of the three battalions [of] militia of the City and Liberties, with the artillery Company, (with two twelve-pounders and four six-pound brass field pieces,) a troop of light horse, several companies of light infantry, rangers, and riflemen, in the whole, above two thousand men, who joined in one brigade, and went through their manual exercises, firings, and manœuvres, &c., &c., in the presence of General Lee, the Continental Congress, and several thousand spectators, then all marched into town to the Coffee House.

12. For public occurrences, see *Pennsylvania Packet*, No. 190.

20. Went to the Factory past eight; stayed till twelve. Just then-about, the three battalions, with the troop of horse, train of artillery, and three companies of light infantry, rangers, &c., marched by the Factory, having been reviewed this morning by General Washington and the members of the Congress.

27. About eight, Brigadier General Sullivan set out from hence, to join the American army, near Boston: he was escorted by the light infantry of the three battalions, and by many other officers and gentlemen, a few miles. ...... An express arrived this day, with sundry occurrences, from the Boston camp. For particulars, see the *Evening Post*, Nmub· 67.

30. This being monthly meeting, it's said J... P... took much pains in endeavoring to persuade the auditors, and they their acquaintance, by no means to keep the 20th of next month as a day of prayer and fasting, but to keep open shop and houses. This was, in plain terms, saying, You may frolic as much as you please on that day, but don't, by any means, suffer yourselves to be humble, or pray on that day, because it is appointed by the delegates for that service, to pray and worship God. This he pressed them to observe, that so they might not be like what he called the world's people. Here is another flagrant testimony to the decay of primitive Christianity, viz., " Pray without ceasing,"— " In the time of trouble, call upon me," &c., &c.

JULY 1. My son Christopher sent me a present of a small keg of pickled oysters, and requested my coming to sup at his house this evening, the which I complied with, and spent the evening in innocent, cheerful conversation with John Adams, Thomas Cushing, Samuel Adams,[1] and Robert Treat Paine, delegates from Boston.

2. Afternoon, two o'clock, an alarm spread of a man of war, full of troops, seen at Bambay Hook, coming up. This alarmed the City, but it proved to be a false report.

7. To Grace Hastings's ; stayed there till church was done, there being a sermon preached at Christ Church to the First Battalion of the City Militia, by Jacob Duché.

9. It is said that some day last week, there was a meeting of the Quakers in this city, wherein it was agreed that a collection should be set afoot in that society, for the relief of the necessitous of all religious denominations in New England who are reduced to losses and distresses in this time of public calamity, to be distributed among them by a committee of their

---

[1] The name of John Adams is here repeated in the original. I have substituted Samuel, which was doubtless meant.

brethren in New England, and to this, it is said, they recommended to their brethren in their several meetings in New Jersey, to subscribe for [the] said purpose. In the evening came Colonel Dyer, [Silas] Deane, and [John] Jay, three of the delegates, ... who all stayed and supped, and spent the evening very agreeably, till near ten o'clock, it being a fine serene night.

14. The many and various accounts of the slain at Bunker's Hill reconciled, by an account of the return made to General Washington on the fourth instant — of the Provincials, viz., one hundred and thirty-eight killed, three hundred and one wounded, and seven missing, and the best account he had received of the regulars was, that eight hundred were killed, and seven hundred wounded. See *Evening Post*, No. 74, and J. Humphrey's *Ledger*, No. 25.

16. After two, Charles and his wife, and daughter Betsey, came in the chair; just stopped and bid us farewell. They were going to Bristol, to try the water, on account of son Charles's health[1] ...... After they were gone, Samuel and John Adams, two of the delegates, came; stayed some time.

17. Stayed at home till near six; took a walk to the College yard, to see the Dutch butcher ask pardon of one of the companies for speaking disrespectfully of their proceedings[2].

---

[1] The mineral waters at Bath, near Bristol, Bucks County, Pennsylvania, did not go out of vogue until within about sixty years.

[2] The following notice from the Committee of Safety, was published about this time:

Committee Chamber, Philadelphia, July 17, 1775.

The Committee of Safety do hereby recommend it to the good women of this City and Province, that they voluntarily supply the Surgeons or Doctors who have usually attended their respective families, with as much scraped lint and old linen for bandage, as they can conveniently furnish, that the same may be ready for the service of those that shall happen to be wounded in the defence of their country.

Signed by order of the Committee,
WILLIAM GOVETT, *Clerk, C. S.*

20. This being the memorable day in which an unjust and cruel ministry took away all our sea trade, as far as their inveterate malice could reach : the morning was pleasant ; fine sunshine, yet cool and agreeable weather, although a melancholy appearance presented, as all the houses and shops in our neighborhood were shut, and to appearance more still than a First Day produced, as there was no riding abroad visiting, as is generally on First Day. ...... Most families attended divine worship in the different churches and meeting houses of this city. I went to Christ Church, where an excellent sermon was preached on the occasion, from Psalm ——, unto a large and crowed auditory, amongst whom were, I presume, all the delegates. It was an awful meeting, as numbers of wet eyes demonstrated their attention. ...... This afternoon, Robert Taylor called at my house, who said there was nigh two hundred of their militia came up this morning from their parts to church, in their uniforms, as he was. He is a lieutenant.

22. My wife and I took a walk to the place, and, awhile after, came there, Christopher Gadsden, [Roger] Sherman, and Colonel Dyer, three of the delegates, and my son Christopher. Soon after came Dr. Brown, Dr. —— (who was just come from Watertown, to get a thorough insight into making saltpetre. He was sent by the Provincial Congress), and James Cannon, who all stayed and drank coffee, &c.

24. Accounts are that on the eighth instant, two hundred volunteers, from the Rhode Island and Massachusetts forces, had burnt and destroyed the regulars' guard-house, [and] brought off two muskets and accoutrements, with one halbert : this done without [the] loss of one of our men. This was an advanced post, and gave the regulars an opportunity of discovering our operations at Roxbury. On the eleventh instant, a party of men from the Roxbury Camp went to Long Island, in Boston harbor, and brought off fifteen of the regulars

prisoners, between twenty and thirty horned cattle, and about one hundred sheep. The prisoners were sent from the head-quarters yesterday, to Concord. The same account says that General Gage's troops are much dispirited; that they are very sickly, and are heartily disposed to leave off dancing any more to the tune of Yankee Doodle, and that General Gage had sent many reputable housekeepers in Boston, to prison, for refusing to work day's work on board the men of war, and the fortifications.

25. Account was brought last night, that a vessel from Hispaniola had brought and landed, for our use, seven tons of gunpowder, being about one hundred and thirty casks; put under the care of the Committee of Safety.

26. It's said that a person was sent to prison this forenoon, for attempting to spike the guns in the State House Yard. Account is arrived from Georgia that the people there, hearing of a parcel of gunpowder's being on board a ship just arrived from London, went, landed and secured it for their own use. It's said that it amounted to thirteen thousand pounds, and that the Georgians have appointed delegates to attend the Continental Congress, and [who] are daily expected. A gentleman who got off [from] Boston, July 10th, says that the inhabitants were numbered, and amounted to six thousand five hundred and seventy-three — the soldiers, women and children, to thirteen thousand six hundred. Three hundred Tories are chosen to patrol the streets, forty-nine of a night. Very sickly: from ten to thirty funerals a day, but no bells allowed to toll. For further occurrences, and names of the officers killed and wounded, see *Pennsylvania Journal*, No. 1703.

27. This day, was launched, up town, a [gondola,] as another of [the] same construction, was launched last week, down town, each of them to row with —— oars, to carry ——, cannon, ——, men, and small arms.

29. This week, by accounts, we have received here, under safe custody, fifteen tons of gunpowder, and the same quantity [is] hourly expected, as also a parcel of small arms. Account is received of the Lexington affair's [having been heard of in England] by the return of Captain Darby, who carried it to England in twenty-seven days. See *Pennsylvania Ledger*, No. 18. ...... In this evening *Post* is the character of General Putnam, with some material occurrences. See No. 81.

30. Yesterday morning, set out from this town to the eastward, six wagons, each carrying one ton of gunpowder, escorted by twenty-four of the light infantry, and some riflemen of the first battalion as far as Trenton, then the escort was to be changed by some others at Trenton, and so proceed. This morning, it's said a pilot boat came up to town, loaded with gunpowder.

August 3. Yesterday, several of our delegates went out of town, by virtue of their adjournment to the fifth of next month.

4. Accounts from Boston are of the distress of the inhabitants there, beef being at 1*s.* 4*d.* per lb., butter 1*s.*, and so in proportion; that the Provincials had burnt the Light House at the entrance of Boston harbor, pulled up the piles that were for marks for the shipping, &c., but they first took away all the furniture, fifty weight of powder, and several casks of oil; that eight transports were arrived with about sixteen hundred men; exceedingly sickly in the town, so that every soldier that now arrives seems to add to their distress. From Virginia, that Lord Dunmore had seized a ship, and £900 out of one of the custom houses, for his own use; that thereupon the people had seized all the money in the other custom houses (amounting to about £1674 14*s.*) and treasury, and that the Provincial Convention had stopped all exports (except tobacco) from the 5th inst. With us, Michael Hillegas and George Clymer, of this City, are appointed Treasurers, and Dr. Franklin, Post Master General of the United Colonies of North America.

These appointments are by the Hon. Continental Congress. ...... Called as I came home at Stephen Collins's, whose wife had just received a letter from her husband, but no material news except the extremities of the people in Boston, and of four deserters who had just come over [to] them, and the arrival of one hundred and six of our riflemen.

5. Accounts by the Constitutional Post yesterday are, that about 3060, being parts of nine regiments, were arrived at Boston, and that, by appearances, General Burgoyne is in a deep settled melancholy, walks the streets frequently with his arms folded across his breast and talking to himself, and that General Gage is often out of his head, and that he and Admiral Greaves had publicly quarrelled, so that he told Gage it was a cowardly action to burn Charlestown.

6. Yesterday was published [a] copy of [the Address of] the Delegates of the United twelve American Colonies to the people of Ireland, dated July 28th, 1775, signed by John Hancock, President. There is also a rumor now propagated, that General Gage has resigned the command of the troops to General Howe, and that £50,000 sterling is remitted, in specie, to Boston, to pay and increase the wages of the soldiery, and that orders are [sent] to the Governor of Canada to attack our frontiers.

9. From Richmond, in Virginia, we hear that the convention sitting there has prohibited the exportation of grain and provisions of all kinds, after the fifth of this month, and [have resolved] to embody three thousand men, exclusive of officers, and three troops of horse, to be stationed in the lower end of the Colony, and that between four and five hundred men are to be raised and quartered at the different forts on the frontiers, &c., and that sixty young gentlemen are to be sent from that colony to serve as cadets in the army at Boston, &c.

For Sundry material occurrences, see *Pennsylvania Journal*, Numb. 1705.[1]

11. About four, the Constitutional Post arrived ; also, about six, an express arrived from the camp, with sundry advices, among which were that the regulars were attempting to repair the light house that was burnt down, upon notice of which, Major Tucker was sent to command three hundred men, who landed under a severe heavy fire, and then attacked them, killed the commanding officer, with ten or twelve of the others, on the spot, and took the remainder, about thirty-five in number, prisoners, and ten tory carpenters [and] demolished all their work. While he waited for the tide to carry them off, a large number of boats from the men-of-war came up to reinforce the regulars, on which ensued a smart firing. Our troops, however, got safe back with their prisoners, with the loss of one man killed and two or three wounded ; that the riflemen at the camp had picked off ten men in one day, three of whom were field officers; that of six sail of transports sent to the eastward of Casco Bay, for forage, with one man-of-war, while the parties of them were ashore in the country, a number of the inhabitants possessed themselves of five of the transports by making all aboard prisoners, to the amount of

---

[1] The following advertisement was published at this time :

To the Spinners in this City and County.

Your services are now wanted to promote the American Manufactory at the corner of Market and Ninth Streets, where cotton, wool, flax, &c., are delivered out. Strangers who apply are desired to bring a few lines from some respectable person in this neighborhood.

One distinguishing characteristic of an excellent woman, as given by the wisest of men is, that " She seeketh wool and flax and worketh willingly with her hands. She layeth her hands to the spindle, and her hand holdeth the distaff."

In this time of public distress, you have now, each of you, an opportunity not only to help to sustain your families, but likewise to cast your mite into the treasury of the public good. The most feeble effort to help to save the state from ruin, when it is all you can do, is as the widow's mite entitled to the same reward as they who, of their abundant abilities, have cast in much.

near four hundred soldiers and seamen, and secured the ships out of the reach of the man-of-war.

12. Last night, arrived the Georgia Packet, from Georgia, in which came passengers the Hon. John Houston, Archibald Bullock, and Dr. Zubly,[1] delegates appointed to represent that colony in the Continental Congress. ...... To the Coffee House to see Major French, Ensign ———, and ———, who were come from Dublin in the ship ———, Captain ———, with ——— suits of clothes for the ——— Regiment, which our people secured.

16. For sundry particular and material pieces of news, both foreign and domestic, with the Congress's Petition to the King, see *Pennsylvania Journal*, No. 1706. ...... Past five, took a walk to the State House, election being held there for one hundred men for City, Southern and Northern Liberties.

17. Accounts from Boston are, that the transports were returned and brought with them from Fisher's and Gardiner's Islands, two thousand one hundred sheep, about one hundred head of cattle, seven tons of hay, [a] parcel of hogs, one thousand pounds of cheese, &c. Oh! shame on the tory party!

18. Past seven, to meet [the] Committee in the Philosophical Society's Room, where this evening were met forty-nine members, who proceeded to [the] choice of chairmen, when Joseph Reed, George Clymer, Thomas McKean, and Samuel Meredith were appointed to that service, Jonathan B. Smith, Secretary, Robert Strettle Jones and Peter Loyd, Assistants to him. Agreed that the stated weekly meeting be held on Tuesday evening, at seven o'clock, at this Philosophical Society Room, while convenient; that all the members who are not present when the roll is called over, being twenty minutes after the time appointed, pay sixpence, and if absent

---

[1] A clergyman, native of Switzerland.

all the evening, one shilling ; and if any member met leave the company before business is over, without leave of the chairman, such are to pay five shillings ; that in all future debates, no person be suffered to give his sentiments on any particular but what is concluded in speaking twice on the same subject.

19. There is account from Boston that General Gage has demolished Castle William and sent all his family to England, and that the whole of the army would evacuate Boston soon, but it was thought his rage would carry him so far as to destroy it first ; that four captains of the regulars had resigned their commissions to General Gage, being ashamed of such base and cruel proceedings, and that several officers were gone for England ; that the Provincials had taken a number of prisoners on board several vessels that they had taken ; that several of our companies of riflemen were arrived at the camp, and, by the computation, there are twenty-five hundred of Gage's men killed and died since the Battle of Bunker's Hill, &c. ...... To the Committee, as there was a special meeting appointed to receive an answer from the Committee of Safety, respecting the Soldiers' clothing that was imported in Blair McClenagan's ship from Dublin, in which, their answer, they assumed it was their province to detain [them] and had them now in their possession until the meeting of Congress to dispose of them, as they, the Congress thought proper, upon which a Committee was appointed to go and examine the said packages, to see that there was no other kind of goods, and report next Third Day meeting. Complaint was made by G. Schlosser of his having stopped a piece of linen of a pedler,[1] who thereupon applied to [Isaac] Hunt, the lawyer,[2] who issued out a summons against

---
[1] On the 27th of September, 1774, the Congress unanimously resolved that from and after the First of December, 1774, there should be no importations from Great Britain or Ireland of any goods, wares, or merchandise, and that they should not be used or purchased, if imported after that day.
[2] Isaac Hunt was the father of Leigh Hunt, poet and essayist.

him for the said piece, upon which a motion was made to send for the said Hunt, who after first notice refused, upon which a line from the chairman brought him. He owned the doing of it, but insisted it was according to the rule of his profession, and could see no injury he had done. A good deal was said to him upon the imprudence of such proceedings, upon which he requested time to consult his client, and then he would give the Committee his answer whether he would proceed in carrying on the suit against C. Schlosser, or withdraw and discontinue the action, at the next meeting, which was granted him.

21. Took a walk down town to see Benj. Betterton, who, last Seventh Day, in a jovial humor, jumped ovre a man's shoulders, but on taking the ground, a small stone, it's said, was there, which turned his leg so that he broke it about the small. When I thus visited him, he lay in great pain, but pretty much composed and [with] but little fever.

22. At seven I went to meet the Committee; came home past ten, sundry debates detaining till that time. The one respecting Blair McClenagan's ship is referred to the determination of the Congress, as we could not overrule their resolve of June ———; the other respecting [Isaac] Hunt, who would give no positive answer whether he would prosecute the suit against George Schlosser or no, but requested to have the minutes of this meeting in writing, with leave to give his answer in writing, the which was looked upon to be only evasive, so it was determined, *nemine contradicente*, that his answer was not to satisfaction.

24. Called by the way at the Coffee House, advice being brought that the man-of-war below had seized Captain Mifflin's snow, from ———, detained her, and had confined both captain and mate. He seemed to be insolent, his mild behavior, so much before applauded, was now all absorbed in ill-will and rancor; he ex-

pressed himself in conversation, it's said, respecting our Committee of Safety far from politeness, but in low, obscene language, and closed it with this speech as a specimen, "That he did not value all their gondolas or Committee of Safety a ———;" so much to show the mild, complaisant gentleman! ...... I went to the Manufactory where we made a board, but before business, Thomas Tillbury spoke and behaved himself very wrathful and rude in his expressions, because it had been urged by some of the managers, that none of us, while in that station, should engage and set up a manufactory for themselves, but if they had concluded so to do, they should have informed the other managers and declined acting as manager in this, from that time. This was the cause of his rancor and ill-will, which, at last I found, was chiefly levelled at me, because I had insisted on the impropriety of serving two masters, self and this manufactory, &c., &c. Came home past nine, T. Tillbury going away very wrathful before eight.

25. Paid Crugillus Vanzening 48s. for hauling twenty-four cords of wood; paid Jonat. Malsbary for twenty-four cords of wood, at 12s. 9d., and cording £15 10s. Paid Robert Tompkins 51s. 3d. for three cords of wood, at 11s. 6d., cording and hauling, &c., &c. Paid for carrying and piling the said wood, with rum, &c., &c., &c., 40s.[1]

26. At five, I went to the Coffee House, being called there to meet the sub-committee on account of Isaac Hunt's case, and, after some conference, agreed to meet at said place next Second Day morning, at nine o'clock. ...... For several material pieces of news respecting Gloucester at Cape Ann, and the Asia man-of war's firing on New York, see *Evening Post*, Numb. 93, &c.

28. At nine, I went to [the] Coffee House, met the Committee respecting Isaac Hunt; went away at

---

[1] These accounts were in Pennsylvania Currency. $2.66⅔ made a Pound.

eleven. ...... After dinner went with William Rush to Kensington, to see the gondola launched.

29. Past eleven, went to [the] Committee Room at [the] Coffee House, in order to enquire, with my other brethren, into the conduct of Captain Clay, who had brought in with him two officers as passengers of whom he had made no report to the Committee, before they were gone from this city to New York. Upon hearing what he had to offer, and finding things not clear in his favor, it was referred over to the weekly meeting this evening. ...... At near seven, went to the Committee Room; stayed there till past ten.

SEPTEMBER 1. Wagons loaded with flour and flaxseed almost constantly passing for this week past, in order to ship off.

6. For sundry public occurrences, respecting damage by [the] storm last week, and other pieces of news, see *Pennsylvania Journal*, Numb. 1708. Between eleven and twelve this forenoon, about thirty of our associators waited upon and conducted Isaac Hunt from his dwelling to the Coffee House, where having placed him in a cart, he very politely acknowledged he had said and acted wrong, for which he asked pardon of the public and committed himself under the protection of the associators, to defend him from any gross insults from the populace. This, his behavior, they approved him, and conducted him in that situation, with drum beating, through the principal streets, he acknowledging his misconduct in divers places. But as they were coming down town, stopping at the corner where Dr. Kearsley lives, to make his declaration, it's said the Dr. threw open his window, snapped a pistol twice amongst the crowd, upon which they seized him, took his pistol, with another in his pocket from him, both of which were loaded with swan shot. In the scuffle, he got wounded in the hand. They then took Hunt out of the cart, conducted him safe home, put Kearsley in,

brought him to [the] Coffee House, where persuasions were used to cause him to make concessions, but to no effect. They then, with drum beating, paraded the streets round the town, then took him back to his house and left him there, but as the mob were prevented by the associators, who guarded him, from tarring and feathering, yet after the associators were gone, they then broke the windows and abused the house, &c.

8. Past eleven went to the Committee at [the] Coffee House; stayed till one. It appeared there in conversation, that Samuel Rhoads, mayor, had on the sixth instant, called upon Major Bayard and Captain ———, to order out their battalion, in order to disperse the people assembled at the Coffee House on the said day,[1] &c., &c.

9. This being the day appointed by the Congress for the shipping to depart this port, it's been a busy time with many of the merchants to complete their loading, but with their steady application and industry, they have complied with it, and it's computed that about forty sail went down with this evening's ebb.

13. After my wife came from Market (she went past 5), she ordered her girl, Poll, to carry the basket with some necessaries to the place, as she was coming after her, they intending to iron the clothes. Poll accordingly went, set down the basket, came back, went and dressed herself all clean, short calico gown, &c., said she was going to school, but presently after, the negro woman, Dinah, came to look for her, her mistress having mistrusted she had a mind to play truant. This was about nine; but madam took her walk, but where, she is not come back to tell.

16. I arose before six, as I was much concerned to see my wife so afflicted on the bad conduct, as before, of her girl, Poll, who is not yet returned, but is skulking and running about town. This, I understand, was the

---

[1] See entry of October 3d.

practice of her mother, who, for many years before the death, was a constant plague to my wife, [and] who left her this girl as a legacy, and who, by report, as well as by my own knowledge for almost three years, has been always so, down to this time ...... About eight, word was brought that Poll was just taken by sister Lynn, near the market, and brought to their house. A messenger was immediately despatched for [her,] as she could not be found before, although a number of times they had been hunting her. Brought home, I suppose, about ten.

18. As I went down town, called at [the] Coffee House, an express being arrived from Ticonderoga ...... Thence to my son's, and spent some time with Samuel and John Adams; from there, I called at Christopher Gadsden's lodgings, spent some little time with him; from there to the place and drank balm tea with my wife. Came home about dark, and spent the evening there.

19. Some of our militia, in number ——, with —— wagons, money, and coarse clothing, set out for the camp, near Boston, commanded by Major Cooks and Capt. Cowperthwaite ...... At two, I went to [the] manufactory by invitation, to consult with some of the managers respecting the employment of three, (it's said) complete spinners on the machine and cotton weavers, &c. &c.

20. Past three went to the place, where Samuel Adams, Governor Ward, John Adams and Christopher Gadsden and son came, drank coffee, and spent the afternoon in free conversation.

21. Went to the manufactory, where was a full board of managers. Business went on with temper and good humor, as Mr. Tillbury was absent.

25. Past ten, went to meet [the] sub-committee at [the] Coffee House, where fifteen of the vendue masters attended, and were qualified agreeably to the resolve made by [the] Committee.

27. Past eleven, went to [the] Committee Room, at [the] Coffee House; from there, went with last night's resolves to the Congress at the State House, in company with John Benezet.

28. About one, went down to [the] wharf to see the gondolàs sail by, the delegates being aboard, with a great number of others. Two of them, about Masters' wharf, each carried away a mast.

OCTOBER 1. From New York, of Sept. 28th, "There is a report in town that two thousand Canadians have posted themselves between St. John's and Montreal, to cut off the communication between the town and Carlton's garrison."

2. After breakfast, went to [the] State House. Election began past ten.

3. Yesterday were chosen the following persons, Representatives for this county, Joseph Parker, 3077 votes; John Dickinson, 3122; Michael Hillegas, 3111; George Gray, 3107; Thomas Potts, 3103; Samuel Mills, 3098; Robert Morris, 1882; Jonathan Roberts, 1700. Sheriffs, William Dewees, 2985; John Bull, 1602. Coroners, Robert Jewell, 2213; William Moulder, 1602. Past three, I went to [the] State House. Election for two burgesses then-about was begun. I stayed there till near five. ...... N. B. Samuel Powell was elected Mayor this day in the room of Samuel Rhoads.

4. Yesterday were elected Burgesses for this City, Benjamin Franklin, 775 votes; Thomas Mifflin, 724 votes. ...... This afternoon, Benjamin Franklin, Thomas Lynch and Benjamin Harrison, three of the delegates, set out for Boston, being appointed to the service of consulting and advising with the gentlemen in the Provincial army. ...... This day arrived, Ship Aurora, Capt. Reed, from London, as did the Ship Clementine, Capt. Brown, from Scotland, and Ship King of Prussia, Capt. Potts, from Rotterdam. The two last with passengers.

6. About six, was called to [the] Committee Room, where were twenty-nine members, some of whom by information had been down to Chester after some letters which they were informed were going to England, in the possession of Christopher Carter, who had been partner with —— Spikeman, in Market Street, which said person they found, and then recovered [the letters] by threats of detaining and bringing him up to town, and after recovering said letters, in two parcels, one of them directed to Thomas Corbyn, and the other to Mrs. McCalla, and taking his qualification to the whole of them, and of whom and by whom he received them, they then discharged him, and brought the letters, which were now read, and as they appeared to be base and cruel invectives against the liberties of America, and calculated by wicked men to inflame the minds of the people in England against the Colonies in general, it was directed that three of the authors be immediately taken into custody, which was immediately put into practice by securing Dr. Kearsley, James Brooks, and Leonard Snowden (a Quaker), brewer in Pemberton Street, and they were confined under a guard in the State House until next morning. A seal was also put on the Doctor's desk, and a guard placed at his house. All this done by eleven o'clock. N. B. James Brooks was taken up at the Doctor's, and Snowden at the Doctor's street door.

7. Notices called the Committee to meet at ten. According I went and met them, there being about seventy members. After some time being met, report was made that there was reason to apprehend that there was a great number of inimical letters on board the snow Patty, bound to London, upon which a sub-committee was sent down in a pilot boat to examine and bring them all up that were suspected, and also all persons on board that were suspected. This being done, a resolve was brought in by three of the Committee of Safety from

the Congress, dated the sixth instant, ordering that all suspected persons that were found to act inimical to the rights and liberties of America that fell under our discussing and notice, should by us be delivered over for trial of their offences to the Committee of Safety, they only being invested with that power and not we — we having no right to hear or determine any case of that kind.

This produced a warm debate for some time, and, at length, upon motion seconded, whether the present papers, relating to Kearsley, Brooks, Snowden and Ordale (Minister of Burlington in the Jerseys), should, by a Committee appointed, be carried to the Committee of Safety for their sole judgment and determination, the same motion was carried by a majority of the whole, except one and myself. Past two, the Committee broke up.

8. About two, was brought to town, Christopher Carter with a number of letters from on board the brig Black Prince. He was put into prison, where the three before mentioned[1] were sent by the Committee of Safety, last night, till further examination.

9. Went at ten o'clock to the Committee at the Philosophical; stayed till twelve, in which meeting, fifteen members were chosen to assist the Committee of Safety in the trials of Dr. Kearsley, Leonard Snowden, J. Brooks, [and] Christopher Carter, whose trials then came on before the Committee of Safety and those fifteen members, at the Lodge Room, and continued till just dark before finished ...... N. B. The four persons before mentioned were conveyed from prison and back there again by a guard of associators, not less than fifty, with drums, fifes, &c., &c.

10. Dr. Young called at my house, requesting me to endeavor to collect a small supply for Mrs. Cleamuns, a woman driven from Boston with several children, whom

---

[1] Kearsley, Brooks, and Snowden.

they purposed to send and settle for the present amongst a set of his friends near Albany, if a small contribution could be made here for her, so as to convey her there, and to help her a little at first settling down. I accordingly set out and waited upon some who threw in their mites.

11. Past ten, I went out collecting for Mrs. Cleamuns, and collected, yesterday and to-day, with my own mite, the sum of £3 2s. 6d. which I paid unto herself. ...... Ship ———, Capt. Robison, arrived from London, brought account that Richard Penn was arrived at London, who carried the Congress's petition to the King, but that it was not delivered when he sailed, but was to be in a few days after.

12. At six went to the manufactory; stayed there till near nine. We were pleasant and agreeable, as sundry humorsome spirits were present. ...... For sundry pieces of news, see *Evening Post*, Numb. 113.

14. Took a walk down town and spent some time, viewing two of the gondolas. ...... We have had many fears for a day or two past, respecting a piece of news from Boston, how that on the fourth instant, had sailed from there, a fleet, consisting of one sixty-four, and one twenty-gun ship, two sloops of eighteen guns, and two transports, with six hundred men — their destination a profound secret, but that they had taken on board two mortars and four howitzers, with other artillery fitting for bombardment of a town. This, we thought, might be to visit us.

17. Near six, went to [the] Committee Room (Society Hall); came away past nine. In that time a petition from the privates, requesting this Committee's assistance respecting the General Association recommended by the last Assembly and adopted by the Congress. Upon motion, a Committee of nine were appointed to meet to-morrow, consider and prepare a draught by way of petition to the Assembly, now sitting,

to enforce that resolve, but first to present it to this Committee, who are to meet the nineteenth, at this room, to consider the contents. At said time, a motion that a petition be also presented to the Assembly, praying them to take the saltpetre works into their care. The same was then written, read and approved of, signed by George Clymer, Chairman, and delivered to Joseph Parker, to present to-morrow.

18. Near twelve, went to the Committee Room, at the Coffee House, being on the committee for settling the conditions of security for vessels taking provisions from one colony to another.

19. Near six, I went to [the] Committee Room at [the] Society's Hall, where news was brought by —— West, of the Jerseys, that a Transport ship was stranded at Brigantine Beach, near Egg Harbor, that some of the men had come on shore, said she was from Boston, and that, on her stranding, they had thrown all her gunpowder and small arms overboard. Now as this account was imperfect, the committee proposed sending an express directly, but Major Cox and Captain Ash proposing to go, if agreeable, their proposal was readily accepted of, and although it rained hard, and [was] very dark, yet they intended to set off immediately, in order to send back a true account, and if needful, to stay and assist that part of the country.

20. James Cannon visited me this morning, respecting a petition the Committee of privates intended to send to the Assembly. I gave as my judgment that no time should be lost, as I was apprehensive that the Assembly might soon adjourn, in order to prevent any application to them respecting a General Militia Law.

24. Near six this morning, Dr. Kearsley and James Brooks, under a guard of eight of the Light Horse, left this City for the different jails allotted them in this Province. ...... To Ashton's Ferry, as fifteen, called recruits of Gage's army, that were on board the ship stranded in

the Jerseys were brought, under an escort of the Jersey militia, and delivered to ours here, who took them to our prison. ...... Past two, went and met part of [the] Committee at [the] Coffee House; from there went in a body to Carpenters' Hall, in order to attend the funeral of Peyton Randolph (who had departed suddenly, after dinner, last First Day, at the country house of Richard Hills); then proceeded to Christ's Church, where a sermon was preached by Jacob Duché; then to Church Burial Ground.

25. At three, went to [the] Committee at Society Hall, being on the appointment of twelve members, to hear and examine Captain Hastings, and the mate of the ship Rachel and Francis, which was stranded at Brigantine Beach on her voyage from Boston to New York, respecting her cargo.

28. About three, went down town; called at John Lynn's; from there to Benja. Marshall's; stayed till near six in company with John Hancock and lady, Samuel and John Adams, [Thomas] Cushing, [Eliphalet] Dyer, Treat Paine, [John] Langdon, Silas Deane, and another delegate not known to me; drank coffee there; from thence, through the rain to the manufactory, by appointment, to consider a memorial to present to the Assembly.

29. Near six in the evening, went to meet the Committee at the Philosophical Hall, being called to attend by ticket from the Chairman, in order to consider a "Memorial presented by the People called Quakers" on the twenty-seventh instant, to the Assembly now sitting. This Committee accordingly met (present seventy-two members) and, without one dissenting member, agreed that the said Memorial should be counteracted. Agreeably thereto, a Committee of seven members, to wit, McKean, Clymer, Smith, Jones, Delany, Wilcox and Matlack, were appointed to prepare a draught for that purpose, to be brought to this Committee to-morrow

evening at six o'clock, for their approbation, in order to be presented to the Assembly the thirty-first instant, in the morning.

30. At six, went to meet [the] Committee at [the] Philosophical Hall, by ticket, where the Remonstrance to the Assembly in opposition to the one presented by the Friends, was read and approved of by the whole body that was there met, being seventy-four members, and we were ordered to meet in a body at this house, and so proceed to present it to the Assembly to-morrow morning at nine o'clock.

31. Just before nine, went to meet the Committee at the Philosophical Hall. At ten, went, two by two, being sixty-six in number, to the State House. Our chairman, George Clymer, and Mr. McKean presented our Petition to the Speaker of the House, who ordered it to be read while we were all present, which was done accordingly.

NOVEMBER 1. Near twelve took a walk to [the] Committee Room at [the] Coffee House; came back near one, having come to a resolution by the sub-committee then met to request the Chairman to call the Committee this evening, in order to know why the arms ordered to be made last June, were not done, nor yet set about, and strictly to inquire who is guilty of that omission. ...... Yesterday arrived the King's Proclamation, dated London, 23d of August, 1775, wherein he has declared all the Colonies to be in open rebellion, and therein includes all his subjects within his realm that hold or maintain any correspondence with us by any ways. This day, authenticated accounts were brought of the burning and destroying of the town of Falmouth,¹ consisting of between three and four hundred houses, by the man-of-war, which, it's said, fired three thousand balls into it, which set it a fire.

3. Account just brought by express, of the surrender

---
¹ Now Portland, Maine.

of Fort Chamblee to Major Brown, on the Fourteenth of October, in which was a great quantity of ammunition, provisions, warlike stores, &c., with the colors of the Seventh Regiment or Royal Scotch Fusileers, which were brought to the Congress.

6. Near five, son Benjamin accompanied me to Col. Hancock's lodgings, in order to see the ensigns or colors taken at Fort Chamblee; found him and his lady at home, spent an hour or two with him very agreeably.

7. Came back at one. News just brought, by the way of Fairfield, of the taking of St. John's Fort by storm, with the loss of two hundred Provincials.

13. This morning, set out from this city for Canada, Robert Treat Paine, Thomas Lynch [and] Philip Livingston.

15. Yesterday [an] express arrived, with the account of the surrender of the Fort of St. John's, on the Third instant.

17. Account just brought of four vessels' being just taken by our friends at the eastward; one ship loaded with wood and hay, two with live stock, viz., cattle, sheep, hogs, geese, turkeys, ducks, &c., and some hay. One was a brig stranded, out of which were taken to the camp, one hundred and eighteen pipes of Madeira wine. It's said that this belonged to Philadelphia.

21. In company with Sampson Levy, Thomas Combs, and my son Benjamin, we viewed the inside of the new prison;[1] thence into Chestnut Street, to view the arrival of Lady Washington, who was on her journey to Cambridge, to her husband. She was escorted into the City from Schuylkill Ferry, by the Colonel and other officers, and light infantry of the Second Battalion, and the company of Light Horse, &c.

24. After dinner, as I had heard some threats thrown out, that if the ball assembled this night, as it was pro-

---

[1] Corner of Walnut and Sixth Streets.

posed, they presumed that the New Tavern would cut but a poor figure to morrow morning, these fears of some commotion's being made that would be very disagreeable at this melancholy time, in disturbing the peace of the City, I concluded, if possible, to prevent, in order to which, I went to Col. Hancock's lodgings, and finding he was not come from Congress, and the time grew short, being three o'clock, I walked up to the State House, in expectation of meeting him. That failing, I requested the door-keeper to call Samuel Adams, which he accordingly did, and he came. I then informed him of the account received of a ball, that was to be held this evening, and where, and that Mrs. Washington and Col. Hancock's wife were to be present, and as such meetings appeared to be contrary to the Eighth Resolve of Congress, I therefore requested he would give my respects to Col. Hancock, desire him to wait on Lady Washington to request her not to attend or go this evening. This he promised. Thence I went and met the Committee at the Philosophical Hall, which was large and respectable, being called together for this purpose only to consider the propriety of this meeting or ball's being held this evening in this city, at the New Tavern, where, after due aud mature consideration, it was then concluded, there being but one dissenting voice (Sharp Delany), that there should be no such meeting held, not only this evening, but in future, while these troublesome times continued, and a Committee was appointed, immediately to go to inform the directors of this meeting, not to proceed any further in this affair, and also to wait upon Lady Washington, expressing this Committee's great regard and affection to her, requesting her to accept of their grateful acknowledgment and respect, due to her on account of her near connection with our worthy and brave General, now exposed in the field of battle in defence of our rights and liberties, and request and desire her not to grace that company, to which, we are informed, she has an invitation this evening, &c., &c. Came home near six. After I drank coffee, I went down to Samuel Adams's lodgings, where was Col. Dyer. Spent some time pleasantly, until Col. Harrison came to rebuke Samuel Adams for using his influence for the stopping of this entertainment, which he declared was legal, just and laudable. Many arguments were used by all present to convince him of the impropriety at this time, but all to no effect; so, as he came out of humor, he so returned, to appearance.

25. At half past eleven, went to the Committee Room at the Coffee House; came away near two. At this time, Major Bayard, one of the four gentlemen appointed to wait on Lady Washington, reported that they had acted agreeably to directions, that the lady received them with great politeness, thanked the Committee for their kind care and regard in giving such timely notice, requesting her best compliments to be returned to them for their care and regard, and to assure them that their sentiments on this occasion, were perfectly agreeable unto her own.

27. About ten, Lady Washington, attended by the troop of horse, two companies of light infantry, &c., &c., left this City, on her journey to the camp, at Cambridge.

30. Near nine, called by invitation at Paul Fooks's, he having illuminated for the taking of Montreal.

DECEMBER 10. As to public occurrences, I refer to the weekly papers which I take, and [as] to what passes worthy of notice in sub-committee, the minutes of that board will relate, as will the minutes of the General Committee, and the minutes of the American Manufactory, to which records I refer the inquisitive. I acknowledge now, the receiving, a few days past, sundry presents from my friend Paul Fooks, viz., a neat window-blind for my library room, two quarts of old French brandy, and a plate of choice red herrings.

21. Within a few days past, arrived several small

cargoes of gunpowder, Capt.———, fifteen hundred weight; Captain Walter Stevens, six hundred and eighty pounds, forty-nine muskets, thirteen silver handled hangers; two schooners, Rebecca, Captain Farey, the Ranger, Capt. Cruse, both from Eustatia, twenty-three hundred pounds of powder in fourteen half barrels, and sixty-six quarter barrels, twenty-four neat swivel guns, and one hogshead of different sized pistols. ...... Near four, went to meet some of [the] Committee members at Major Morgan's, in order to see to settle the price for some powder, and the twenty-four swivel guns.

23. Lent Dr. Young an octavo volume, *Salmon's Collection and Paraphrase, on the Works of the Philosophers, Geber and Hermas,* No. 97.

26. For public news, see *Dunlap's General Advertiser,* Numb. 218.

29. After dinner (half after one), went to the Carpenters' Hall to meet as many of the subscribers to the American Manufactory of Wool, Cotton, Flax, &c., as were pleased to attend, in order to settle sundry affairs relating to the said company. Came away from there about six.

30. For public occurrences, see *Pennsylvania Ledger,* Numb. 49.

31. Sundry pieces of news last night in the *Evening Post,* Numb. 147.

1776.

JANUARY 3. News brought to-day of a skirmish between the Pennsylvanians and the Connecticut people[1] in which Jesse Lukens was killed.

6. At four, went to meet [the] Committee at [the Philosophical Hall (per notice sent). The business was to enquire respecting the conduct of Parson Smith and Tench F......, they having, as reported, spoken and acted very disrespectfully of the Congress and all our

---

[1] In the Wyoming country, then claimed by both provinces.

proceedings. John M......, who was [present] and had given notice of said Smith's conduct, being called upon, used such equivocal and unmeaning expressions, beneath the dignity of a member of society, much less a member of this Committee and of Safety, in order to exculpate the said Smith, that no hold could, at present, be taken of him. The other was put off till next Third [day] evening, and six members appointed to make enquiry respecting his and other persons' proceedings in the prosecuting of the contest at Wyoming ...... News brought this evening of three tons of gunpowder arrived at Egg Harbor or Cape May, thirty-nine tons near the camp, and six tons at New York.

7. It's said, an express arrived from Rhode Island on the Fifth instant to the Monthly Meeting of Friends in this City, the contents of which has induced their members to sit pretty constant for these two days past. What they may hatch or bring forth, Time will make manifest. By yesterday's post, [a] letter from [the] camp before Quebec, dated [the] sixth of last month, gives an account that Gen. Montgomery had joined Col. Arnold with some artillery and about three thousand men; that our men were in high spirits, and were now well clothed with the regimentals destined for the seventh and twenty-sixth regiments, which were taken at Fort St. John's; that they were making preparations to attack the enemy, who are in close garrison, but, it's thought, could not hold out long, as they intended, after they had summoned them to surrender and they refused, immediately to endeavor to take it by a general storm. See *Evening Post*, Numb. 150.

8. This morning arrived, *via* New York, the King's Speech to both houses of Parliament, 27th of October, 1775; also, account of three hundred large barrels of gunpowder landed not far from New York to the Eastward ...... This afternoon, news came of the Schooner, Charming Polly's arrival at Chester, with sixty tons of

saltpetre and Sloop Trial with one thousand pounds of powder.

9. At breakfast, I was visited by Paul Fooks's housekeeper, who informed that their boy, Neal, had heard his sister Rosanna Thompson, who lived at [Richard] Bache's, [say] that James Brattle, servant man to James Duane, one of [the New] York delegates, was employed by Governor Tryon, to collect and send him all the news he could find, on board the Asia, for which he should be well rewarded and also be preferred to some post, in consequence of which, he had written to him, and in particular the day our fleet sailed with their number, &c. On this information, I called upon some of our Committee at [the] Coffee House. Joseph Dean went with me, but could gain nothing. We returned. Then John Bayard went with me to Joseph Reed's : he not at home ; thence to see him at [the] Committee of Safety : not there ; thence to [the] Court House ; found him. After taking his advice, went to Hall's[1] Printing Office ; took [Richard] Bache home with us ; called his maid ; examined her. She seemed confounded, but, on the whole, denied it. From thence to [the] Coffee House, where consulting Major Cox, he joined us two. We went to [the] State House ; called out Mr. Duane ; informed him ; he seemed confounded ; requested us to attend him to his house. We did. He called his man, examined him, took him up stairs and made search, all to no purpose. We then went, took him with us to Paul Fooks's ; examined the boy who persisted. We brought the boy back to the Duane's lodgings ; sent for the young woman, who, upon seeing her brother, confessed that what he had said was true. James was called and interrogated, but all to no purpose. Then Major Cox and Mr. Duane took him up stairs again, and while they were employed in that business, he slipped down stairs, out through the

---

[1] Hall was first the partner, afterwards the successor of Franklin, in the printing business.

yard, and [they] have seen no more of him. Major Bayard and myself waited for them in the parlor. Thus he escaped.

13. Went to Bell's; bought a pamphlet called *Common Sense*.

15. By the New York Post, which arrived Seventh Day night, at nine o'clock, account that Admiral Shuldam was arrived, and five hundred fresh troops at Boston, from Ireland. The regiments were the fifty-fifth and seventeenth; that two regiments had gone to Halifax, and two had pushed into the River St. Lawrence to try for Quebec. An account, by a deserter from Boston, on the Third instant, was that a fleet consisting of nine transports, with three hundred and sixty men, was ready to sail under convoy of the Scarborough and Fowey men-of-war, with two bomb vessels and flat bottomed boats, said to be for Newport, Long Island, or Virginia; and that five thousand militia had joined General Washington, and taken the places of those soldiers who would not stay beyond their time of service; that they were good troops, and the whole army impatient for an opportunity of action.

17. Near seven, Christopher Gadsden, and son came to take their leave, they being to embark for South Carolina to-morrow.

18. Yesterday arrived an account of our forces' attempting to take Quebec, but repulsed with the loss of Gen. Montgomery, and some more officers of note, upon which the Provincial troops were immediately drawn off, but as the accounts at present remain uncertain as to the particulars, we are impatiently waiting for substantial accounts from that quarter.

20. In the evening, met a few friends of America at Fountain Tavern, in Chestnut Street, in order to consult and consider of proper persons to be elected Committee men at the next election in this City for that purpose, as the time of this Committee expires the Sixteenth of

next month. From there, I visited some of the delegates, with Silas Deane, Col. Floyer, and the two new ones from Connecticut.

22. About nine, I went to meet [the] Committee at [the] Philosophical Hall, by summons, in order to answer the request of Congress, which was to make application to the inhabitants of this City and Liberties, for a number of blankets to enable the battalions who are under orders to march for Canada, as none were to be purchased in the stores. This request was immediately complied with, and the members formed themselves into companies accordingly and set out on the business.

23. Cold morning. Snow fell in the night. Went past eleven to [the] Committee Room; came home before one; took a walk to the barracks, as Capt. Dorsey's company marched out of town with their baggage this forenoon. ...... Near six, went to [the] Committee Room at [the] Philosophical Hall. Came away about nine. It was there concluded to break the lock that F...... and Sons had put upon their store door, take out their goods and sell them to-morrow at public vendue, the which I would have the Committee of Safety do, but it was overruled.

24. After dinner took a walk down town to see our floating battery, man-of-war, &c.; came home; then went to John Bayard's vendue.

25. Past nine, went to [the] Committee Room, at [the] Philosophical Hall, by notices, in order to consider of ways and means to provide arms for some of the marching companies for Quebec.

26. Went to [the] Committee Room at [the] Philosophical Hall, by call per ticket; left it at twelve, it being to consult who should be nominated as Burgess, in the room of Thomas Mifflin, at camp. Two were proposed, viz., Joseph Reed and George Clymer, but the first was, by vote, carried to be put. ...... At ——, went to the State House with my ticket.

27. Joseph Reed, our Chairman, [was] elected yesterday one of our Burgesses, in the room of Thomas Mifflin, resigned.

28. Notwithstanding the severe cold weather for some days past, yet several companies of our First Battalion have marched from town for Canada. By the Post, last evening, we learn that two large transports, laden with provisions and ammunition, bound for Boston from England, are taken and carried into Newburyport.

30. After five, went to the Committee Room, Philosophical Hall; came away past nine. ...... At this meeting, complaint was made against John Drinker, hatter, for refusing taking Continental money, who, being sent for, acknowledged he did, and that in point of conscience, he refused it, upon which he was to be censured agreeably to the resolve of Congress published [January 11th, 1776], but to be referred for one week, in order for him to consider well of it.[1]

31. Near six, went to [the] Committee Room at [the] Philosophical Hall, being called by ticket. At this meeting, Thomas and —— Fisher were sent for, upon a complaint of their refusing the Continental Money, to which complaint they made no objection, by acknowledging the complaint to be just and true, and said that from conscience's sake, they could not take it in future; upon which they were ordered to be censured in the public papers next week.

FEBRUARY 2. After dinner, spent some time writing something by way of Address to the Congress, to be laid before the sub-committee, this evening, for approbation, at the Coffee House Room. ...... Went and spent till near nine in conversation with Samuel Adams.

---

[1] Congress ordained that persons refusing to receive the Continental Bills of Credit, or who should obstruct and discourage the currency and circulation thereof, should, on conviction, be deemed, published and treated as enemies of the country, and be precluded from all trade or intercourse with the inhabitants of the Colonies.

3. At eleven, went to Thomas Lawrence's; signed the Remonstrance, to have it presented to Congress, but as they had adjourned to Monday, it was referred to be presented then. This morning, Capt. Mason arrived in town, having left his brig, loaded with arms, ammunition [and] saltpetre, off the Cape.

6. News brought of General Clinton's arrival at Governor's Island, near New York, with six hundred men and two men-of-war, and also of General Lee at New York, with fifteen hundred men.

13. After dinner, I went to the State House Yard to see the volunteers for New York turn out of each of the four battalions of the Associators.

15. This afternoon, came account of Gen. Clinton with the transports' sailing from New York and the Narrows. This prevented our Battalion of Volunteers from going hence to New York.

16. Past six, went to [the] State House; gave my vote for Committee men.

19. Near ten, went to [the] Philosophical [Hall]; met the Committee; went from there to [the] State House. Past eleven, joined and went in procession with Congress, Assembly, Committee of Safety, Corporation, &c., to the Calvanist Church in Race Street, where a funeral sermon was delivered by Dr. Smith, on the death of Gen. Montgomery.

22. Paid 3*d.* poor tax for the Northern Liberties.

23. Past one, went to son Charles's and dined with Governors Hopkins and Ward, Silas Deane, Col. Lewis, Mr. Brown, Badcock, Paul Fooks, and a stranger. After dinner, spent the afternoon in conversation; drank coffee there; I then went to Col. Hancock's lodgings; stayed some time with him and his spouse. I then went and met the Managers of the Prison Society[1] at Armitage's came away past nine.

---

[1] The Society for alleviating the miseries of prisoners.

26. Half past eight, went to [the] Coffee House by appointment from [the] General Committee; met Hoar, Mead, and Matlack; after agreeing upon [a] Memorial to Congress, went with [it] to James Searle's, he being one appointed; found him at home poorly. After all signing the Remonstrance, the three before mentioned and myself waited upon Col. Hancock and delivered it to him, to present to Congress. ...... Took a walk to see the battalions. ...... Past seven, went to Samuel and John Adams's lodgings; stayed till past nine.

28. Went to [the] Committee Room at [the] Philosophical Hall and met Committee, by ticket, in order to procure a Convention to be called, the which, after some debates, was agreed to, but the mode of doing it was referred to a meeting to be called to-morrow evening.

29. At past five, went to the Committee Room, Philosophical Hall; came away past eight; at which the time for the Convention's being called was concluded, viz., the Second of April next, to meet in this City.

MARCH 2. To [the] State House, they being choosing a Burgess in the room of B. Franklin.[1]

4. Spent the afternoon at home, chiefly writing till five o'clock, when [I] went to meet [the] Committee at [the] Philosophical Hall (called by notices), in order to take into consideration the Report of the Committee of Correspondence respecting the propriety of suspending the calling of the Provincial Convention for a few days in order to see the event of sundry petitions now before the House of Assembly. Accordingly, the suspension was agreed to.

5. My wife rose early in order to attend her servants at the place. Fine pleasant morning, but gloomy wind, southwardly. Breakfasted alone. Visited by William Clifton and William Bradford; invited to attend the sub-committee at ten this forenoon, at [the] Coffee

---

[1] David Rittenhouse was elected.

House, in order to consider of the powder, saltpetre and arms brought yesterday in brig Hannah, Capt. James Neale, from Holland.

6. Near seven, went to the Committee Room, called by ticket to consider means to prevent the high prices of sundry kinds of goods, viz., Rum, Sugar, Molasses, Coffee, Pepper, Salt, Cocoa, Chocolate, &c. Came home past ten, after passing sundry resolves.

9. After five, went to [the] Coffee House; stayed there till after the fight of —— Carson and Price in the street, first with sticks, then with fists, but parted. Past seven, the fire-flat was set fire to, which answered the purpose to admiration of the persons present, which were a great number collected on that occasion before the Coffee House and down to the wharf. From thence went to the Committee Room at Philosophical Hall, called by notices to consult and consider the most expeditious way to collect hard money to send to Canada. The Committee, taking it into consideration, concluded to meet in each several district next Second Day at nine, and there appoint sub-committees to go through the City and try what sum they can exchange Continental money for into gold and silver for that service. From there, walked down Market Street to Front, and found the raft still burning. It was said it burned till one in the morning. This afternoon came to town, the Prussian General, as he is called, from the camp.

13. After dinner, went to Dr. Young's. Stayed there hearing him read a piece as answer to Common Sense, called Plain Truth, but very far from coming up to the title. ...... Examined Cassandra's answer to Cato's two letters in *Hall and Seller's Gazette* this week, No. 2464.[1]

15. Paid —— Bright, 3s. 10d. for lamp and watch tax. Past five, went to James Cannon's. Drank

---

[1] The Essays of Cassandra, which, I learn, were highly esteemed, were written by James Cannon.

coffee there with Timothy Matlack; stayed in conversation till near seven. (Dr. Smith said these words in the presence of James Davidson, Timothy Matlack and Cannon — That Great Britain would mortgage America for as much money as would enable her to conquer it.)

17. For sundry pieces of material news, see *Evening Post*, No. 180.

18. After dinner, went down to Samuel and John Adams's lodgings; not at home; I left there with the maid the works of George Stonehouse, neatly bound and lettered, viz., *Universal Restitution, Scripture Doctrine, &c., Universal Restitution further defended, &c., Christ's Temptations Real Facts, &c.*, as a present. From there I went and visited Governor Ward, in the small pox. ...... Near seven, went by appointment to meet eleven of the sub-committee, who with me had before valued, at Jacob Winey's six hundred and ninety-four guns, bayonets, gunpowder, &c., the which said Winey now objected to, when after hearing his objections we confirmed our former settlement, to wit, that, the Committee of Secrecy pay the sum of £3 15*s*. per piece, when they are put in proper order by the Commissary, and buy the cannon powder, at £17 10*s*. per cwt., provided upon trial it be good. The charge of repairing was what Winey objected to, being £80 5*s*.

20. Went at nine o'clock to meet a Committee by appointment, to draw a Remonstrance to the Assembly, requesting to rescind their directions to our delegates.[1] ...... Then went to Paul Fooks's: stayed some time there with General Baron De Weldke, the Prussian. ...... Near seven, went to [the] Committee Room, Philosophical Hall, called there by summons; came away about nine. At this meeting, Benjamin Sharpless Tanner was complained of [for] refusing the Continental Money. He was sent for, and acknowledged the charge.

---

[1] See *postea*, note to June 8th.

He was requested to think and give his final answer whether he would recant or no, at our next meeting.

23. Down town to see the Province Ship launched.

24. For public occurrences, see *Evening Post*, Numb. 183.

26. This morning, about two o'clock, departed my honored and worthy friend, Governor Ward, by the small pox, which he bore with manly and great patience. His loss will be deplored by all the true friends of liberty in these colonies, who knew his merits. ...... Dined at home with Thomas Paine. ...... We hear, that on the seventeenth instant, about nine in the forenoon, the Ministerial army evacuated Boston, and that the United Colonies are in actual possession of the town, and that they [the British] have left effects by their sudden departure to between Thirty and Forty Thousand Pounds.

27. At three, went to [the] Committee Room at [the] Philosophical, being appointed to meet there in order to go in a body to the funeral of Gov. Ward from his late lodgings in Lodge Alley. We went there and accompanied the corpse to the new building in Arch Street, where an excellent discourse, suitable to the occasion, was delivered by Samuel Stileman. After service, the corpse, in same procession, was carried to the Baptist Meeting House, in which he was interred.

28. News brought of the defeat of the Ministerial party in North Carolina. See *Pennsylvania Journal*.

31. A complete relation of the taking possession of Boston is in the *Evening Post*, Numb. 186.

APRIL 1. About three, went to James Cannon's. Spent good part of this afternoon and evening till eight there, in conversation with Thomas Paine, Dr. Young, James Wigdon and Timothy Matlack. Came away about eight, by the cry of "Fire"; went home; thence up town where the malt house, and new front house of Robert Hare was in flames. Went with Col. Roberdeau to the powder magazine, where a number of us attended with an engine, which played upon the magazine and other huildings adjacent for fear of sparks.

5. Dined at home with James Cannon. We then went to Paine's; stayed some time; thence Cannon and I went to Dr. Young's; not at home. We went up to Kensington; found him and several friends there at work on board the frigate building by Messrs. Eyre. We joined them in assisting what we could till night. Then came home.

6. Near two, set off for Kensington, in order to assist with a number of fellow citizens in getting the lower deck beams on board the frigate building by Messrs. Eyre. I presume there came not short of one hundred, who stayed till they were all put on board (in which were included three parts of the Light Infantry of First Battalion, who came in warlike array). Came away just at dark.

9. Near seven, went to [the] Committe Room at [the] Philosophical Hall; came away before ten; at which meeting, Townsend Spikeman attending, owned he refused and could not take the Continental money. He refusing to appeal, his case was ordered to be published.

11. After dinner, went to Kensington, where a number of inhabitants met, in order to assist in getting the lower deck beams in the ship that was building for man-of-war, by Bruce and Company.

16. News confirmed of our fleet's arrival at New London, and of the arrival of Gen. Washington at New York. Some particulars, See in *Evening Post*, Numb. 193. ...... Near seven, went to [the] Committee Room at [the] Philosophical Hall; came home past ten. Great debate about rescinding the prices some time past affixed to sundry articles by the Committee. This debate arose from a Remonstrance, now presented by sundry citizens.

18. Near seven, went to [the] Committee Room at [the] Philosophical Hall; called by summons, where

the rights and powers of the Committee were discussed
and prove to be invested in them by the votes of Congress and the call and nomination of the people at large,
and that the regulations they had entered into were well
founded. Yet in order to promote peace and harmony
at this time, a vote was passed (contrary to mine and
many others' present approbation) that a Remonstrance
be sent to Congress requesting them to explain some
former Resolves. A Committee was appointed for that
purpose, to draught it and bring it to the next meeting
for approbation. At this meeting, after Committee was
over, many stayed and appointed sixteen members present to confer with the Committee of Privates and the
Patriotic Society, respecting the candidates for Burgesses
on the First of May next. Agreed to meet to-morrow
evening.

19. Near seven, went to William Thorn's school
room, Videll's Alley ; met a number of persons appointed to consult upon persons proper to be returned as
four Burgesses from this City, on the First of May.
Came away past nine, having adjourned to seven to-morrow evening at same place. I was chosen Chairman,
J. Cannon, Secretary.

20. Went thence to James Cannon's. Past seven,
went with him to William Thorn's school room, as by
appointment last night. Came away about ten.

21. Many, I understand, were the private meetings
of those called moderate men (or those who are for reconciliation with Great Britain upon the best terms she
will give us, but by all means to be reconciled to or with
her), in order to consult and have such men carried for
Burgesses at the Election (First of May) as will be sure
to promote, to accept and adopt all such measures.
These are the schemes that are now ardently pursued
by those men.

23. Near eight, I went with J. B. Smith to Col.
Hancock's, to deliver a Remonstrance from the Com-

mittee to Congress (we being appointed for that service), the which he received very politely and promised to perform and favor us with the result of Congress thereon.

25. Went to Jacob Schriner's; met sundry persons there; went thence to the sign of Rotterdam in Third Street; stayed till the ticket was settled for Inspectors, and three persons to put into practice the Resolve of Assembly for disarming Non-Associators. ...... Thence, to meet the Committee at William Thorn's school room, where we concluded and fixed the ticket for four Burgesses, viz., George Clymer, Col. Roberdeau, Owen Biddle [and] Frederick Kuhl, but to be kept a secret from the public till after our next meeting on Second Day night, at that place [at] seven o'clock.

27. Past two, went to Kensington, where a number of persons, not much short of one hundred and fifty, were collected, in order to get the upper deck beams into both the frigates building there. The same, was completed, without any accident's happening, by six in the evening. I then came away with Frederick Kuhl, James Davidson and James Cannon, to whose house I went and drank coffee.

28. After supper, Joseph Lecond and myself took a walk down to Plumstead's wharf, in order to see what readiness the two ships of war were in, as they were under sailing orders, occasioned by an express, arrived about three this afternoon, who left Lewistown about six last night, sent by land from Henry Fisher, giving an account that the man-of-war, the Roebuck, pursuing a vessel, had, that afternoon, run ashore on the Brandywine [shoals] and was then, to appearance, fast. The vessels were nigh ready, as we learned, and would sail in the morning.

May 1. At nine, A.M., went to William Thorn's school room by appointment; from thence to my sons'; thence to [the] Coffee House and so home; from there down to [the] drawbridge; thence to the State House; stayed till one; went in company with Thomas Paine and dined at son Christopher's. Went back to the State House; engaged till past five; then went with James Cannon to his house; drank coffee there; then we returned to the State House; stayed till eight; then I came home, eat supper and went back. Stayed till past ten, the Sheriff having proclaimed to close the poll in half an hour. This has been one of the sharpest contests, yet peaceable, that has been for a number of years, except some small disturbance among the Dutch, occasioned by some unwarrantable expressions of Joseph Swift, viz., that except they were naturalized, they had no more right to a vote than a Negro or Indian; and also, past six, the Sheriff, without any notice to the public, closed the poll and adjourned till nine to-morrow and shut the doors. This alarmed the people, who immediately resented it, flew to the Sheriff and to the doors and obliged him again to open the doors and continue the poll till the time above prefixed. I think it may be said with propriety that the Quakers, Papists, Church, Allen family, with all the Proprietory party, were never seemingly so happily united as at this election, notwithstanding Friends' former protestation and declaration of never joining with that party since the club or knockdown Election. (Oh! tell it not in Gath, nor publish it in the streets of Askalon, how the testimony is trampled upon!) About midnight, casting up the poll, it turned out thus, viz., Samuel Howell, 941; Andrew Allen, 923; George Clymer, 923; Alexander Wilcox, 921; Thomas Willing, 911; Frederick Kuhl, 904; Owen Biddle, 903; and Daniel Roberdeau, 890.[1]

4. Took a walk alone, down to the old fort, viewing the preparations making along the bank of our river, viz.,

---

[1] It thus appears that the Tories and Moderates elected three of their candidates, Messrs. Howell, Allen and Wilcox, the Whigs but one, Mr. Clymer.

fire boats, building frigates, cheveaux de frises, &c. ......
Post from New York this morning. For news, see *Evening Post*, Numb. 201. This day, were executed on our commons, William Bales and James Jones, for street robbery, and John Woodward for the murder of his wife.

5. This day arrived the Brig Lexington from her cruise of —— weeks; she having carried away her foremast in being chased by two King's ships for eight hours, who were convoy to [the] fleet of soldiers (where bound was uncertain). Upon this loss, he prudently returned, passed the man-of-war at our capes, who fired one gun at him, which he returned as he passed her. It's said a French vessel with twenty-four tons of saltpetre [and] thirteen tons of powder, from Port Orient, hearing of the man-of-war at our capes, put into Egg Harbor, and is there safe secured by our people.

6. About twelve, alarmed by account of the men-of-war's coming up. Our alarm gun was fired, the flag hoisted; sundries much alarmed. ...... News just published of forty-five thousand English and Foreign Troops expected to be sent into America.

8. Near two, went to [the] Coffee House; the City alarmed with hearing a great number of heavy cannons firing down the river. The drums beat to arms, and a number of volunteers went down in boats in order to assist, as the report was that the Roebuck, of forty, and the Liverpool of twenty-eight guns, with tenders, were got above New Castle, standing up the river.

9. After dinner, went to [the] Coffee House, where various reports were circulated, how that the Roebuck ran aground, &c., that upon the whole, it appeared that little damage has been sustained on our side, but as no express has arrived this day, we are in suspense. Near five, I went and drank coffee at James Cannon's; afterwards he and I took a walk to the State House Yard. There, we heard the fight was renewed by the constant discharge of heavy cannon.

10. Various accounts of the affair down the river, between the men of war and our gondolas, but nothing that's certain, save our men conducted themselves valiantly, and obliged the men-of-war to fall down below New Castle, being handled very roughly.

11. Little further accounts from below, but agreed that no person was killed or wounded by the enemy, that our officers of six of the gondolas have done their duty with credit, both officers and men having distinguished themselves nobly and gained great reputation. The others not showing the same bravery and resolution, I hope will be enquired strictly into. Great numbers of families have moved out of town this last week.

13. Then back to James Cannon's. Stayed there till past ten, in company with Paul Fooks, Thomas Paine, Dr. Rush, Benjamin Harbeson, Timothy Matlack, James Cannon, &c. Appointed to call upon sundry other persons, to meet to-morrow night, at Burnside's school-room at eight, to take in consideration and to concert a plan necessary to be adopted on the meeting of our Assembly, next Second Day. ...... This afternoon, Col. Thomas Mifflin, in company with his wife and attendants, arrived in town from New York.

14. Went to James Cannon's; spent some time in [the] College Yard with him and a person from Cumberland county, respecting public affairs. ...... At eight, went with Paul Fooks [and] Thomas Paine to Burnside's school room. Met several there agreeably to appointment. Agreed to draw up [the] heads of a Protest to be brought to-morrow night for approbation ...... This day came an account, *via* New York that "the Assembly of Rhode Island in their May sessions have passed an Act absolving the inhabitants of that colony from their allegiance to the King of Great Britain."

15. Part of several pieces of the men-of-war, beat off by our gondolas the other day, was brought to the Coffee House this day. ...... Past seven, went and met a large

number of persons at the Philosophical, by appointment (Col. McKean in the chair), where was debated the resolve of Congress of the fifteenth instant, respecting the taking up and forming new governments in the different colonies. Adjourned, past ten, till three tomorrow at said place.

16. At ten, went to [the] Committee at [the] Philosophical Hall, by appointment, to consider what may be necessary respecting the Quakers on the next Fast Day. The same was maturely considered, and upon the whole, a handbill was ordered to be printed and dispersed, as also to be published in the *Evening Post*, Numb. 26, for all people to refrain from treating any Friend on that day, who should open their shops, with any kind of ill treatment whatever. ...... At four, to the Philosophical Hall, to meet a number of persons, to consider what steps might be necessary to take, on the dissolution of government, as published this day. It was concluded to call a convention with speed; to protest against the present Assembly's doing any business in their House until the sense of the Province was taken in that Convention to be called, &c., with the mode and manner of doing these several things by or on next Second Day. Then adjourned to Seventh Day morning next, at six o'clock. ...... Dispersed a number of handbills, as published this day....... It's said by a letter from New York, that our people had possessed and destroyed part of the lower town of Quebec and made a breach in the walls of the upper town, about the Twenty-third of last month.

17. This day is what was appointed for the Fast to be kept through this Continent. Our neighborhood extremely quiet, observant and composed, in compliance with the resolve of the Honorable Congress, yet there was some noise in some few other parts of the City. ...... Account just brought that one of our small vessels, called the Congress, has taken a prize, carried her into Sandy

Puxton in Virginia, with three hundred half-joes, and that the Commissioners and the Hessians are arrived at Halifax.

18. About nine, the New York post came, brought account by letter from Albany that they had account dated the Fifteenth instant, that our forces raised the siege of Quebec upon the appearance of four men-of-war, leaving all their provisions, a number of cannon and two hundred sick and wounded men. ...... Went about seven to [the] Committee Room at [the] Philosophical Hall. ...... Came away past nine. The call of this meeting was to consider a letter from Joshua F...... and Sons, respecting a load of saltpetre lodged in the Committees' store, it being shipped contrary to resolve of Congress in Dec. 1774, but as their letter now was a Jesuitical contrivance to impose upon the country and deceive the Committee, a true state of the case was ordered to be published. A request was brought to this Committee, from a large company of the City and Liberties, that a general call be made of the inhabitants of the City and Liberties, to meet next Monday at nine o'clock forenoon at the State House, in order to take the sense of the people respecting the resolve of Congress of the Fifteenth instant, the which, after debate, was agreed to, only five dissenting voices.[1]

20. At ten, went to [the] Coffee House, thence to [the] State House Yard, where, it was computed, Four thousand people were met, notwithstanding the rain, and then, sundry resolves were passed unanimously except

---

[1] On the Tenth of May, 1776, it was Resolved by Congress to recommend to the several Assemblies and Conventions of the United Colonies, where no Government sufficient to the exigencies of their affairs had been established, to adopt such a government, as should, in the opinion of the Representatives of the people, best conduce to the happiness and safety of their constituents in particular and of America in general. A preamble to this Resolution, agreed to on the Fifteenth of May, stated the intention to be, totally to suppress the exercise of every kind of authority under the British Crown.

one, and there was one dissenting voice, to wit, Isaac Gray. Near twelve, all was completed quietly and peaceably. ...... Went to [the] Committee Room at [the] Philosophical Hall, where were confirmed the resolves at the State House, and directions, with proper persons appointed to go with the said resolves to the different counties.

22. N. B. Yesterday, arrived in town Major General Gates from New York.

24. Yesterday, about two o'clock P. M., came into [town] from New York, General Washington, as did his lady, the day before. Past ten, went to meet [the] Committee at [the] Philosophical Hall, called by notices. Here was an Address to Congress concluded on, in answer to the Remonstrance that was, or is intended to be, sent from the Assembly, to counteract our proceedings last Second Day at the State House. This was to be delivered as soon as their Remonstrance was read in Congress. This paper or Remonstrance of their's was carried by numbers, two by two, into almost all parts of the town to be signed by all (tag, longtail and bob), and also sent into the country, and much promoted by the Quakers. See the copy in *Evening Post*, Numb. 209.

25. Thence to James Cannon's, who was gone out this morning with Tim. Matlack, Benjamin Harbeson, Lieutenant Chambers [and] William Miles to meet sundry county members at Norrington[1] this afternoon. ...... Account arrived by express of our privateer Franklin's taking and carrying into Boston a store ship of three hundred tons, having seventy-five tons of gunpowder, one thousand stand of arms, &c., &c. See *Evening Post*, Numb. 210.

26. Sundry material advices from England were published in *Pennsylvania Journal*, No. 1746.

27. Past two took a walk on the commons to see the

---

[1] Then in Philadelphia county, now in the county of Montgomery, which was formed in 1784, from the North Western part of Philadelphia county.

review of sundry battalions of militia and the recruits, which were drawn up regularly with the troop of horse and train of artillery. The Generals were Washington (chief), Gates and Mifflin, with the Congress, members of Assembly, a number of clergymen, officers, &c., and a vast concourse of people, with between twenty and thirty of the Indians of the six nations.

28. Past seven, went to the Philosophical Hall and met the Committee there. Joshua F...... and Sons' letter to us, respecting salt, was now referred to Congress for their determination. Three letters were appointed to be written by Committees appointed, viz., one to Cumberland county, one to Philadelphia county, Committees in answer to their's, one to the Managers of the Hospital respecting Thomas F......'s being elected Manager.

30. After dinner, went to James Cannon's. Stopped by the way by Humphrey Marshall. Spent near an hour with him in the street, with two or three of the House of Assembly, on the state of the times. ...... Dr. Young, being returned from Yorktown, came there to see me. ...... Heard his declaration of his expedition, read his letters from the Committee.[1]

31. Past seven, went to the Committee Room at [the] Philosophical Hall; came away past nine, having appointed a Committee to settle the price of salt, find the quantity, &c. Also had sundry letters read from Committee of Yorktown and Lancaster. Went from there to James Cannon's, found a select company of friends of the liberties of America. Stayed and supped.

JUNE 1. Thence to meet [the] Committee at [the] Philosophical Hall, where the prices of salt and teas were settled for the present, and a determination to support the resolve of Congress, dated May 25th, at all

---

[1] Dr. Young appears to have been one of the gentlemen sent into the different counties with the resolves of the town meeting of May 20th. Yorktown or York is the county town of York county, Penn.

hazards. A resolution was come to for presenting a Memorial to the County Court, requesting them to adjourn till the sense of the Province was taken.

2. Visited this forenoon by Paul Fooks, who gave a relation of their meeting last night with seven of the Captains of the Gondolas by appointment, to which I had been invited, and [a] relation of Captain Mugford's death. See *Evening Post*, Numb. 213. ...... In the evening came Robert Whitehill, member for Cumberland, Paul Fooks, John Payne, ... who stayed and supped.

3. Went to [the] Committee Room at [the] Philosophical Hall, past nine, being by notices, to hear the Memorial read, that was ordered to be prepared to present to the Magistrates of the County Court to be held this day. The same was read and approved of, and Col. McKean was requested to present it. From there, sundry of us went to [the] Court House; thence I went to [the] Committee Room at [the] Coffee House, where two vessels with drygoods and some military stores, oil and sugar, were entered, one from St. Martin's, one from Hispaniola.

4. To [the] State House, in order to hear the examination of [the] Committee of Safety and the captains of [the] Gondolas before the Assembly.

5. This morning, General Washington, General Mifflin, Gates, &c., with their Aids de camp, left this city for New York. Past three, I went to Paul Fooks's. He went with me on the commons, where the Third and the Shirt Battalions [1] were exercising.

6. This day arrived, it's said, at Capt. Craig's, in this City, from on board the Privateers Congress and Chance at Egg Harbor, Twenty-two Thousand, Four Hundred and Twenty Dollars [and] one hundred and eighty-seven pounds of plate, taken by them from three Jamaica ships, those Privateers had taken.

---

[1] Probably so called from wearing hunting shirts.

8. This day, fresh instructions were given by our Assembly to their delegates in Congress, Yeas 31, Nays 12.[1] Sundry pieces of intelligence see in *Evening Post*, Numb. 216. This afternoon, came up to town, the ship Juno, Capt Saml. Marston, being one of the prizes taken by two of our Privateers. She was bound from Jamaica to London, with rum, sugar, molasses, &c.

10. Near twelve, went to [the] Committee Room, at [the] Coffee House, where we entered Sloop Sally, from Saint Eustatia, with one thousand and twenty bushels of salt. Came away about one. Just about this time, part of the Fourth Battalion seized a Jew, for mal-practice, cursing the Congress, declaring his willingness to fight against them, &c., &c., but upon their treating him roughly [he] excused himself by informing against Arthur Thomas, a skinner, who, he said, instructed him in those points. Now, as this Thomas was one [who] had been frequently complained of ever since Dr. Kearley's affair, and with whom it's said, he now corresponds, the mob flew to his house. Not finding him as he ran away on their appearance, they wreaked their vengeance on his house, furniture, cash,

---

[1] These fresh instructions rescinded those given in the previous November (to dissent from and utterly reject any proposition that might lead to a separation from Great Britain), and authorized them to "concur with the other Delegates in Congress, in forming such farther compacts between the United Colonies, concluding such treaties with foreign Kingdoms and States, and in adopting such other measures as may be judged necessary for promoting the liberty, safety and interest of America, reserving to the people of this colony the sole and exclusive right of regulating the internal government and police of the same."

The concluding paragraph of these instructions is as follows:

"The happiness of these colonies has, during the whole course of this fatal controversy, been our first wish: their reconciliation with Great Britain our next. Ardently have we prayed for the accomplishment of both. But, if we must renounce the one or the other, we humbly trust in the mercies of the Supreme Governor of the Universe, that we shall not stand condemned before his throne, if our choice is determined by that overruling law of self-preservation, which his divine wisdom has thought fit to implant in the hearts of his creatures."

skins, breeches, &c., &c., &c. ...... Down to where the First Battalion exercised; stayed till the resolves of Congress, Fifteenth of May, and the resolves made the Twentieth at the State House were read, then [it was] proposed whether they should support them at all hazards. The same was agreed to unanimously, except two officers in the Foot, two officers in the [Light] Infantry and about twenty-three privates in the [Light] Infantry. From thence to the Second Battalion, where the same was read and agreed to by all except two privates. The same I understand was done by Col. McKean's and Col. Matlack's [Battalions] to a man, this day.

12. Past seven, to Committee at Philosophical Hall, called upon special business, viz. to settle the number of members to meet the country members on the Conference to be begun [the] Eighteenth instant.

13. Rose this morning soon, a Committee of five being appointed to meet at seven at [the] Coffee House in order to pick out twenty-five members to be returned to the General Committee to serve in Conference.

14. Yesterday an express came from Harry Fisher of a numerous body of Tories assembled in Sussex County,[1] who were intrenching and had cut off the communication by land to Dover. ...... Powder and ball were sent from here under escort of a company of Col. Matlack's Battalion. It's thought this trick of the Tories was concerted in this place in order to give disturbance and break our measures, but they will find, I hope, that the pit they dug, they themselves will fall into. ...... At James Davidson's till past seven. Then went to [the] Committee Room, where the appointment for the twenty-five members was settled by ballot, who were to attend the Conference as Deputies from this City and Liberties on the Eighteenth instant. The persons were, B. Franklin, Thomas McKean, S. Delany,

---

[1] In the State of Delaware.

John Cox, John Bayard, G. Schlosser, C. Ludwig, J. B. Smith, James Milligan, B. Loxley, C. Marshall, *Senior*,[1] Joseph Moulder, F. Gurney, T. Matlack, J. Schriner, J. Deane, J. Barge, Dr. Rush, S. C. Morris, William Coates, S. Brewster, J. Blewer, William Robinson, G. Goodwin, William Lowman.

15. Yesterday, the members of the Assembly, to the number of thirty-three, adjourned to August the Twenty-sixth, sundry country members being gone out of town.

17. Went to [the] Committee Room at [the] Philosophical Hall, at eight [A.M.] in order to consider the mode of opening the Conference, to be held to-morrow in this City by the Delegates appointed from the different Counties. Some proceedings proposed, but referred till to-morrow morning to be fully concluded. ...... Went to [the] sign of [the] Harp and Crown, Third street, being one appointed by [the] Committee to meet and consult with the Captains of the Gondolas respecting their complaints and intentions of resigning their commissions.

18. Met [the] Committee at [the] Philosophical Hall, agreed upon the mode to open the Conference at ten this morning, but to meet at nine in order to introduce some of the country members, who are strangers. Returned home till nine; then went, as agreed, to meet the Delegates from the different counties at Carpenter's Hall, where Thomas McKean was chosen President, Joseph Hart, Vice-President, Jonathan B. Smith and Samuel Cadwalader Morris, Secretaries.[2] Adjourned till three P.M. ...... Past three, to Carpenter's Hall, but as [the] Chester and Northumberland delegates were not arrived, adjourned till nine to-morrow morning. ...... Past seven, to [the] Committee Room, came away near

---

[1] The writer of the Diary.

[2] For the minutes of the Provincial Conference, see the volume on the Convention of Pennsylvania, published in 1825, at Harrisburg, by John S. Weistling, page 35 to page 45.

ten. Agreed at the meeting that George Bryan take upon him the collectorship, as per resolve of Assembly, May ———. Account was brought of Thomas Lightfoot, ——— Myng, and two or three others, who were called to an account at Germantown by the populace for speaking and acting inimical to the Congress and American liberty in general.

25. Went to meet the delegates at Carpenter's Hall. Broke up and finished the conference past one.[1] Went and dined with several of the Country and City members, with General Wooster, his Aide de Camp, &c., at the sign of the Indian Queen.

27. Yesterday morning, Capt. McCutcheon was examined by our Committee on the information of James Steward, the Pilot, and by them sent to [the] Committee of Safety, who committed him to prison for his attempting to engage him for fifteen shillings sterling per day to go and pilot the Asia from the Narrows into our river.

28. The declaration agreed in conference to be taken by those elected to sit in Convention[2] is highly censured, and as it's represented, and not unjustly, that I strenuously supported it, I am blamed, and was buffeted and extremely maltreated by sundry of my friends, as I thought, and who, I believed, were really religious persons and loved our Lord Jesus Christ, but now declare that no such Belief or Confession is necessary, in form-

---

[1] The Provincial Conference, besides calling a Convention "for the express purpose of forming a new Government in the Province on the authority of the People only," made provision for raising 4500 militia in obedience to resolutions of Congress of the Third and Fourth of June 1776, for establishing a Flying Camp in the middle colonies.— See Weistling's *Pennsylvania Conventions*, page 43.

[2] On the Twenty-first of June the Provincial Conference "Resolved that no person elected to serve as a Member of Convention shall take his seat or give his vote until he shall have made and subscribed the following declaration, I ——— ——— do profess faith in God the Father and in Jesus Christ, his Eternal Son, the true God, and in the Holy Spirit, one God, blessed for evermore; and do acknowledge the Holy Scriptures of the Old and New Testament to be given by Divine Inspiration.

ing the new government. But their behavior don't affect me, so as to alter my judgment in looking upon such a Confession to be essentially necessary and convenient.

30. Sundry pieces of news are circulated about town, viz., that six or seven sail of men-of-war [are] at our capes with a large store ship, intending to proceed up our river; that the brig ——, Capt. Newman, a Privateer, lately from this City, was taken going out of our capes; that General Howe, with sixty sail of vessels, was arrived at Sandy Hook and had landed a troop of horse; that Governor Franklin of the Jerseys was sent prisoner to Hartford in Connecticut; that most or all of our forces were killed and taken in Canada; the remains were arrived at Crown Point; that the Quakers in England had gotten a security and indemnification from the crown for all their approved friends' estates in America.

JULY 1. Information was received from ——, a comb maker, of not less than four different clubs of Tories in this City, that meet frequently. Sundry names were also mentioned of some that attended those clubs. The four places mentioned were, one at Widow Ball's, Lombard Street, one at [the] sign of [the] Pennsylvania Farmer, kept by Price, another at Jones's beer house on the dock, and one at the sign of the King's arms. Past ten, went to [the] Coffee House; thence to [the] Court House; the trial of the ships Juno and ——, which, I am informed, were both condemned. The said Jury insisted that the King's Arms in [the] Court Room should be taken down. The same, I am informed, was done.[1]

2. Past seven, went to Paul Fooks's; spent some time with him (who says he is a relation to the present Chevalier, Charles) and the Engineer, who is going to build a grand battery and fort of thirty-six heavy cannon

---

[1] The Historical Society of Pennsylvania has in its possession the English Arms painted on wood in the time of Queen Anne.

at Billingsport. ...... Past seven, to [the] Committee Room at [the] Philosophical [Hall]; none been there; went to John Lynn's; stayed till near eight; then returned; broke up past ten. At this meeting, six besides myself, were appointed a Committee of Secrecy to examine all inimical and suspected persons that come to their knowledge. ...... This day, the Continental Congress declared the United States Free and Independent States.¹

3. Near nine [P. M.] went to meet the Committee of Privates with others at Thorne's school room, where three speakers, viz., James Cannon, Timothy Matlack [and] Dr. Young flourished away on the necessity of choosing eight persons to be proposed to the people for their concurrence in electing them next Second Day for our representatives in Convention. The speakers expatiated greatly upon the qualifications they should be possessed of, viz., great learning, knowledge in our history, law, mathematics, &c., and a perfect acquaintance with the laws, manners, trade, constitution and polity of all nations, men of independent fortunes, steady in their integrity, zeal and uprightness to the determination and result of Congress in their opposition to the tyranny of Great Britain. Sundry names were proposed, out of which eight were collected to lay before the meeting tomorrow evening,— Joseph Moulder in the chair.

4. Accounts from New York are, that, Friday last, one of General Washington's guard was executed in a field near that City for mutiny and conspiracy, he being one of those who had formed a plot to assassinate the staff officers, blowing up the magazines and securing the passes of the town on the arrival of the Tyrant George the Third's fleet before this City. It's said that the number of transports from Halifax now arrived at Sandy Hook, amounts to one hundred and thirteen sail. It's

¹ See Appendix (D.)

thought General Howe's also in the fleet; that our troops from different parts of the country on their way and there arrived will amount soon to Twenty-five thousand men. ...... To the Committee Room at Philosophical Hall; came away past eleven [P.M.] An express was sent off from this Committee near ten o'clock by request of a Committee of Congress, with a letter to the meeting of officers at Lancaster, in order to request them to expedite the six thousand men appointed to compose the Flying Camp, and to march directly for Brunswick in the Jerseys, the place appointed for the rendezvous of those troops. The said Committee of Congress requested this Committee to meet a Committee of the members of New York, Jerseys, Lower Counties, officers of the Five Batalions and Safety, at seven to-morrow morning, at [the] State House, to take into consideration what may be necessary to be done in this critical situation. It's said that through the vigilance of our brethren to the Eastward, seven transports with Scotch rebels (soldiers) are taken and secured safely. See *Evening Post*, Numb. 227.

6. Past ten, I went with Jacob Schriner, Boehm, Kuhl [and] Leamington to collect awnings to make tents for the militia, going into the Jerseys; finished our district by one o'clock. ...... Near eight, went to committee, Philosophical Hall, where eight members were voted for and carried by majority, some of whom I have no objection to, but would not rise, nor agree to support at the election some others. Agreed that the Declaration of Independence be declared at the State House next Second Day. At [the] same time, the King's arms there are to be taken down by nine Associators, here appointed, who are to convey it to a pile of casks erected upon the commons, for the purpose of a bonfire, and the arms placed on the top. This[1] being Election day, I opposed

---

[1] This is, the next Second Day (Monday).

the motion, only by having this put off till next day, fearing it would interrupt the Election, but the motion was carried by a majority.

8. Warm sunshine morning. At eleven, went and met [the] Committee of Inspection at [the] Philosophical Hall; went from there in a body to the lodge; joined the Committee of Safety (as called); went in a body to [the] State House Yard, where, in the presence of a great concourse of people, the Declaration of Independence was read by John Nixon. The company declared their approbation by three repeated huzzas. The King's Arms were taken down in the Court Room, State House [at the] same time. From there, some of us went to B. Armitage's tavern; stayed till one. I went and dined at Paul Fooks's; lay down there after dinner till five. Then he and the French Engineer went with me on the commons, where the same was proclaimed at each of the five Battalions. ...... This day, the eight members for this City, and the eight members for this County, to serve in Convention, were elected very quietly at the State House.[1] Fine starlight, pleasant evening. There were bonfires, ringing bells, with other great demonstrations of joy upon the unanimity and agreement of the declaration.

10. For sundry pieces of intelligence, See *Pennsylvania Journal*, Numb. 1753. Dined at home alone, as my wife was at the place. Past five, went and called at John Lynn's; thence to Benj. Harbeson's about the soldier's camp kettles; thence to James Cannon's; drank coffee there; stayed till past nine. There were John Adams, Paul Fooks, Dr. Young, Timothy Matlack,

---

[1] For the City of Philadelphia: Benjamin Franklin, Frederick Kuhl, Owen Biddle, George Clymer, Timothy Matlack, James Cannon, George Schlosser, David Rittenhouse.

For the County of Philadelphia: Frederick Antis, Henry Hill, Robert Loller, Joseph Blewer, John Bull, Thomas Potts, Edward Bartholomew. William Coates.

&c. Thence home. Starlight and pleasant. There was a small gust this afternoon; blew hard, but little rain or thunder. (No Poll)

11. Went this morning with Benja. Harbeson to Col. Cox's store; ordered twenty four-gallon iron pots to William Rush's work shop to have bales put to them, to send for the use of our forces going into the Jerseys. Yesterday, several companies went from here by water to Trenton.

12. Past six, I went down to Mulberry wharf. Numbers of militia going upwards, as many have done this morning for Trenton.

14. Yesterday, came to town, about eighty prisoners, taken at St. John's on their way, it's said, to Cumberland County. Three or four companies of militia gone off this morning for Trenton. Sixteen shallops, with Maryland troops, going to Trenton, amounting, it's said, to eleven hundred. Two or three companies arrived from Cumberland County; rest till to-morrow; going to Trenton. The whole, it's said, in high spirits.

15. Past three, took a walk to the State House; thence to the causeway leading to Kensington. ...... More of the militia, with the artillery, went for Trenton this day, and Col. Montgomery's men from Chester came to town and used part of [the] College as barracks.

17. Past eight, I went to Benja. Harbeson's; we went [and] called upon Captain Davis, then we waited upon Gen. Roberdeau, as by appointment at [the] Committee last night, respecting troops to be left to secure this City in the militia's absence.

18. Account that our troops were marched yesterday from Trenton to Woodbridge, and that the men-of-war and tenders that passed New York up North River were roughly handled by our forts. It's said, they had above forty men killed. ...... Col. Roberdeau took his leave of me, going to set out for camp, about seven. (This night our girl was brought home. I suppose she was hunted out, as it's said, and found by Ruth, down Passyunk Road.

Her mistress was delighted upon her return, but I know of nobody else, in house or out. I have nothing to say in the affair, as I know of nothing that would distress my wife so much as for me to refuse or forbid her being taken into the house.)

19. Near twelve, John Payne called and took his leave of me, being going to camp as Secretary to Gen. Roberdeau. Several companies of Col. Montgomery's Battalion from Chester left this City last night, to proceed to Trenton on their way to camp. This day came letters to Congress from Gen. Lee at South Carolina, giving an account of the defeat of Gen. Clinton and the fleet in Charleston, June 18th, last. See *Evening Post,* Numb. 234.

20. I went to wait upon Capt. Peters, some complaint being made to me as Chairman of [the] Committee, of a company of negroes, that meet by the barracks, in order to get a guard from him to attend some of the members this evening to try to apprehend some of them. ...... Waited on and acquainted some of the Committee that a guard would be ordered to attend them if wanted and called for. ...... The gentlemen appointed this day, in Convention, for Provincial Delegates in Congress, were B. Franklin, votes, 78 ; Robert Morris, 74 ; James Wilson, 74 ; John Morton, 71 ; George Ross, 77 ; Col. James Smith, 56 ; Benja. Rush, 61 ; George Taylor, 34.

21. Sundry more troops went out of this City yesterday for camp in the Jerseys. ...... Between twelve and two this day, two companies of our Artillery, with field pieces and baggage wagons, went out of town, as also went twelve shallop loads of the troops from Maryland, with fair wind and tide for the Jerseys, and one company of ——— Battalion came to town from Carlisle [and] went to our barracks.

23. This day, the Convention chose and appointed the following persons as Committee or Council of Safety,

viz., Samuel Morris, *Sen.*, Samuel Howell, *Merchant*, David Rittenhouse, Samuel Morris, *Jun.*, Thomas Wharton, *Jun.*, Joseph Blewer, Owen Biddle, James Cannon, Tim. Matlack, Jonat. B. Smith, Nathaniel Falconer, Frederick Kuhl, Henry Keppele, *Jun.*, George Gray, Samuel Mifflin, John Bull, Henry Wynkoop, Benja. Bartholomew, John Hubley, Michael Swope, Daniel Hunter, William Lyon, Peter Rhoad, Daniel Epsey, John Weitzel [and] John Moore; a poor set for that important post at this time.[1]

24. For sundry pieces of news, See *Pennsylvania Journal*, Numb. 1755. Sundry papers to write and endorse for different persons from this City and from [the] Committee of Cœcil County, Maryland, who were going to the Northward.

25. I was called up by Jacob Schriner and Philip Boehm, to consider what steps will be necessary to take in order to apprehend a company of negroes and whites, it's said to the number of thirty or forty, who meet in the night near one Clynn's in Camptown,[2] near the barracks. After some consideration, it's concluded that some persons in that neighborhood keep watch, and when they are met, come and give information to Schriner or to Boehm, who are to go to the main guard at [the] State House, for a file of their men, who have orders to attend when called upon such occasions. Near twelve, called upon to consult at [the] Committee Room at [the] Coffee House, measures to be taken respecting Mrs. Arrall, who left this City this morning, it's said, for New York. There being great reason to suspect that she is carrying on an intrigue between our enemies here and aboard the fleet, it was thereupon agreed by the members met, to send an express to overtake her at Princeton, to-night, and bring her and her papers back, the which was done.

---

[1] Mr. Marshall must be understood to speak of the Committee as *an unit*; several of the persons here named being his particular friends.

[2] Part of Kensington formerly bore this name. Kensington now composes a great part of the Eighteenth and Nineteenth wards of Philadelphia.

26. Called out of bed early, as some of our Committee got information last night that Mrs. Arrall, the person sent after by express, was not gone, but was to go in the coach this morning. Four of them attended, waited till she got in the coach, then requested her to walk into the house and to have her bundle brought in. They accordingly detained her and brought her to my house. Sundry of the Committee being called, she was examined, her bundle also, but no letters found. Upon the whole it appeared she had been a little unguarded in conversation, and had no concern with Henry Shaff in the package of cambrics and lawns, found at his lodgings; upon which she was discharged, about ten. ...... This afternoon, came to town and passed by our door to the barracks, two companies of clever fellows, one from [the] back parts of Lancaster, the other from York County, [under] Col. William Rankin. It's said that three or four shallops left this City to-day, with troops for the Grand Army at Amboy, Elizabeth Town, &c.

27. Waited upon by sundry gentlemen going to the Northward. Gave a pass to John Spear, of Baltimore, on the recommendation of Brigadier General James Ewing and Col. Bartram Galbraith.

28. Wrote two passes, one for the Rev. Henry Muhlenburgh, *Jun.*, and one for John Gartley, both having a desire to go to New York.

29. About nine, wrote four passes; for Henry Woodrow, for Gabriel Springer, William Hemphill [and] John Stow: these three last of Wilmington, New Castle County, on the strong recommendation of Andrew Tybout; the first by a written recommendation of sundry of his neighbors in the Northern Liberties.

30. Three or four companies of militia came to town yesterday from [the] back parts of Cumberland, York, and Lancaster Counties; went to barracks.

31. Gave a pass to John Caruthers, he going to join

the army for three weeks, the time allowed for the masters to be absent from College duties.¹

AUGUST 1. News to-day of the ship —— (sent out by Congress), 's being in the river, from Marseilles in France, with ten tons [of] gunpowder, one hundred and eleven stand of arms, thirty-seven and a half tons of lead [and] one tierce of flints.

2. Yesterday, Arthur Thomas was brought to town, under a guard from Bucks County, he and his son (who made his escape), being, on information, concerned in helping —— Kerchland to make his escape out of prison. The information was given by —— Hale in Lombard Street, who was employed and did procure horses for him to go off with. Account last night was, that the Congress, Privateer, Captain Craig, of this port, has taken and brought into Egg Harbor a brig from Nevis. It's said to be worth near Twenty Thousand Pounds.

5. Waited on by Capt. Hysham, Capt. Simpson, and John Leamington, who had thrown the twelve —— of Green Tea, as directed last Committee night, into [the] Delaware; upon which, I copied the resolve, with direction to the printers to publish it and the affair in next newspapers.

7. Yesterday, arrived here, the ship Friendship, Capt. McCoy, of four hundred tons, sent in by the Reprisal, loaded with sugar, rum, &c., bound from Granada for London.

8. This day, came to town, the King's Speech, dated 23d of May (also, near nine, our Poll returned home from her cruise).

10. Wrote a discharge for William Carstins, servant to Speigel (Barber surgeon), confined in [the] workhouse, for which, as there is a dispute between this

---

¹ The teachers of Philadelphia appear to have been distinguished for their patriotism. We may add the name of Mr. Caruthers, about to spend the August holidays in camp, to those of Charles Thomson, James Cannon, and James Davidson.

master and the former, Speigel gave bond to me, in behalf of [the] Committee, for this man's appearance when a proper Judicatory is settled.

11. Several shallops, with troops for the camp, went from town yesterday, as [others] did also this morning [at] flood.

15. Sundry vessels left this City with the flood with troops for the camp.

15. Every day this week, numbers of soldiers going to the camp.

17. Yesterday being the expiration of the time of the Committee of Inspection and observation, the Committee, in obedience to the resolve of Convention of the Ninth instant, concluded still to act, agreeably to the said resolve.[1] See *Evening Post*, No. 244.

18. Yesterday were published three resolves of Congress respecting the return of the Associators from the camp in New Jersey, without leave. See *Evening Post*, Num. 246. The same was printed in handbills. ...... About two o'clock, about eleven or twelve sail of shallops, with soldiers for camp, went past.

24. This evening were published, the Messrs. Shewell, for breaking the rules of Congress and Committee. For that and some pieces of news, see the *Evening Post*, Numb. 249.

26. Came home past nine. Moonlight and pleasant. I met part of the First Battalion of Philadelphia Militia, just returned from camp in the Jerseys. ...... Yesterday, came to town, several companies of forces from the back counties, from Maryland, &c.

27. Past eleven, the Second Battalion came to town. ...... Past seven, went to [the] Committee Room,

---

[1] The term was extended upon the ground that the Associators, who composed a great majority of the Electors, might be absent at camp at the expiration of the Committee's year, and it would be highly inexpedient that the City or Counties should be without Committees, or that they should be partially elected.

Philosophical Hall ; came home past ten. ...... [At] this meeting, Samuel G...... was sent for, to answer for his not producing satisfaction respecting two chests [of] green tea, which refusal he still persisted in, and as he had treated those members who before waited on him with great violence and contempt, and called the Committee, robbers, and that he would prove them so, &c., &c., the same six members were to wait on [the] Committee of Safety to-morrow morning. ...... Third and Fifth Battalions come and coming from camp.

29. My wife rose early to visit the wharves for wood; all bare. One vessel with twenty-three cords of hickory and oak just sold before she came, altogether for twenty-nine shillings for hickory, twenty shillings for oak. ...... An account brought of an engagement between our forces on Long Island and the enemy, in which our forces repulsed them, but many [were] killed on both sides ; General Sullivan and Lord Sterling among the missing. See *Evening Post*, Numb. 251.

30. My wife rose early to visit the wharves on account of winter's wood. ...... Yesterday, went from here a great number of troops for Trenton, on their way to the camp. It's said near three thousand.

31. I rose past six, as our folks began to get in their winter's fire wood and were piling in the yard, as also my customers came soon this morning about salt, passes, disputes, &c , &c., &c. ...... Paid £10 for eleven and a half cords of oak fire wood. Paid for hauling, carrying, and piling, 42s. 10½d. ...... News brought to-day of our forces upon Long Island's taking away all their guns, stores, &c., except some large ones, which they spiked, and left the Island in good order and went to New York; Lord Sterling and General Sullivan prisoners. The enemy lost two Generals, supposed to be killed, as our people knew nothing of them when the flag came to enquire.

SEPTEMBER 2. At nine, went to [the] Committee

Room, Philosophical Hall; came home past twelve, been fixing the quantity of salt to be sold to each county, being what was Messrs. Shewell and Joshua Fisher and Sons'.

3. At seven [P.M.] went to [the] Committee Room, Philosophical Hall; came home near ten. ...... At this meeting [it was] proposed to call an election for [a] new Committee for this City and Liberties, and reduced the number to fifty.

4. Yesterday, high words passed at [the] Coffee House, William Allen, Jr., declaring that he would shed his blood in opposition to Independency, and Col. John Bayard, in the support of Independency. Allen's behavior was such that William Bradford immediately complained to Samuel Morris, Jr., as a member of the Commitee of Safety, of the abuse offered by Allen to the public.

5. For public occurrences, See *Pennsylvania Journal*, No. 1761.

7. It was said yesterday by —— Livingston, that three members of Congress, viz., Benjamin Franklin, John Adams [and] Edward Rutledge [had gone] as Deputies to Gen. or Lord Howe, to hear what he had to propose to the Congress. Gen. Sullivan left this City yesterday, to return agreeably to his parole with Gen. or Lord Howe. Yesterday arrived a Bermudian vessel with twenty-five hundred bushels of salt.

8. It's said that two more vessels are just come in with salt; quantity, it's said, two thousand bushels.

9. A number of the troops, it's said, from the counry, went out of town yesterday. Those gentlemen, delegates, mentioned to go out on the Seventh, to converse with Lord and General Howe, did not go till this morning. It was General Sullivan that went thenabouts, from this City.

10. For sundry public occurrences, see *Dunlap's Genral Advertiser*, Numb. 255.

11. Yesterday was published the proposed Plan or Frame of Government for the Commonwealth or State of Pennsylvania (Printed for consideration), in twelve small pages, folio, containing forty-nine Sections. For particulars of the engagement in South Carolina, see *Pennsylvania Gazette*, Numb. 2490.

13. As I stand informed, Samuel Morris, the Elder, resigned his office of Councillor of State, and as there were three before, who had not qualified, the Convention appointed four new members, viz., John Bayard, John Cox, Francis Gurney and Cad. Samuel Morris. ...... Went to [the] Committee Room at Philosophical Hall, where William Wild appeared in support of his Memorial. Upon being interrogated respecting the money, [which,] he had said belonged to the merchants in England, he now declared otherwise, and that the whole sum was his own private property, and in order to prove that, said his letter and cash books would show it, which he could fetch in one quarter of an hour, if requested. Upon this he was desired to fetch them, and the Committee would wait. In about that space of time he returned and declared he had destroyed his letter and cash book and every other book, about ten days ago, which might publicly bring his employers into trouble. Referred to next meeting.

14. Past, or near, six, I went to Col. Hancock's to report William Wild's conduct, being requested to do so, by some members of Committee.

15. Yesterday, Paul Fooks gave at [the] wharf, twenty-five shillings per cord for oak wood; took three cords, and paid two shillings and six pence per cord [for] hauling. This he told me last night.- Yesterday was published an Ordinance for punishing persons guilty of certain offences, particularly by speaking or writing against the United American States, in order to obstruct, or oppose, or endeavor so to do, the measures carrying on by the United States for the defence and support of the

freedom and independence of such States, and also, an Ordinance to compel debtors in certain cases to give security to their creditors. See *Evening Post*, Numb. 258, with sundry pieces of public occurrences. Several companies have arrived in town this week, of stout able bodied men, from the lower counties, the back parts of this Province and some from Virginia. Also a number of recruits in this town set out for the camp to join the main army.

17. Went to [the] Committee Room, Philosophical Hall; came away past nine, having passed a vote to break up this Committee entirely, except eight members to settle Committee's accounts, and the six members that were appointed to see the salt for each county settled. William Wild's money was lodged in Hazlehurst's possession, and Samuel G......'s tea to be put into the hands of [the] Committee of Safety. ...... This day, accounts arrived that the enemy had taken possession of New York on the Fifteenth instant. See *Pennsylvania Journal*, Numb. 1763.

18. Accounts published to-day of the conference between Lord Howe and the three gentlemen sent by order of Congress, and also an account that the enemy were in possession of New York, but no particulars. There is also an Ordinance for rendering the burden of the Associators and Non Associators, in the defence of this State, as nearly equal as may be. *Pennsylvania Gazette*, Numb. 2491.

19. Accounts brought to-day of a skirmish, above New York, with the Forty Second Regiment, a Battalion of Light Infantry and three Companies of Jagers or German Riflemen, whom, after a smart engagement, our people drove under cover of the men-of-war's guns in East River.

23. By letters by post from camp at Harlem, we hear that a fire broke out last Friday evening in New York, which has destroyed a number of houses and two churches,

it is said. For sundry pieces of news, &c., raising eighty battalions in the States, the proportion and method of procedure, counties, &c., the Declaration of the Delaware State in Convention, &c., the gentlemen appointed in the government of the State of New Jersey, &c., See *D. General Advertiser*, Numb. 257, &c.

28. Dined at home with our Miller that supplies us with flour. ...... This day were published, three resolves, by the majority of the Assemblymen now met, dated [the] Twenty-sixth instant, against the proceedings of the Convention now sitting. See *Evening Post*, Numb. 264, where is also the time, mode and form of election in this Province, fixed by Convention, same day. It's said that before the then members of Assembly (being twenty-six) broke up, fourteen against twelve passed a vote for the sum of Five Hundred, or a Thousand Pounds, to be paid our late Governor. The order was immediately drawn, signed by Morton, *Speaker*, sent and the cash received.

30. This afternoon came to town General Mifflin, L. Colonel Penrose and Major Williams, from camp above New York.

OCTOBER 1. Account to-day of a great fire at Basseterre, in St. Kitts, which, with hurricane, chiefly destroyed the town. Particulars not yet come to hand. Since come; see particulars [in the] *Pennsylvania Journal*, Numb. 1769.

2. Accounts of a great number of prizes' being taken by our friends to the Eastward and arrived safe into port ; also a report that General Arnold had lately destroyed most of the enemies' boats at the North and Lake Champlaine, and made prisoners of six hundred English, Scotch and Hessian soldiers, on a small island on the lake. See *Pennsylvania Journal*, Numb. 1765, *Evening Post*, Numb. 265.

4. Accounts brought that election was held in Chester and Bucks Counties, for Assemblymen, Sheriffs, Coro-

ners, be on the First instant, and that some day this week, Joseph Fox and John Reynolds refused to take the Continental Money for large sums due them by bond, mortgage, &c., as it's said. Of Fox's, a record was made by Paul Fooks, from the person that tendered him £240 before two witnesses, due on mortgage.

7. Son Charles came to invite [me] to dine at his house to-day with some friends from Boston, but having an invitation from the owners of sloops Congress and Chance on the Fifth, to dine with them at James Byrne's this day, I went near two, where were betweeen sixty and seventy persons. I came away before six. ...... A vessel arrived this day from Surinam with some powder, lead, some stands of arms and some woolen cloths, molasses, &c.; a vessel from Bermudas, with salt. Arrived this day, his Excellency General Lee from the Southward.

10. Prize ship in the river from Jamaica, with three hundred and ten hogsheads [of] Sugar, ninety casks or puncheons of spirits. She is called the Thetis, Capt. May, taken by [the] General Montgomery Privateer, Captain Hamilton. Also a private brig from St. Martin's arrived yesterday. It's said that General Lee left this City to-day for the army near New York, and that another reinforcement arrived last week from England, at Sandy Hook, consisting of Burgoyne's Light Horse Two thousand Hessians and one thousand British troops are on Staten Island. An account, also, from the West Indies of an insurrection of the negroes in the Island Jamaica, and that martial law was declared. See *Pennsylvania Gazette*, Numb. 2494.

11. A severe Satire, by way of Dialogue, published in the *Evening Post*, Numb. 269, on the proposed plan or frame of government of this Province.[1] Also a Resolve of Congress of the Third instant for borrowing Five Millions of Continental Dollars for the use of the United States, at [an] annual interest of four per cent.

---

[1] See a defence of it in the *Evening Post*, No. 279, November 2, 1776.

12. By letter [through] yesterday *Evening's Post*, Paul Fooks received from Nantz, in Old France, from Mons. Permel, that he had loaded two vessels for Virginia with blankets, coarse cloths, linen, arms, ammunition, &c., also two of [the] same commodities for Rhode Island, and that he had another (besides this, that brought this letter, both loaded with the some commodities) that sail in a few days, which, I hope, will all arrive safe. I think this letter was dated Third [of] August. Two vessels with salt arrived within these two days past, and yet it's said some are selling it at Three Dollars per bushel (so inhuman are some of our citizens to poor people). ...... A wonderful Ordinance published in *Evening Post*, Numb. 270, inviting all masters of vessels, coming with salt to sell it to them for fifteen shillings per bushel. O rare Council of Safety!

13. About eleven o'clock last night alarmed by cry of fire, which proved to be just above Pool's Bridge, near the Magazine, in a baker's shop, but it was soon extinguished. ...... The prize ship, coming through the chevaux-de-frize, got hurt, so that they were obliged to unload and keep the pumps going till arrived in town, then ran her ashore at Hodge's wharf and were busy unloading her cargo this day on the said wharves.

14. Took a walk to the place, stopping as we went to view part of the First Battalion exercise, this being, it's said, the last field day they are to have, as per Act of Assembly, for this year. ...... Two more vessels, it's said, with cargoes of salt. Various pieces of news circulating, but little to be depended upon except that the King's troops have entirely abandoned Staten Island, but where gone, or the reason is not known by the public. Major Keppelé, just come home from Elizabeth-Town Point, which he left this morning, said he was on the island.

16. Yesterday arrived the Continental Schooner Wasp, Captain Baldwin; brought with her a large

Guinea ship bound from Jamaica for Liverpool, having on board three hundred and five hogsheads of Sugar, fifty-one puncheons of rum and other goods. Letter from Harlem, where our companies [are] of the Thirteenth instant, says most of Howe's forces are got about six miles above King's Bridge, and were landed in order if possible to surround our camp, so that a general engagement may be hourly expected to be heard of. For further occurrences, see *Pennsylvania Journal*, Numb. 1767.

17. Another vessel, it's said, arrived yesterday with twenty-five bushels of salt from Bermudas. ...... Past six, went to Philosophical Hall, being called there by invitation in printed tickets, where met a large number of respectable citizens in order to consider of a mode to set aside sundry improper and unconstitutional rules laid down by the late Convention, in what they call their Plan or Frame of Government, where after sundry deliberate proposals, some amendments were agreed to, *nemine c. d.* and ordered immediately to be printed with the reasons that induced this company to make such alterations, to be published immediately for the perusal and approbation of the whole State at large, and that a general town meeting be held at the State House in this City, next Monday afternoon, the proceedings of which to be printed and immediately transmitted to all the Counties in the State. The whole of the meeting was conducted with great order and solemnity, and broke up past ten, in great union.

18. Sundry pieces of news from about New York, but none confirmed, but that our people had landed upon Staten Island, and a heavy firing of small arms had ensued on last Third Day, and as all the Hessians had not left the Island, it was supposed to be an engagement betwixt them and the party of our army that went over. A person who left Head Quarters last Second Day, says that the detachment from Gen. Howe's

army that landed at Frog's Point, had been attacked by a party of Gen. Washington's, who obliged them to retreat under cover of their ships, and that another detachment had also been beat off and prevented from landing on the banks of the North River. ...... This day, thirty-three Tories were brought from New York, and lodged in our New Jail.

19. After breakfast, Anthony Benezet came to pay a friendly visit. We held conversation for near an hour, on religion and politics.

20. In the *Evening Post*, Numb. 273, is this remarkable extract of a letter, dated Dominica, Sept. —, viz., " Capt. Stout, of Antigua, told us that he had heard from Taylor and Bell of that island, that a house that does the government business there had poisoned two kegs of rum, which they shipped in the Creighton, Capt. Ross, and directed for Gen. Howe, in hopes that if the ship should be taken, the Americans would send those to the camp, on supposing them of an uncommon good quality." What a diabolical project! He had it from their own mouth! Oh, dreadful!

21. To [the] Coffee House, where I stayed and saw fifteen prisoners (taken on Staten Island last week, viz., eight Hessians and seven English soldiers) come on shore. Thence to State House Yard, where it's thought about fifteen hundred people assembled, in order to deliberate on the change of sundry matters contained in Form of Government, settled in the late Convention. Col. Bayard being seated in the chair, [we] proceeded to business, which was conducted with prudence and decency till dark; then adjourned till nine to-morrow morning. Chief speakers, against [the] Convention, were Col. McKean and Col. Dickinson; for the Convention, James Cannon, Timothy Matlack, Dr. Young and Col. Smith of York County.

22. Went to the State House, as was appointed last night, where came on the consideration of the Resolves

as begun yesterday, the which, after being maturely considered and put, were carried by a large majority, except the oath appointed to be taken by every elector before he could be suffered to give in his vote for Assembly. This was entirely set aside as it then stood. Committees were then appointed to go to each county, to carry the proceedings and request their concurrence &c. The meeting then broke up peaceably. ...... On the Twenty-first, arrived a schooner with twelve hundred bushels of salt [it's said]. The Twenty-second, was sent in here the Brig Sherburne, Capt. Burnell, with five hundred and eighty-three barrels of oil, being a prize to Brig Hancock, Capt. Newman. An account of an engagement on the lakes, the Eleventh instant, and as the enemy were vastly superior, our people retreated to Crown Point. See particulars, *Pennsylvania Journal*, Numb. 1758.

25. Near twelve, I went to John Lynn's by desire of Major Keppele, who, upon account of his late marriage had requested sundry persons to come visit, drink punch, wine, eat gammon, &c., &c. ...... An account of a large ship from London to Quebec, loaded with Indian goods, viz., duffields, strouds, blankets, ammunition, &c., &c., taken by one of the Eastern privateers, and said ship was arrived at Providence.

25. Near three took a walk to Camping town, where was to be a meeting for [the] Northern and Southern Districts, to consider how to carry on the election on the Fifth [of] next month. Sundries met and agreed amicably.

26. Received this morning of John Nixon, by the hands of George Lehman, £353. 2s. 6d., on account of the Committee of Inspection and Observation for this City and Liberties.

27. About one this morning, alarmed by the cry of fire, which proved to be the Prize Ship sent in here by the Privateer Wasp, which entirely consumed the same

with her valuable cargo of sugar, rum, &c., &c. A number of valuable prizes appear to be taken by our cruisers and safe arrived in sundry ports to the Eastward, among which are a ship and a snow, both bound to New York, loaded with 56,896 [weight of] bread, 8020 [weight of] pork, 256 bushels [of] peas, 257 bushels [of] oatmeal, 16,000 weight [of] beef, 12,064 weight [of] flour, 4101 weight of raisins, 165 gallons of oil, 507 gallons of vinegar, 3500 gallons of spirits, 460 dozen candles; these aboard the snow; ship, same sorts, but more in quantity. See *Evening Post*, Numb. 267, where is the following extract of a letter from Fort Lee, dated 26th instant, viz., " A deserter at head quarters informs, that the loss of the enemy on Friday last, must have been seven or eight hundred; that in the cannonade after the battle, General Howe had his leg very dangerously shattered by a ball, which killed a soldier who stood near him. Last night, a party of rangers, under the command of Major Rogers, having advanced towards Mareneck, were attacked and defeated by a party of our forces, thirty-six were taken prisoners and the number of the slain is supposed to be greater, since sixty arms and as many blankets were found upon the field. As the corps are composed of Tories, this victory is the more glorious. Our army is in high spirits, having outflanked the enemy."

30. Yesterday arrived a Brig, being a prize, it's said, to [the] Hancock Privateer. Account also of some vessels of the enemy's attacking Fort Washington on the 28th, but repulsed with great damage unto two of the men-of-war.

31. Past six, I went to [the] Coffee House, being invited by letter to meet sundry of our citizens to appoint Inspectors and to think of six suitable persons to represent this City in General Assembly. This meeting was conducted with great unanimity and concord, and the proceedings referred to a larger meeting to-morrow evening

at [the] Philosophical Hall. ...... To-day, were launched two ships of war, at Kensington.

NOVEMBER 1. Sundry pieces of news and intelligence are in the *Evening Post,* Numb. 278. ...... Past six, went to [the] Philosophical Hall, called by notices. Met about forty. I was appointed Chairman, but after some conversation on the intent of the meeting, it was concluded, as so few attended, to refer the full discussion of affairs respecting the appointment of six members of Assembly for this City till to-morrow evening, at this place, in hopes a larger company would attend.

2. Transcript from Order of Council of Safety, dated [the] Thirty-first [of] October last, viz: " Complaint having been made to this Council by Christopher Elliot, that John Baldwin, of this City, Cordwainer, had refused to receive in payment the Continental Bills of Credit, issued by order of Congress, thereupon, the said John Baldwin was ordered to appear before this Board, and being informed of said complaint, did acknowledge that he had refused to receive the said Bills of Credit in payment. The Council urged the pernicious and destructive tendency of such conduct, and requested him to reconsider it, allowing him several days to form his judgment and fix his final resolution. This day, agreeably to notice given him, he again appeared before the Council and declared that he was determined not to receive the said Bills in payment, whereupon, Resolved that the said John Baldwin is an ' Enemy to his country, and precluded from all trade and intercourse with the inhabitants of these States:' Resolved that the said John Baldwin be committed to jail, there to remain without bail or mainprise until he shall be released by order of this Council, or some other person lawfully authorized so to do: Ordered that these proceedings be made public." ...... Went to the Philosophical Hall, as appointed, where a large [and] respectable number of citizens were met, and also the following gentlemen were scratched for,

as members to be voted for on the Fifth instant as Assemblymen in this State for this City, viz., George Clymer, Robert Morris, John Cadwalader, John Bayard, Michael Shubart, Peter Chevalier; but some altercation happening, and P. C. declining, Joseph Parker was chosen by voice. Broke up past nine, but, upon motion, it was resolved to answer the request of the contrary party by appointing seven members to hear what they had to say, and draw up the proceedings of this evening and have them printed in handbills and distributed through the City, before or on Election Day, signed by Samuel Howell, Chairman for this evening. ...... (No news from camp as yet.)

5. Went past nine to the State House, being appointed one of the Judges to superintend and conduct the Election, as is usual. Continued there till near two next morning, where all matters in general were conducted with great harmony and concord in the house; two or three small buffetings, I heard about the door in the street, but soon went over. Upon casting up the votes, they turned out thus: For Joseph Parker, 682; for George Clymer, 413; for Robert Morris, 410; for Samuel Morris, Jr., 407; for John Bayard, 397; for Michael Shubart, 393. These six were the elected members. Those six following had votes, each, viz., David Rittenhouse, 278; Timothy Matlack, 268; Jonathan B. Smith, 273; Jacob Schriner, 269; Thomas Wharton, Junior, 268; Joseph Parker, as above, he being chosen by both parties. Votes " For No Councillors," 406; " For Councillors," 211.

6. The members chosen for [the] County of Philadelphia, yesterday, were, Robert Know, 523; John Dickinson, 419; George Gray, 419; T. Potts, 407; Isaac Hughs, 282; Frederick Antis, 275. " For No Councillors," 370; " For Councillors," 133. Sheriff was William Masters, by [a] large majority. For Coroner, Robert Jewel. For sundry pieces of material intelligences, see *Pennsylvania Journal*, Numb. 1770.

8. Past six, went to the Philosophical Hall; called there by notices, to consider a Set of Instructions to be handed to a Town Meeting, which was concluded to be called on Third Day next, nine o'clock, forenoon, at the State House, there to settle them, in order to have ready to present to the members of this City and County at their meeting in General Assembly on the Nineteenth instant.[1] Broke up about nine.

10. A report prevails to-day that on the twenty-eighth, there were killed in that skirmish, of our Enemy, one Colonel, eight officers, and a number of privates; and that thirty Hessian Chasseurs came over to our side, and brought with them a three-pounder brass piece; and that Gen. Howe had drawn off Ten Thousand of his troops, in order to pass at Dobbs's Ferry, and so penetrate through the Jerseys to this City, and that Howe's troops had indiscriminately plundered on Long Island both Whigs and Tories, in particular, Samuel Nottingham, a noted Quaker Preacher and —— Rapelja, who now lies himself in confinement for Toryism, in Connecticut Government.

13. For sundry pieces of public occurrences, see *Pennsylvania Journal*, Numb. 1771.

14. News to-day of Guy Carlton's leaving Crown Point, on the Second [of] October, and returning to Canada; also of the enemy's leaving their lines at York Island and embarking, it's said, in three or four hundred sail of transports; left Sandy Hook, steering for the Southward, and, it's expected, to pay a visit to this City. See *Evening Post*, Numb. 284.

15. Handbills were published last night by order of Congress and Council of Safety, requesting the inhabit-

---

[1] The Constitution of September, 1775, secured to the people of Pennsylvania "*The Right of Instruction*" in the following words, Chapter I, Section 16, The Declaration of Rights. "That the people have a *right to assemble together* to consult for their common good, *to instruct their Representatives*, and to apply to the Legislature for redress of grievances by address, petition, or remonstrance."

ants of this State to put themselves in a martial array, and march by companies and parts of companies, as they could be ready, and march with the utmost expedition to this City.

16. Past three, went below the Swedes' Church to the launching of one of the galleys called the ———. ...... No news respecting the enemy.

18. Account spread to-day of Gen. Howe's taking Fort Washington, last Seventh Day, in the afternoon, but this is not credited but by our enemies, and the timorous and faint-hearted amongst us.

20. The reduction of Fort Washington is confirmed by intelligence received by Congress. For this and other pieces of occurrences, see *Pennsylvania Journal*, Numb. 1772.

21. Visited this morning by Frederick Kuhl, on account of Capt. Moebale, a Danish Officer, in order to intercede with Col. Hancock for a Captaincy in the Marines.

22. News last night of Sykes's new brig, and, it's said, two other provision vessels, taken and carried into New York by our British enemies. Four or five sea vessels came up to-day; there is some salt in one of them. ...... Express just brought account of the enemy's taking Fort Lee on the Twenty-First instant, by surprise, our people being careless. ...... One of those sea vessels, arrived this forenoon, it's said, is a large ship, a Prize from the Montgomery Privateer, but from where did not learn.

23. This was also the stormy day, raised through James West.

26. On the twenty-fourth was brought in, a Prize, the Ship lately commanded by Samuel Richardson. She was taken on her voyage from Barbadoes to Liverpool, by the Continental Sloop Independence, Capt. Young; was mounted with four guns and had on board Twenty Thousand [Dollars], two tons and a half of ivory, one hundred bars of iron.

27. News to-day is, that the enemy intends to make a push for Philadelphia. It's said, part of their force is embarked, either to go up the Delaware and make their attack at both sides at once, or else to amuse the Southern States and prevent their sending any assistance to Philadelphia. See *Pennsylvania Journal*, Numb. 1773.

28. This morning a large and respectable company met at the State House to consider the present alarming affairs of the State. It's said General Mifflin spoke animatedly pleasing, which gave great satisfaction.

30. No news from camp this day, as I could learn, but there is an account of two very valuable prizes' being carried into some port to the Eastward.

DECEMBER 2. This City alarmed with the news of Howe's army's being at Brunswick, proceeding for this place. Drums beat: a martial appearance: the shops shut: and all business except preparing to disappoint our enemies laid aside. I went to [the] Coffee House; then to children's; then home; then back to the Coffee House and other parts of the City; then home; dined there. Our people then began to pack up some things, wearing and bedding, to send to the place. After dinner, I went to [the] State House; conversed with Jacobs, *Speaker of Assembly*, with Robert Whitehill, J. Dickinson, Gen. Mifflin, &c. To [the] Coffee House; then home; drank tea; then down town. Accounts brought that General Lee was near our army with ten thousand men. Various but great appearances of our people's zeal. Came home near nine; then went down again as far as the children's. Some gondolas gone up for Trenton and some companies marched.

3. One gondola just gone past for Trenton; some troops in motion; after dinner ...... [The] Light Horse and some of the Militia went out of town. Numbers of families loading wagons with their furniture, &c., taking them out of town. ...... Drank tea at home; then wen with a number of deeds to son Christopher's; put the

into his iron chest. ...... No news to be depended upon this day.

4. Great numbers [of] people moving, and militia, with Proctor's company and two field pieces, wagons, &c. No news to be depended upon but that one hundred and fifty sail of vessels left New York last First Day, but not known by us whither, and that General Lee, with ten thousand men, was within a few miles of the regulars.

5. After dinner, went in company with Paul Fooks, Thomas Smith, and Leonard Keassler, a begging for old clothes for the naked soldiers coming from camp. In the evening, sent for by Council of Safety. I waited on them. It was to request I would join with some other citizens in providing necessaries for the sick and needy soldiers returning from the camp. I readily agreed.

6. Dined at home; afterwards went in [the] chair with my son to the Bettering House, having sent some of the sick there, in order to provide for their reception; thence to sundry places in the City, as the sick came in very fast this day.

7. To sundry places with some of my brethren, to place the returning soldiers in separate houses and send the very sick and weak to the Bettering House; providing also fire wood and straw with sundries at the different places.

8. Went to our office, appointed in Richard Willing's house, in Second Street; came home to dinner; then went back to the said place in order to provide and give necessary directions for the sick soldiers, &c. News brought of General Howe's intentions of bringing his army by land through the Jerseys to this City. Martial Law declared, and Gen. Putnam constituted chief ruler in this Province.[1]

---

[1] See Appendix (E.)

9. All shops ordered to be shut; the Militia to march into the Jerseys; all in hurry and confusion; News that Gen. Howe is on his march; attend at our office the sick soldiers, &c.

10. Our people in confusion, of all ranks, sending all their goods out of town into the country. News brought that our army had sent their heavy baggage from Trenton [to] this side of the river; the enemy advancing in great order, and was at Brunswick. This day, attended forenoon and afternoon [at] the aforesaid office. Great numbers of sick soldiers arriving into the town.

11. Further accounts of the rapid progress of Gen. Howe. Our Congress leaves this City for Baltimore. The militia going out fast for Trenton: streets full of wagons, going out with goods.

12. News that Howe's Light Horse were at Princeton, and that Gen. Washington, with all his troops, had come over [the] Delaware. Attended forenoon and afternoon at [the] office; numbers of sick soldiers arriving. ...... We sent one wagon load of household goods to the Trap, as did my sons to a place near.

13. Accounts of Howe's army's coming into Trenton, and part of them going [to] and received into Burlington by the Friends there. The Friends here moved but little of their goods, as they seem to be satisfied that if Gen. Howe should take this City, as many here imagined that he would, their goods and property would be safe; other people still sending their goods.

14. Alarming and fresh accounts of Howe's near approach; people hurrying out of town.

15. Accounts that Howe's troops had attempted to cross our river, at several places and several times, but always repulsed, so that he could not effect it. Our troops increasing and in high spirits.

16. Much the same as yesterday, except an account that Gen. Lee was taken prisoner through treachery.

17. Accounts that Howe's army were returning back

to Brunswick, and that many of our citizens were in his camp, having deserted over to him.

18. Great numbers of the Country Militia coming in to go to join Gen. Washington's army. ...... News that our army intended to cross at Trenton into the Jerseys.

19. Numbers of Country Militia coming into town. A large number of our troops left this City to join some in the Jerseys, in order to pursue and attack a number of Hessian troops, who, it's said, had come as far as Moorestown, this side of Mount Holly, in the Jerseys. It's said that the Generals Sullivan and Gates had joined General Washington's army, and that the enemy were fortifying Bordentown.

20. Waited on Gen. Putnam respecting firewood's being cut for the soldiery, as little came now by water. ...... No news stirring to be depended on.

21. Past nine, went to our office, thence I waited upon Gen. Putnam; then back to the office; past twelve, waited upon [the] Council of Safety, respecting their sending hands to cut firewood for the troops in and about the city. ...... News brought that a ship from England, mounting eighteen guns, having fifty-odd officers and two Generals sent to replace all officers here in America that were Parliament men, who were sent for home, was taken by ———, Capt. ———, one of our Continental ships and carried into ———. Great numbers of our Country Militia are daily arriving in this City. This day the *American Crisis*, No. 1, written by T. Paine, was published.

22. No news I heard to day from camp (nor no account of Poll as yet).

23. With Dr. Allison to College, some of the Country Militia being quartered there. ...... Yesterday, it's said, the Brig Andrew Doria, arrived from Saint Eustatia, with goods on account of Congress. It's said she has taken two or three prizes, not arrived; that she ran through the several men-of-war now lying in our Capes.

25. This day, numbers of men came in from [the] back counties, and a detachment of Three Thousand, with Gen. Putnam, was agreed upon to leave this City and pass into the Jerseys to-morrow morning. The men were in high spirits.

26. Waited upon General Putnam respecting some orders for sick soldiers; thence to [the] Council of Safety, on account of the Commissary's refusing to grant rations to poor sick soldiers, coming to town without their officers.

27. News brought this day of our troops under Gen. Washington's attacking Trenton yesterday morning, having beat the enemy and drove them out of town; and that this day were landed in this Province from thence, Nine Hundred and eighteen Hessians; one Colonel, two Lieut. Colonels, Three Majors, Four Captains, Eight Lieutenants, Twelve Ensigns, Two Surgeon's mates, Ninety-nine Sergeants, Twenty-five drummers, nine musicians, five servants, seven hundred and forty-five privates; One thousand stand of arms, and six brass field pieces, twelve six and four pounders, three standards, &c., with all the ammunition for the six brass field pieces.

28. To [the] Council of Safety, in order to procure wood for the Associator's wives, gone to camp. Got an order for Wm. Coats, tanner, to supply them. ...... The news of yesterday confirmed, and that our militia crossed the river into the Jerseys yesterday, and that the Hessian prisoners are expected from Newtown, Bucks County, into this City to-morrow. This morning, Capt. Proctor's company, with two field pieces, ammunition and baggage, left this City for head quarters in Bucks County or elsewhere, as did some hundreds of country militia. It's said Three Thousand went for camp yesterday, headed by Gen. Putnam, all in high spirits and warm clothing.

30. Near eleven, the Hessian prisoners, to the amount

of nine hundred, arrived in this City, and made a poor, despicable appearance. Numbers of the militia, with three field pieces, crossed our river from this City to-day, and many of the prisoners taken on Long Island, returned to this City very poorly and weak. It's said they were allowed but half allowance by Gen. Howe during their imprisonment.

31. More of our poor prisoners coming into town. ...... More Hessian prisoners, with the officers, came to town this evening from the Jerseys.

1777.

JANUARY 1. More Hessians and their officers, with many of their wounded, brought to town this day and evening.

2. A number of sick soldiers arrived from New York, being discharged by Gen. Howe, after a tedious imprisonment, being starved by the enemy. ...... To the office after presenting, by request, to [the] Council of Safety, a petition to them respecting a testimony put forth by the meeting of sufferings, the twentieth [of] last month, signed by J.... P....

3. News flying about of an engagement between our forces and those of the enemy at Trenton. This raises the spirits of the Tory party, who are in great expectation of Howe's success. Published this day the Resolve of Congress and Council of Safety, respecting the establishing of the Continental Currency.

4. The news of the day, and confirmed by express, it's said, just arrived at nine at night, is that Gen. Washington occupied part of Trenton, and Howe the other with the main body of the British army. Our General being informed of Gen. Howe's advancing with four thousand men, went privately at midnight in order to intercept Howe, and meeting with him at Maidenhead,

an engagement ensued early in the morning, when the enemy, standing a smart fire for half an hour, gave way, when Gen. Washington pursued them to Princeton, when the Fortieth Regiment took refuge in the College, which our General summoned to surrender, or else he would fire the building and burn them in it; upon which they all surrendered. They likewise took three hundred prisoners on the road with eight field pieces, &c. He also sent off two brigades to the relief of that part of his army he left behind him to amuse the main body of the enemy at Trenton, which decamped as soon as they heard of Gen. Washington's victory, and filed off towards Pennytown. 'Thanks to God for this victory!

5. Yesterday Gen. Putnam left this city for the camp with five hundred men, and Gen. Irving is to have command of this city in his absence. It's further said that Gen. Washington is appointed sole dictator for the space of six months.

7. The gondolas returned to this city, and brought some Tory prisoners with them, taken in the Jerseys. It was the severe freezing upwards that brought the gondolas down.

9. This afternoon, were brought to town, between seventy and eighty English prisoners (among whom it's said were some of their Light Horse), who were sent to our new prison.

10. It's said that Col. Scott has taken sixty or seventy Highlanders with a great many baggage-wagons, and that part of Col. Smith's riflemen had taken twenty-seven Tories (killed seven) with four baggage-wagons loaded with plunder, part of which, to the value of Seven or Eight Hundred Pounds' worth, they sold at Burlington yesterday. The remainder was brought this day to the city with the prisoners.

12. This morning all the officers and soldiers belonging both to the Continental army [and] the troops of this State or militia (Col. Fleming's Regiment from Vir-

ginia excepted) now in this city, were, by order from the General yesterday, to assemble in the barrack-yard at ten o'clock, with their arms and accoutrements, under pain of being severely punished for neglect. The troops are to draw three days' provisions this day, which are to be immediately cooked. For what end this manœuvre is intended, is a profound secret to the public. By accounts from the Jerseys, we hear that a body of militia of that State, under Gen. Maxwell, attacked and defeated one Regiment of Highlanders, and one of Hessian troops, at Spank's town on this day was a week.

13. A number of Hessians, Waldeckers, &c., prisoners, came to town this evening.

14. A number of sick soldiers coming in. Visited to-day by Dr. Shippen, Jr., who being chief physician for the army here, proposed the taking of the sick soldiers from the sundry houses in this city, where they are now placed, into the House of Employment to-morrow. This proposal I communicated to the Council of Safety (who had requested me to take charge of the sick soldiers about a month past), in order for their determination, but received no answer this evening, as they were very busy.

15. To the Treasurer Nesbit's and Co. Received Five Hundred Pounds, by order of [the] Committee of Safety, for the relief of the sick soldiers.

16. This morning marched out the Virginia Ninth Regiment for the Camp. ...... Just come to town ...... a number of Light Horse from Virginia. I counted with officers seventy men, well accoutred. About noon was brought to town, a number of prisoners. ...... This afternoon, was buried from the City Tavern, Gen. Mercer (who died in Princeton of the wounds received there the third instant) with all the honors of war, on the south side of Christ Church Yard, his body having been brought to town the Fifteenth instant for that purpose.[1]

---

[1] His body now lies in Laurel Hill Cemetery.

17. After breakfast, went to the office, where the members present last night, met and agreed to send two members with our application to the Council of Safety. The members were Thomas Leach and William Ball, who brought for answer to us that we should proceed in our appointment as before, without paying any regard to Dr. Wm. Shippen's notices, &c., upon which we resumed our former care and regard to the sick soldiers and prisoners. This forenoon, Capt. Wm. Shippen was interred with military honors in St. Peter's Church Yard, he being killed in the engagement the third instant, with Gen. Mercer, and brought to this city with him to be buried here with his family. ...... Set to cut some sheets of Continental money as I had done some evenings before, for the convenience of having cash to defray [the] expenses of the office, and to supply, in part, the wants of the wives of the Associators of Captains Bower's and Brewster's companies, now in the Jerseys.

18. This day sundry troops left the city for the camp; also it's said that fourteen hundred militia men arrived in this city from Maryland and our back counties, as did a number of sick soldiers from New York. Yesterday was published the second number of the *American Crisis* by Common Sense, author of the first. Sundry pieces of news to-day, but none to be depended upon from the camp, except that Gen. Washington had his headquarters at Morristown, and Gen. Sullivan with his advanced guard at Chatham, about five miles distance, and that Gen. Howe was at Amboy and the heights of Brunswick with his army, and had sent Gen. Lee[1] prisoner with a very strong guard, consisting of all his light-horse and infantry from the latter to the former, three days ago.

19. This week past, went out of this city, three or four companies of the Virginia light-horse, commanded by sundry captains, for our camp at Morristown.

---

[1] Gen. Charles Lee.

20. A number of the militia came to the city to-day from [the] country, as did some, say two companies, of light-horse from Virginia. In the evening were brought thirteen Tories, it's said from Crosswick's in the Jerseys, under a guard.

21. Deal of floating ice in the river so as to prevent the plunder of a number of Tories in the Jerseys (part of which, it's said, to the amount of thirty-seven wagons, is arrived at Wm. Cooper's ferry, &c.), from being brought over to this city. ...... It's said that several hundred soldiers arrived in town from the lower parts of this Province and Maryland, and that several more Tories are brought in this day from the Jerseys, among whom is Col. Charles Read.[1]

22. About twelve came into town from Morristown in the Jerseys, the Second Battalion of City Militia, commanded by Col. Bayard, with their baggage wagons, &c. ...... A number of troops from the back parts came to town this day, it's said, eight hundred; as did also Gen. Thomas Mifflin from the camp. It is said that Gen. McDougall, with a detachment of about fifteen hundred New Englandmen, has taken possession of Fort Washington. The number of [the] garrison who are prisoners of war is trifling, but the military stores are considerable.

23. Accounts from the army are that within these three or four days, there have been several skirmishes in the East Jerseys, in which our troops have always beat the enemy. About three miles up the Raritan from Brunswick, a party of our army attacked a large body of the enemy and took near six hundred head of cattle, upwards of fifty wagons, fifty or sixty butts and casks of oil, and a number of English horses of the dray breed, which were so emaciated that they were scarce able to walk.

---

[1] From the twenty-first of January to the early part of April, Mr. Marshall was confined to his house by a severe attack of illness.

24. Last evening, came from the camp, the Light Infantry of [the] First Battalion of City Militia, also were brought the remains of Ensign Antony Morris, Junr., who was killed at Princeton, bravely supporting the cause of Liberty and Freedom; buried this afternoon in Friends' burial ground in a very heavy shower of rain, and without military honors, it being the request of his relations to the General that he should be so interred. This morning, came to town, three or four of our field pieces with the train. In the afternoon also arrived from twenty to twenty-five of our City Light Horse, being dismissed from camp with the thanks of Gen. Washington, as part of the Virginians had joined him, and one company of the said corps arrived in this city yesterday on their way to Gen. Washington's camp. ...... It is again asserted for a fact that New York was taken last Thursday night by the Continental army.

25. Great quantities of backwoodsmen coming to town this day; so many that with what were here before, an order was issued for the billeting of them in the non-associators' houses, which was put into execution in our part of the City. This day, some companies of troops left this City for the Jerseys, as yesterday did the Virginia Light Horse for the camp. This afternoon was interred in the [old Presbyterian] burial ground [Col. John Haselet of the Lower Counties] with military honors, attended, it's said, by great numbers of people of different ranks. This afternoon, set out for Easton, the Commissioners appointed to confer with the different tribes of Indians to be assembled there, on a treaty.

28. N.B. The Lottery for these States began selling their tickets this day for the First Class.

30. The accounts of the cruelty and wantonness of our enemies, the English, could scarcely be believed, were they not authenticated by proper witnesses; another instance of which is the news of the day, that being in possession of Rhode Island (a town of about seven hund-

red houses), and which made no resistance, yet after plundering the inhabitants indiscriminately, Tory and Whig, [they] set it on fire and consumed it. Further particulars expected.

FEBRUARY 1. This day was published the King of Britain's Speech to both Houses of his Parliament, dated October 21st, 1776 (No Poll). For public occurrences, see *Evening Post*, Numb. 308.

4. This day was published the Law of our Assembly enforcing the Continental Currency and the Bills of Credit emitted by Resolves of the late Assembly, making them a legal tender, and for other purposes therein mentioned.

6. The news of the day, as I am informed, is the electing of five members by our Assembly to represent this State in Congress. The gentlemen elected were Dr. Franklin, Robert Morris, William Moore, Jonathan B. Smith and Gen. Roberdeau.

7. A number of troops from the back counties, Maryland, &c., which were placed in Non-Associators' houses in different proportions, as to the fitness of their houses.

19. Account is that six or seven sail of trading vessels are in the river, amongst which [are] two from [the] French West Indies with sundry passengers, &c.; one a prize from our Privateer Rattlesnake.

20. Thomas Salter came and paid me, as I think, a religious visit, as our conversation turned upon that point calmly and soberly till near dusk.

21. On the Fourteenth instant, the following persons were elected at the State House, Thomas Wharton, Jr., Councillor, and Col. Bull, Col. Moore, Major Lollar and Col. Coates, members of Assembly for Philadelphia County. It's said the Hon. John M'Kinley is appointed Governor and Commander-in-chief in the Delaware State.

22. Gen. Farmoah, French officer, came to town some days past, and amongst other things informed P. Fooks, that some days past Gen. Howe sent a flag to

Gen. Washington, proposing a cessation of arms for three months. Gen. Washington answered he could not grant it, as he was prepared and ready to receive him in battle, when he pleased.

23. I am informed that yesterday afternoon Major S...... and near sixty-six Tories were brought from the Jerseys into this City, under a strong guard (some of them in irons) and confined in the New Jail. Our Assembly have appointed James Wilson, Delegate to Congress in addition to our members, and George Clymer as Delegate in the stead of Wm. Moore, who resigned.

27. This day, it's said, were brought to this City, six brass field pieces with their proper appendages, that were taken from the Hessians at Trenton in December last.

MARCH 3 to 7. I was severely handled by a pleuritic pain in my right side. This continued both day and night for the whole of this week. I was blooded, blistered on my side, some nights could not lie down, but obliged to sit up all night, yet to the praise of God be it spoken, his Good Spirit wonderfully assisted me under this grievous affliction, so that I comforted myself in the heavenly support, I now witnessed to be daily administered. Blessed be thy name, Amen.

9 to 21. Exceeding weak, so that I was scarcely able at times to read. I was generally more or less visited every day by numbers of acquaintances, but in particular by Whitehill, Bonham, Thorn, Foster, and also by Paul Fooks, this being the first of his going out. Thus I have been visited by this disorder, which brought me on through length of time down to this day by weakness, so low, that death appeared at times not far off, yet through the mercy of our great God, and through the vigilance, industry and care of my wife (who really has been and is a blessing unto me) I still live, to his eternal praise, in hopes I may dedicate the remainder of

life unto his honor and praise, who has thus preserved me, to whom be glory now and forever more, Amen.

31. This day was hanged Molesworth, being convicted of treasonable practices against this State.[1]

APRIL 7. Eat breakfast soon, as my wife was getting ready to go a journey with my son Christopher as far as Lancaster, in order to view a house and lot that were to be sold by Col. Cox, in order for me and my family to remove there as I am so poorly in my health, and to be out of the difficulties, should this City be invaded, as I was not capable of rendering any assistance. They went on horseback about eleven o'clock.

13. Account came of Ship [Morris] from France's being chased by three men-of-war for a whole day. [The Captain] finding he could not get clear ran her aground and blew her up, after securing all her papers and crew. But Captain Anderson himself staying too long was lost with the ship. [Account by] express from Lewistown to-day, that left it yesterday, of the Roebuck and two other ships' standing up the Bay. By an order of Congress in conjunction with [the] board of war, a number of persons in each ward were appointed and went upon duty this day through this City to take account of all provisions of every sort, with rum, wine, sugar, spirits, &c.

14. I had my books that I sent to College last fall, brought home this day. It's said that nine men-of-war are in the river.

16. Near five came Paul Fooks, Dr. Phyle and Col. John Cox, who brought the Deeds for the house in Lancaster, and executed his to me, for which I then paid him, he then promising to acknowledge the same with his wife, when she came to town, of which he desired those gentlemen to take notice and remember this his promise.

JUNE 6. Paid John Whitehill £48 for hauling five

---

[1] See the *Life of Gen. Joseph Reed*, for a full account of this person.

loads of goods to Lancaster; two from Philadelphia, three from the Trap.

9. This afternoon severe thunder struck the steeple of Christ Church; carried away some parts of the ornaments of the Crown on the top of the rods.

16. All this day at Benjamin's ...... Kitty and Charles both gone to town on the news of the enemy's marching from Brunswick in two divisions, &c.

27. Arrived at our house in Lancaster near seven. I was really tired, the road so hilly and stony, and I being so poorly.

JULY 11. Sundry Philadelphians, who moved here last winter to live, have returned back with their families this week; not pleased.

13. We have had some difficulties to encounter here, as the people here have taken offence against the Philadelphians, who some of them, have not behaved prudently, so that at last the country folks would scarcely bring them anything to market. But I'm in hopes, as some are gone and some more going, that the harmony that once subsisted will return again. I've not been able to get a load of hay or of wood, as yet, nor pasture for my horse. Had not my wife bought a load in the spring, and we sent some bushels of oats stowed in our bacon, he must have suffered, but we have a lot adjoining to us; though small, it serves to turn him in just to stretch his legs. A bushel of bran or shorts can't be procured, but [I] am in hopes after harvest, we shall get supplied, as I intend to visit some of the farmers. I just give this note by way of memento, to remember some of our difficulties. Yet I must say that the people of note, that I have had the pleasure of seeing and conversing with, have behaved extremely polite and kind to me, and some of the females have come and visited my wife and more have promised.

14. I went this morning and visited several of our Philadelphia friends, and at the same time in company

with our friend George Schlosser, reminded them, as well as some of our Lancaster friends, whom we visited, of the distress poor Dr. Young (deceased)'s family was left in, most of whom, to their honor be it remembered, gave me what they thought proper, in order for me to remit it for their relief, the which I accepted and kindly thanked them on the family's behalf. ...... This day, Dr. Kennedy sent me two wagon loads of firewood, he calls them cords. I let him have two entirely new Octavo volumes of Brooks's *Practice of Physick*, for which he is to pay me when I settle for this wood and what more he brings me.

26. At breakfast, received an affectionate letter from son Christopher, giving particular account of the situation of all their families. The account afforded us comfort and satisfaction. In it [he] informed [me that] brown sugars were raised in town to £30 per hundred, requesting that if I could at 4*s*. per lb. I would get one hundred weight; on which I went to town, but the news of the prices had reached some here. However, I got, after traversing about, a neat hundred at 4*s*. per pound, and thirty pounds extraordinary at 5*s*. per pound.

29. After dinner, went to visit sundry town's people, also to hear what news from Philadelphia, as several persons from there this day or two past had reported that Gen. Howe with the English fleet was expected there daily, nay, that the fleet was really in the Delaware river. These reports gave great uneasiness respecting our friends there, but I could find nothing further as no express here was yet arrived.

30. There has been for these two weeks past in agitation by the friends of the States of America in this place, a plan in order to form a Society under the name of the Civil Society, in order to assist the present plan of government, whereby each member will be called upon to take the Oath or Affirmation of Allegiance or leave the State. This meets great opposition from a

Junto, who call themselves Moderate men, and [maintain] that no man should be compelled to be honest.

31. Advice by express yesterday from Philadelphia, was that one division of the enemy's fleet was seen off our capes, steering for them; that Congress had demanded Four Thousand Militia from the States to join the Continental Army, which was marching towards Philadelphia in three divisions, one by Reading, one by Trenton ferry, but the main body with Gen. Washington to Corryell's ferry, to join as occasionally.

AUGUST 1. I afterwards spent some time in religious conversation with a Menonist Preacher at Dr. Neff's. In the afternoon I was visited by another named Benja. Ereson, Jr., who brought me their Confession of Faith to peruse. ...... No news of any moment by the post last night, except that the enemy was seen off the Capes, that Philadelphia was pretty quiet, and the Militia all ready to turn out. Brown Sugar at 7s. per pound. ...... News that some of the enemy's ships were got to Reedy Island; whether true or not remains doubtful.

2. Just heard from [a] passenger in the Stage Wagon arrived last night, who left Philadelphia Fifth Day morning,[1] that the alarm guns were fired as they came away, and the citizens in great hurry and bustle. ...... Express arrived to-day for six hundred wagons to go directly for Philadelphia, and for the Lieutenant of the County to have the militia ready for marching, as two hundred and fifty sail of vessels were seen off our Light House, standing in for the Capes.

3. It's said that news is come from Philadelphia that Howe's fleet has entirely left the Bay, and gone they don't know where.

4. Came back before dinner. I was much disturbed after I came, our girl Poll driving her same stroke of impudence as when she was in Philadelphia, and her

---

[1] Thursday, July 31st. The Stage Wagon was two days traveling sixty miles.

mistress so hoodwinked by her as not to see it, which gave me much uneasiness, and which I am determined not to put up with.

5. No news but that in short, the Enemy on the Thirty-first was off our Capes, but suddenly moved away; that Gen. Washington with some of his troops was in Philadelphia, but most of them at Germantown and the Falls; the militia in motion in order to give the enemy, if they came up the river, which had been suspected, a warm reception; every thing of clothing and eatables extremely dear. In the evening I went down into town; learned that the County Court was opened this day in a very regular manner, and the business conducted decently.

8. Our Court broke up yesterday with great decorum.

14. News from Pittsburgh by express this day from Gen. Hand, that the fort was like to be invested by three thousand Canadians, Indians, Regulars, &c., and that we had but eighty men in [the] fort, and about eight hundred could be collected soon.

15. To writing, being engaged at times for this week past in correcting the Annals of the Brethren at Ephrata, left with me by Peter Miller and Obed when here to visit me.

20. I gave to James Cannon, to carry to the Widow Young, the donations I collected in this place, which, with my own, amounted to Seventeen Pounds, six shillings.

21. I was at Dr. Neff's, where James Webb, a mason, came for some medicine, who related that about four years ago, about six in the morning, he saw in the sky before the door the likeness of a great snake without a head, who shaking his tail made all about there to tremble, and that at [the] same time fiery balls were seen to fly about at Germantown.[1] This he interpreted was our

---

[1] See Appendix F.

present war, which we carried on without any head, and so we should come to nothing. This afternoon I finished my correcting of the manuscript or History of the Brethren at Ephrata, containing four hundred and eighty-eight quarto pages. N. B. The said Webb asserted that our present Assembly were not regularly chosen, as they were voted in by a parcel of soldiery and apprentice boys; therefore, their laws were not worth regarding.

22. Went and agreed with Joseph Walter, the barber, to call and shave me twice a week at thirty-six shillings a year. ...... This day, it's said, that Capt. McCullough has taken upon him to examine all strangers passing through here respecting taking the test, which several complied with and took the same, but John Hollingshead refused, for which he was committed to the Jail of Lancaster. No news yet from Howe.

23. By express last night the militia on their march down were countermanded, on account of the Indians' breaking in on the frontiers. ..... In the evening came George Schlosser and Benja. Harbeson, who brought account of the defeat of Lieut. Col. Bern by Gen. Stark on the sixteenth instant, who commanded a body of mostly militia, who wholly routed his army and took a great number of prisoners. For particulars, see *Pennsylvania Journal*, Numb. 1804.

24. Sent our negro woman and girl Poll to Friends' Meeting. Wife and I stayed at home to keep the boys out of the orchard. After dinner I took a walk with Capt. Markoe to the barracks; stayed there till the English, Scotch and Irish prisoners, to the number of two hundred, marched out under a strong guard to Reading.

25. To [the] barrack; waited till our division of Hessian prisoners, consisting of three hundred and forty-five, marched out under a strong guard (with some women and baggage wagons, as the prisoners yesterday had done), for Lebanon.

26. News that Gen. Washington, with half his army and light horse, passed through Philadelphia [on] First Day morning, on their way for Wilmington, and that Howe, with his fleet, was seen off Eagle Point, but had not landed. On First Day morning [the] bellman went round this town, calling upon the inhabitants that had Hessian prisoners, to take them to the barracks and receive receipts for them, but very few obeyed.

27. News this morning is that Howe has landed his men about eight miles from the Head of Elk. It's said that he sent one of his men to this town for a Hessian man and woman, by name; that he found them last night, and they three set out for his camp this morning. This made some people here uneasy, as they were not sent after, but as no horse could be found, Capt. Markoe lent his horse, without bridle and saddle. (It's from him I had this relation this morning.) A parcel of Hessian prisoners sent off this day under guard for Lebanon.

28. News brought that the persons sent after, the Captain and the man, were overtaken and brought back. I then went into town just as Samuel Henry, William Atlee [and] Michael Hubley, were going to the prison to examine them. These gentlemen invited Capt. Markoe and myself to attend them, which we did, when on the examination, both   Hewey, the pretended officer, and   Wood, pleaded innocency, and as their examination was written and the reasons for apprehending them also, the which was immediately sent to Gen. Washington at head quarters, their trial was postponed till an answer comes from the General, and they were ordered in the mean time to be confined apart.

29. Yesterday there went from this town under guard, three hundred and sixty-five Hessian prisoners for Carlisle and adjacent places.

30. A great stir this morning in town, occasioned by some [men] of Col. White, of the Georgia Regiment's robbing him last night. They were pursued and taken.

Part of the cash was recovered, but his trunk, with all his papers, more money, his commission, &c., not to be found, though searched after all this day. ...... In the evening we again went into town to hear news, but none for certain, but that the enemy was in possession of Cœcil Court House and Head of Elk; that our army was at Christiana, but that our Light Horse had been down to visit them, had a skirmish and taken some few prisoners.

31. News of the day, little; that Howe was getting his men on shore at Elk; that thirty deserters had come over to us; that in some skirmishes, our people had taken about forty prisoners; that Gen. Washington was at Wilmington. ...... No further news, but that a number of wagons, with the Congress materials of printing, press, types, &c., were just arrived from Baltimore.

SEPTEMBER 6. This afternoon, the two thieves, who stole Col. White's cash and trunk, were marched about a mile and a half out of town, in order, it's said, to be hanged, but upon the Colonel's lady's intercession, it's said, they were pardoned from death, but received two or three hundred lashes each, well laid on their backs and buttocks. A great number of spectators, it's said, were assembled.

8. News came yesterday of a conspiracy amongst some of the garrison of Fort Pitt, in conjunction with some of the settlers on Red Creek, to deliver up the fort to the commander of Detroit, who with some Indians, was invited to come; but this discovery has, it's to be hoped, baffled their hellish scheme.

10. Received two letters from Ed. Milne, covering newspapers and Remonstrance of sundry Quakers and other disaffected persons to the United States of America, to the Congress and to the President and Council of this State, one of them signed by three or four, the other by twenty-one. A written list was also handed about, containing the names of forty persons. News from the

army, viz: that Howe was advanced to New Garden,[1] and had taken a number of cattle.

11. News was that the enemy advanced towards the Concord road to Philadelphia; that part of our army was gone to Chad's Ford; that several deserters were gone for Philadelphia; some, very few, come here; that some of the Virginia forces coming to our assistance had crossed [the] Susquenannah to the amount of one thousand; others on the road. From Fort Pitt that one or two persons were apprehended, coming there from Detroit, on one of them were found some papers, particularly one with the list of names of those in the fort and in the neighborhood, who had declared their allegiance to George the Third. One of the persons, by the name Wm. Gallaher, formerly a pedler, had made his escape, for whom a reward of six hundred dollars is offered.

12. I went into town, an alarm being spread that some of Howe's Light Horse had been seen at Pequea Church, about eighteen miles from Lancaster. This set sundry people (by report) to pack up their goods and some sent them out of town into the country. As there were so many flying reports and no certainty, a subscription was proposed and carried immediately into execution, for hiring three men to go as express to where the army was, to bring certain accounts, which was immediately put in practice, and three were dispatched. ...... Met Col. Calbreth, who was just come from Philadelphia. By him learned that the news in the morning was the lie of the day, as he had traveled the road and saw none of the enemy, nor had they been there where reported. He had with him a Proclamation published by the Executive Council, inviting all persons to assist against the common enemy. This was read at Major Wertz's where many of us were collected.

---

[1] Chester County, Pa.

13. Came home in the evening. Just then, came to his family, Capt. Markoe, who was present at the engagement on the eleventh instant, near to Concord Meeting or Chad's ford, between, as he computes, three thousand of our troops under the Generals Maxwell, Sullivan and Sterling, and eight thousand of the enemy, which began in the afternoon and continued until dark, in which great numbers were slain on both sides, but that our people behaved most gallantly, until ordered to retreat, as the ground would not admit of our troops' coming to a general engagement, as the enemy were in possession of an eminence that overawed our camp, so they rested for the night. The loss on either side was not as yet ascertained.

15 Election this day for Burgesses for this borough, when Henry Dehaff and George Ross, were chosen. News of the day is that the Friends sent out of town[1] as prisoners were stopped at Pottsgrove by the Pottses there, and they would not suffer them to proceed any further, upon which a company of militia was ordered from Reading to take them in charge and convey them to their destined post. It's said that Gen. Putnam, with three thousand men, was expected to have been at Philadelphia yesterday; that Gen. Smallwood with his forces, near two thousand, was at Nottingham meeting house yesterday, and was there to be joined by some more forces from the Eastern Shore; that three thousand Jersey forces were to cross [the] Delware at Cooper's ferry, this day.

17. Near twelve, express arrived from camp; brought account that in the action last week, our people had between four and five hundred men killed and wounded; that our enemy, the English, had near two thousand killed and wounded, nine hundred of which were killed in the action; that we had not one-half of our people engaged, but that the enemy had treble our numbers, and

---

[1] Philadelphia.

the flower of their army, yet our people held them in play till dark, retreated about six hundred yards, and lost seven or eight field pieces; that they were in no wise intimidated but in high spirits, eagerly longing for a fair opportunity. It's said they have been joined since by four thousand troops, but from where could not learn. It's further said that, four or five hundred volunteers from Virginia, were at Yorktown[1] yesterday, on their march to join Gen. Washington's army. It's also said that James Rankin, who ran away last week from his habitation in York county on account of his being accused of forming a scheme to destroy all our magazines of ammunition, arms, tents, baggage, provisions, &c., in Lancaster, Carlisle, York, Reading, &c., was taken about sixteen miles from our enemies' camp, and secured, but where I could not learn.

19. No post come; supposed to be prevented by the enemy on the road, as it's said, they were near Downingstown, and our army near French Creek, yesterday. This morning numbers of people came out on the hill near our place, in order, it's said, to hear the firing of the cannon between our people and the enemy, but I could not say that I heard any. ...... After dinner, went into town; saw two companies [of] Lancaster militia march forward towards the camp. One of our expresses came in; brought a letter dated at Red Lion, yesterday, two o'clock, A.M., giving account that the enemy were on full march for Philadelphia, and that they intended to follow them in a few minutes, so that an engagement may be hourly expected.

20. It's wonderful to hear and to see the progress and fertility of the lying spirit, that moves about in and through the different classes of men in this place, attended with such twistings, windings and turnings, that it seems impossible to fix any truth upon them. ...... Two letters from son Christopher and his daughter, letting us know

---
[1] York, Pa.

that they were all well, but much terrified as the enemy were pushing that way towards Swedes' Ford, and that Gen. Washington had sent into their neighborhood and the Trap, about eight hundred wagons with stores and sick soldiers, &c., and [they] were then momently expecting to hear the dismal sound of cannon, and were also at a loss what they should do on these momentous occasions. ...... We sat late, conversing on these melancholy times.

21. Near five, came and stood for some considerable time at [the] corner of B ...... 's house, the said B ...... and James W ...... Sen'r, in a strong and zealous conversation. The nearness of, and the harmony of, their two spirits, I was surprised with. The zeal that animated them was powerful and strong; gestures and motions, various and frequent; love and attraction by shaking and holding hands was conspicuous. Upon the whole, I was satisfied by their behavior that they were, though different in the principles of religion, by the outward profession, yet now animated by one spirit — the same that would enslave and reduce the freedom of America.

22. News of the day is that the enemy have formed a design to surround and take prisoners Gen. Wayne's Brigade. For that purpose, about one in the morning of the Twenty-first instant, a number of them without noise till they entered our lines, then setting up a prodigious hideous noise, attacked our people with swords and bayonets; and as our people were some sleeping and off their guard, they were thrown into confusion, yet made a good retreat, losing neither cannon nor baggage. It's said that we had about one hundred killed, wounded and taken prisoners, and that the enemy suffered equally with us, notwithstanding their number and the surprise.[1]

23. Just after dark visited by Col. Ross, who said he

---

[1] This has since been known as the Paol Massacre.

had slept at my son's [the] night before last; that they were all well, but in trouble as the enemy were as nigh to them as six miles; that they had no time to write, as they were sending some of their valuable goods further into the country, viz: over Oley Hills.[1]

25. Visited by Capt. Hervey, who came to enquire after news, but none was stirring but the lie of yesterday (as I had heard), which was that Howe had crossed [the] Schuylkill and entered Philadelphia, the twenty-third instant, without any opposition; nay further, that the City was all in flames. This, Mrs. Taggert told me, a man had said before her door yesterday. Thus are many of the people in this place imposed upon. ...... Came into town President Hancock, and some others of the Delegates.

26. News of the day was that Howe was got into Philadelphia; then, no; then he had crossed Schuylkill; then that he had returned back; so that there was nothing to be depended upon.

28. News of the day is that three thousand of Howe's army, under G^l. Cornwallis, entered Philadelphia last sixth day, in the afternoon.

29. Took leave of sundry of the Congress, who were setting off for Yorktown. ...... Many of the inhabitants of Philadelphia came to-day and yesterday to this place, as did our President or Governor, the Executive Council and the members of Assembly, who met here this day in the Court House. News of the day is that Gen. Burgoyne and his army are defeated,[2] himself wounded, and Ticonderoga retaken; that part of Gen. Howe's army encamped on the commons facing the Bettering House;[3] that Gen. Cornwallis had made his head

---

[1] Berks County, Pa.

[2] Burgoyne was defeated on the 19th of September. He intrenched himself on the following day, and was finally defeated and compelled to surrender on the 7th of October.

[3] This building stood upon the square between Spruce and Pine and Tenth and Eleventh Streets. It was taken down about forty years since.

quarters at Widow Norris's. The remainder of the British army encamped along the road to Germantown, and ours were behind them.

30. News of the day is that last seventh day, four men of war came to anchor off our fort,[1] in order to take it, and the cheveaux de frise, but were repulsed so as to leave their anchors behind them, and get away as fast as they could, being much mauled, &c., by the fort.[1]

OCTOBER 1. It's said that Major Miller, with a party of men, had made an excursion from our army to the Rising Sun on [the] Germantown Road. On return, met some Hessian troops, engaged them, killed nine [and] brought off six prisoners with their accoutrements.

2. Went into town with Col. McKean, who had just called at our house. I visited sundry Delegates and Assemblymen in Lancaster, having a desire that in conjunction with [the] Executive Council and the Assembly, some good regulations might be made here in order for our protection and for our comfortable living here. ......
R. Whitehill, Dr. Phyle and self, took a walk to view a number of Virginians encamped upon the commons, ... thence into the main street near the prison. Met a large number of prisoners just brought into town from Bethlehem, going to-morrow for Virginia.

3. Spent some time in conversation with sundry persons, respecting a Dutchman called Motchs, who said he came from Philadelphia, had a printed pass from G¹. Howe, yet the Magistrates here, with the President and Executive Council, all suffered him to pass on his journey to York, and then to Philadelphia, as he said. ......
Three or four hundred Virginians left this place to-day.

4. News of the morning is that [James] Brooks (the conspirator with Dr. Kearsley), who has been long confined in this jail, made his escape last night, and this day Caleb Johnson, a Friend and inhabitant of this place,

---
[1] Fort Mifflin.

was examined before the Council and sent to the prison, as being privy and accessory to his escape. ...... News of the day, to be depended upon, was that the day before G¹. Howe entered Philadelphia, being the twenty-fifth [of] last month, a number of Tories, said to amount to four or five hundred, went out in parade to Germantown, returned and triumphed through the streets all the night, taking, securing and sending to prison all they could find that they looked upon or termed friends to the Free States of America, amongst whom, was and is the parson, Jacob Duché. My son Benja. writes on the First instant, that most of the Generals were viewing the hill near his house, in order, if occasion [required] to make a stand; that they were moving down, and that part of our army and scouts were at Germantown; and that the Generals, Read and Cadwalader, being out on a scout the thirtieth [of] last month, called at the house of Thomas Lewsley,[1] a miller, who not knowing them, told them that those two Generals were but a little way from there, and that if they (as he took them for two of [the] British Light Horse) would pursue, they might easily take them, for which end he gave them a very fine horse, which they brought away. My son on [the] back of his letter, dated First instant, says, just now a British Light Horse [man] passed here a prisoner, taken last night with despatches of consequence to G¹. Howe, and is sent with them to G¹. Washington.

5. Viewed part of [the] Virginia Battalion, with colors flying, wagons, &c., marching for camp, and I am informed that a division of three hundred took the same route yesterday, *via* Reading. ...... About noon, another party of Virginians, amounting to near three hundred, with wagons, passed through here on their march to the camp.

6. Went into town; spent chief [part] of the after-

---

[1] Thomas Livezey, resided on the Wissahiccon Creek in Roxborough Township at "Livezey's Mill."

noon there in conversation, respecting public occurrences, as the express had just come in; brought account of a parcel of our army's moving in three divisions last Sixth Day night, eight or nine miles, and [that they] attacked our enemy near five next morning near Chestnut Hill; threw them into disorder and drove their grenadiers with others into Germantown, where they took refuge in churches, houses and meetings, with their cannon (of which our people had brought none with them) and as the main body of the enemy advanced our little party retreated back to their former ground in good order, taking one piece of cannon with them, and all their wounded. Accounts say that we had killed, wounded and prisoners on our side about four hundred, and that the enemy had nearly fifteen hundred in killed, wounded and prisoners.

7. About twelve o'clock, marched out under a guard of one hundred and twenty militia men, one hundred and twenty-three prisoners of English, Scotch and new levies, for Virginia, with baggage wagons, &c. ...... The account it's said, to-day brought from Philadelphia by some of the Friends from their Yearly Meeting, of the engagement last Seventh Day, is that we had two thousand men killed, wounded and taken prisoners, and that our enemies suffered in the same proportion; further, that our late Governor, John Penn, is appointed Governor, and Andrew Allen, Lieut. Governor. Between two or three hundred Virginians marched through this town to-day for our camp. ...... Came to town, this evening, a company of Light Horse from North Carolina, near upon fifty, with their wagons, &c.; put up their horses at the Continental stables.

8. In my son's letter are many instances of the wanton cruelty they exercised in his neighborhood, amongst which is the burning of the house where Col. Reed did live, the house where Thompson kept tavern, with every thing in it, all the hay at Col. Bull's, fifteen hundred

bushels of wheat, with other grain, his powder mill and iron works; destroyed all the fences for some miles, with the Indian corn and buckwheat, emptied feather beds, destroyed furniture, cut books to pieces at Col. Bayard's; at one place emptied some feather beds, and put a cask of yellow ochre, cask of Spanish Brown [and] cask of linseed oil, and mixed them all together. So brutal and cruel are all their steps marked, it would be tiresome tracing them with a pen. ...... Yesterday, after many day's waiting, a sufficient number of members of Assembly met, so that they have made a House and entered upon public business.

11. News of the day is that the slaughter in Howe's army this day week was very great; that the Generals Agnew, Grant and Erskine, are among the slain, and another General officer badly wounded; these, by report, were principal officers in Howe's army; that on the Eighth instant, Washington's army being refreshed marched downwards to Philadelphia, and that he was reinforced with four thousand men from the Northward, besides a number of Virginians, within the space of eight or ten days, so that an engagement may be hourly expected. Our Council and House of Assembly continue still sitting here, as does the Congress at York.

12. News of the day is variously represented, viz: that our army was got to within nineteen miles of Philadelphia; that Gen. Lee was exchanged (for Prescott); was expected soon to be at camp; that Saml. Shoemaker acted as Mayor of Philadelphia, and had publicly declared in the Market Place, in order to inform the inhabitants by order of Genl. Howe, that Congress money should not be received in any payments; that sundry of the English troops had repassed [the] Schuylkill, but for what intent, it was not known; that Gen. Putnam had retreated from Fishkill, as Burgoyne had received a supply of troops.

13. News just come, *via* Reading, that Fort Mont-

gomery was taken by the enemy, with all its stores, and five hundred men made prisoners, and with a loss to them of one thousand men killed; that they had burned two frigates that were unfinished in the North River. After dinner, Gen. De Kalb set out for the camp. The Assembly broke up this day, having completed their session, having first appointed twelve Commissioners to act in conjunction with the President and Council, during [the] recess of the Assembly, and to the end of next session, unless ordered otherwise by the next Assembly. ...... In the above Commission, I was appointed one, but upon being informed, I went and requested another might be put in my room, which after some altercation was not granted nor put they any other in my place, as the law had been already passed for that purpose.

14. I went into town, this being Election Day, as appointed by the Constitution. The following gentlemen were elected in Lancaster, viz: Wm. Brown, Alexander Lowery, Philip Mastiler, James Anderson, John McMullen [and] Ludwick Lauman. The election was conducted with great order and sobriety. ...... News was that our enemies had erected [a] small battery on Province Island, which our gondolas destroyed, took fifty-four prisoners, and one hundred muskets, two officers, a captain and lieutenant, with the cannon that they had mounted.

15. Bought this day (for and per order of my son Charles), of Adam Zantzinger, fifty-six pounds of Muscovado sugar, for which I paid him nine shillings per lb. ...... News of the day is, it's said, an express about noon, on its way to Congress, who also had despatches to our President and Council, giving them information of the total rout of Burgoyne's army; great numbers of them slain, say three hundred, as many taken prisoners, with all their tents, baggage, &c., with two twelve and six six-pounders, brass guns, and that they were in full pursuit of the runaways; Generals Clinton and Arnold, both wounded, but not mortally.

By report of several, a most prodigious heavy firing was heard yesterday, great part of the day, account of which is impatiently expected by the honest hearts.

16. I am informed that yesterday were brought to this jail, three or four persons from Chester County, two of them named Hunter, who, by receipts found upon them, appear to have been as suppliers of Howe's army with sheep, cattle, &c. The others are called Temple, who appear to have been concerned as directors of the roads to Howe's army, and informing against sundry persons to him as good friends to the United States, and other inimical practices.

17. News by express from [the] Northward, confirms the above intelligence, and adds that it was Burgoyne's Aide-de-camp [who] was taken prisoner, with most of the Artillery officers and head officers of the Grenadiers with the Q. Mr. General, and a number of inferior officers. Among the slain is Genl. Frazer. It's further said that the taking of Fort Montgomery cost abundance of blood on both sides. On the English side, were slain Gen. Camphiel, Major Stillé, Major Grant, Capt. Steward, with many other officers; and that our forts on [the] Delaware hold out bravely, the men in high spirits on the fifteenth instant.

18. News of the day is that some of our militia under Gen^s. Smallwood and Potter, had taken a large drove of cattle near Chester, that was driven for the use of Howe's army; that the enemy had entirely evacuated Wilmington; that our river was yet in our possession, although daily cannonaded by the enemy's shipping, but as bravely repulsed; that Lord Howe in a sixty gun ship was arrived at Chester; that provisions were very scarce and dear in Philadelphia; beef three shillings and nine pence[1] a pound, butter seven shillings and six pence,[2] no money passing but hard and Pennsylvania old money; that full

---

[1] Fifty Cents.
[2] One Dollar.

confirmation of Gen. Burgoyne's defeat was brought this day to Congress from Gen. Gates, who was then in full pursuit of his flying army; that numbers of them came into us with heavy complaints against Burgoyne's behavior, and that he had written a polite letter to Gen. Gates, requesting him to take care of his hospital.

20. By letter from son Benja. by the express, is a full account of the surrender of Gen. Burgoyne and his whole army to Genl. Gates, on the Fourteenth instant; to march out on the Fifteenth to a place appointed, with the honors of war, there to ground their arms, and then as prisoners to be sent to Massachusetts Government. On the Eighteenth a feu de joie was fired in our camp on this glorious acquisition; at the same time an alarm was that the enemy under Howe was in motion to attack our army, who received the news with great joy and moved with great alacrity to receive them. It was remarked that when Gen. Washington received the account of Burgoyne's defeat, he stood silent for some small time. ...... As it was rainy weather, we all went to bed past eight. Wind blew fresh and stormy. Near nine, alarmed by Timothy Matlack, who came to inform me that an express [had] just arrived in town with the news of Howe's quitting Philadelphia, and that Gen. Washington was in full pursuit of his army.[1] This was joyful news indeed. I then went to bed, but had not lain long when Major Wertz came with boy, candle and lantern, on the same errand. I then arose and conversed till he went away; then to bed. Not long there before Robert Taggert came with his lantern. After he was gone, I went to bed. Not being easy, Dr. Phyle arose. We dressed ourselves, went into town; met with many heartily rejoicing; then to Jorden's; stayed in large company till near twelve; then home in the rain to bed, before one.

---

[1] This news was premature.

21. In the evening went into town, having first prepared our front windows with conveniency of fixing candles for the illumination this night, on account of Gen. Burgoyne's defeat. A further account came this evening, and was read in the Court House room, where the principal inhabitants (with many others, strangers, &c)., were collected to spend the evening in [a] kind of festivity on the occasion, which was conducted with great sobriety and prudence. ...... There were many patriotic healths drunk, and a cold collation. The part of the battalion under arms, that were in the borough, paraded the streets, fired a feu de joie, with many manœuvres; drums, fifes, playing in the room. I came away with a great many others about nine; fine pleasant night, but cool. The account read was that the prisoners were, first, Lieut. Gen. Burgoyne, seven Brigadier Generals, two Majors, two Lieutenant Colonels, a number of captains and inferior officers, five thousand privates, fifteen thousand stand of arms, forty pieces of brass cannon, ammunition, tents, all their baggage, &c. No further account from Philadelphia to be depended upon.

22. This afternoon, were brought to town *via* Reading, thirty English and five Hessian prisoners, taken in the last skirmish at Germantown, brought by some of the militia and lodged in the jail, also three light horse and four jagers, who were out on a scout, who were also confined with the other prisoners. It's further said that a very heavy cannonade was heard on the outside of this town, most part of this afternoon.

23. Our neighbors this morning remarked a constant heavy firing all this forenoon, which was distinctly heard near twelve. I listened and heard a heavy firing from E. S. E., as I apprehended it, to be platoon or broadside firing. There are just brought to town from Chester County, about forty of the men that were wounded in that affair on the Brandywine (in seven wagons). ...... Almost constantly engaged in my mind respecting the

situation of our good friends, relations and associates in Philadelphia, whose distress from the Tories I commiserate.

25. News of the day, it's said, is by two expresses, one the confirmation of Gen. Burgoyne's defeat; the other that twelve hundred Hessian Grenadiers, under the command of Count Dunop, and sundry other principal officers crossed [the] Delaware at Cooper's ferry, marched through Haddonfield down to Redbank, from there attacked our fort, nay, it's said, some got over the abattis, but were repulsed with a great number slain, many wounded, among which the above named officers, who were taken prisoners, and one hundred and eighty others (and twelve brass cannon), the rest dispersed; and that our fleet had bravely repulsed the men-of-war, and that our fire rafts had set three of their men-of-war on fire, and two were thereby blown up and destroyed. One of said vessels, it's said, was the August, sixty-four gun ship, and the other the Apollo. This day was published a Proclamation, reciting part of an Act passed the Thirteenth instant, constituting a Council of Safety, and vesting the same with certain powers. The persons so named in said Act were John Bayard, Jonathan Sergeant, Jonathan B. Smith, David Rittenhouse, Joseph Gardiner, Robert Whitehill, James Cannon and Wm. Henry of Lancaster. This day was published an Address from [the] said Council of Safety, to the inhabitants of Pennsylvania, dated at Lancaster the Twenty-third instant.

27. It's said that five hundred militia men marched this day for camp, notwithstanding the heavy rain, which continued till bed time.

29. News to-day but little. It's said that our brave fellows still keep our fort and cheveaux de frise; that our army is on the Skippack road, near Morris's mill. Letter from Reading to Col. Morgan says, that Dr. Potts wrote to his wife, confirming the defeat of Bur-

goyne's army ;. that the person who brought said Potts's letter, writes that he saw Burgoyne with several Geneals and other officers at Albany, as he passed through there.

30. This day I paid Conrad Wold £117 for one hundred and seventeen gallons of whiskey, ordered by my son Christopher and Thomas Rees, and sent them. ...... News of the day, as reported by Wm. Young, servant to Robt. Erwine. He says he left Philadelphia last Saturday ; that our enemies report that they lost one thousand killed, besides a number wounded, at their attack at Redbank ; the inhabitants in Philadelphia in great distress for provisions, as the soldiers seized all that was in the market, and were also seizing and taking away out of people's cellars and yards all their firewood ; that the defence on the river was maintained with great vigor, having destroyed three of our enemies ships, viz : sixty-four, thirty-four and twenty-eight gun vessels ; that Gen. Howe had a bridge at Ogden's ferry, was fortifying this side [of the] Schuylkill, and for that purpose had two thousand men there.

31. The news of the day is that the particulars of the surrender of Burgoyne and his army were gone by express to Congress last night, but the account was not vet returned, though several accounts were handed about, but none authenticated. ...... An invitation made by the President at Major Wertz's, to which was invited scarcely any other but a parcel of Tories in this place, some of them inhabitants, and some who reside here from Philadelphia. Poor Dr. Phyle and some of his principles, were not counted worthy to taste of the dainties, and thereby they escaped being intoxicated and made drunk, and next day sick, &c.

NOVEMBER 1. After breakfast, I was engaged good part of the day in patching and mending the old out house, at this place, through the want of workmen, obliges me to be a jack of all trades, as the saying is, and good at none.

2. I received a letter by the post, from my son Benja., dated yesterday, giving an account that both his and his brother's family were well, and had not, and hoped should not have, cause to remove from their present habitations by our enemies, as they were now in the environs of Philadelphia; that there had been no firing on the river since the two ships were blown up, and that Gen. Washington had sent off a train and company of Artillery with three hundred men to reinforce the fort at Redbank (yesterday); that they had for several days the most violent storm of wind and rain scarcely known; that the creeks were so risen that the water was up within a foot of Thomas Rees's parlor floor, &c., in which time of rain our poor soldiers suffered excessively by the storm, but were now recruited and in high spirits, and, it's thought, would move downwards to-day or to-morrow; that the poor inhabitants of Philadelphia are in a dreadful situation for the want of provisions and firewood, and it's said that the gallery-men have got up a number (thirty) of cannon and other things out of the wreck of the ships, &c.

5. Afterwards went into town, as our Quarter Sessions began yesterday, and were conducted with great order and decorum. This day, came to town on their way to York, the Generals Sterling and Mifflin. ...... News of the day is, by letter from Dr. Shippen at Reading to Thomas Smith here, that last First Day, the ship Eagle of sixty-four guns attacked our gondolas, but ran aground, on which our people boarded her, got her off and took her, and also that they had taken fourteen boat loads of provisions and other goods, going to Howe's army, and that our people had retaken Rhode Island, and made eight hundred prisoners, with their stores and ammunition, &c. Sundry of our new Assembly came to town yesterday and to-day, but not sufficient to make up a house to do business.

6. I have been favored with [the] sight of [a] copy

of Jacob Duché's letter to Gen. Washington, which the
General transmitted to Congress. It's dated [the]
eighth of last month, the which contains a panegyric
upon himself, an applause of the General, then proceeds
to the most illiberal, scurrilous, and invective language
against the Congress [and] the supporters of the United
States in every department of government, then proposes
a total surrender of our all into the hands of Howe, and
the other Commissioners that were formerly appointed
by the King and Council; then calls upon Gen. Washington to pronounce this at the head of his army, as the
only means that can be taken to preserve all America
from utter ruin and devastation, and thereby the General
would alone be the deliverer and savior of his country,
&c. &c. &c. Yesterday came Mary Brown's son, who
came the night before from near Germantown; told me
that he had seen his mother and Mrs. Owen there, who
had come out of Philadelphia just before on parole, to
procure some provisions, which, they said, were very
scarce and dear in the city. Mrs. Owen told him to
tell me, when he saw me, that the enemy had destroyed
all my fence round the garden, at [the] country seat,
put soldiers into that house and my dwelling house in
town, and that Paul Fooks had taken away all my books
out of my house before they took possession, and had
them carried to his own dwelling house, and being found
there, as if his own property, &c.

8. News to-day corresponds how that Gen. Cornwallis,
with a number of his army attacked Red Bank, the sixth
instant, where he was repulsed. His loss in killed,
wounded, and prisoners amounts, it's said, to six hundred.

10. A number of militia marched through this town
for Gen. Washington's camp, as did likewise, it's said,
near seven hundred on their return from camp to Virginia,
their times being expired. The accounts from Philadelphia are very distressing, on the many exercises the
Whig inhabitants have to encounter with, being much

pinched for wood and provisions, besides the inhuman behavior of the Tory crew in that City. Account is brought that two spies were detected in Red Bank fort, and were hanged immediately, one of which confessed the fact; said they were employed by Sam¹. Shoemaker, Paul Reeves and Sam¹. Garrigus, *Sen.*, to procure information.

11. News of the day is that Col. Morgan's Regiment of riflemen was arrived at Gen. Washington's camp, and that part of Gen. Gates's army had crossed North River, at Fishkill, and may be expected to join our army in a few days, and that Gen. Clinton's army was expected to join Gen. Howe's.

13. It's said that eight hundred Continentals and three hundred of the militia from Virginia, are now on their march to join our General Washington, besides five or six hundred from North Carolina, and Cumberland County militia, just now passing by to head quarters. This [day] came to town and encamped in the woods near Conestoga Creek, Two hundred Continental troops from North Carolina, on their march to Gen. Washington's camp.

14. News of the day is that Col. Morgan's Riflemen were sent down to Tinicum Island; that Gen. Gates, with his army, had crossed at Corryel's ferry; that several of our people, of the prisoners under Gen. Howe, that were confined in Philadelphia, had perished for want of nourishment, provisions being so scarce and Howe so cruel unto our people. This day some companies of militia men came into this town, on their way to join Gen. Washington.

17. News of the day is that six thousand blankets, with watch coats, shoes and stockings, were arrived from the eastward at our camp. It's further said, that three thousand of Gen. Putnam's division crossed at Dunks's ferry last week on their way to Gen. Washington's camp; that Dr. Kearsley, prisoner at Carlisle, died there some

time last week, and was buried in their church, which disgusted many of the Church party in that place, so that they declared against going to that church any more.

18. News of the day is that Fort Mifflin was evacuated after removing the guns and stores, last Seventh Day night; and that Elizabeth Shipley, a public Friend, who fled from Howe's army, at Wilmington, said these following words just before she died, " Hold out Americans, hold out Americans, your cause is good, and God will give you your country."

20. Breakfasted with our standing family, James Davidson, who was going to set off on account of [the] Executive and Council of Safety, in order to examine their salt works in the Jerseys, and also to purchase salt in that State for the use of this State, if to be got on moderate terms.

21. I went to town, in company with Robert Whitehill, to Council Chamber, where John Brown of Philada. was sent a prisoner from Congress, who, by his own confession, said at the request of Thomas Willing, he had received orders from Gen. Howe, to propose to some members of Congress, that if they would rescind Independency, he would withdraw his fleet and army, would put the States into the situation they were in [in] seventeen hundred and sixty-three, and grant them more than they have asked, and would establish the paper currency. With this verbal message, he said he came, by desire of Thos. Willing, and communicated the same to Robert Morris. The Council, having considered maturely the nature of the offence, unanimously agreed to commit him to the common jail of this county, under strict confinement, for the present. ...... Yesterday, our Assembly made a House [and] proceeded to business, after choosing James McLean, Speaker. This morning they, with the Council, elected Thomas Wharton, President, and George Bryan, Vice President, for the ensuing year.

22. About half after seven, before I arose, hearing a great noise like an empty wagon going over a gutter. When Robert Whitehill arose, he asked if I had heard the earthquake; he said it made the house shake to the foundation. The same was felt by Dr. Phyle. As they lay up stairs, and we below, they felt the shock more sensibly. This was felt by many, whom I heard talking of it in town. ...... News of the day, that Gen. Cornwallis, on the sixteenth, with three thousand British and Hessian troops, marched from Philadelphia to Chester, there went on board [a] transport (having crossed [the] Schuylkill at [the] middle ferry); on the Eighteenth, went to Billingsport, disembarked the Nineteenth and proceeded to attack Red Bank Fort; that Col. Procter, with artillery, had gone down to Province Island, and Gen. Greene, with three thousand of our troops, was to cross some days past, at Bristol. Potatoes in Philadelphia, at sixteen shillings a bushel, beef seven shillings and six pence per pound, and a chicken at ten shillings, so great is their distress.

23. News to-day that the English Ambassador, Stormont, had left Paris. On his arrival in England, stocks fell fifteen per cent; that the King of Prussia had ordered the Port of Embden to be open for American privateers.

24. News of the day is that Gen. Burgoyne's troops had mutinied on their march, so that the guards were obliged to fire on them, killed several, which obliged the rest to be still and quiet. Near forty Light Horse came in from Virginia, on their way to head quarters.

26. News of the day is that [the] fort on Red Bank was evacuated on the approach of Gen. Cornwallis, with his forces; that our people destroyed great part of our fleet, fire rafts, floating battery, &c.; that the enemy had burnt Woodbury, but that our gondolas had passed the City and got up the river; that the enemy had burnt Isaac Norris's house, Jonathan Mifflin's, Peel Hall, and

sundry other houses; that they had also destroyed Spring Garden; that provisions still continued scarce and dear in the City; [that] our people, who are prisoners, are cruelly used; that part of Gen. Gates's forces had arrived at camp.

27. Past four, I went by appointment of Council, in company with Col. Bayard, to confer with the clothier General respecting the clothing of the troops of this State; then returned to Council. Came home at dusk. ...... News to-day is that the Generals Washington, Sullivan, and some others had crossed [the] Schuylkill last Third Day on a reconnoitering over a bridge they had near Spring Mill; that last Second Day a heavy firing was heard, which, by report, was an engagement in the Jerseys between our forces there and the enemy, but was not decided as both maintained their ground in order to renew the fight next morning, ... that our out-scouts near Fair Hill, had attacked and driven the enemy's pickets into the City; waited in hopes they would have been succored, and so have brought on a general engagement, as our army was ready to have engaged, had the enemy come out, but they contented themselves with remaining in their lines.

30. This morning James Young, Esq., set out for camp, on a commission from the President and Council, he, with Col. Bayard, being appointed to enquire into the complaints made that the troops of this State are in a ragged condition, while the other troops are well equipped; also to see sundry clothes distributed amongst them that are in real want, from a parcel now collecting in this county, some of which are sent and more going, and also to make a true report to Council of the state of our army, and of the reasons of the complaints made respecting the scarcity of provisions.

DECEMBER 2. Yesterday were read in Council, the Thirteen Articles of Confederation and Perpetual Union of the United States; also a letter from Robert Morris to the President and Council, requesting the enlargement of John Brown, and proposing to be his security in any sum that they should require. The same was put to vote, and carried unanimously that he should still be retained a prisoner.

3. A letter was read in Council from G. Wood of Bedford County, dated [the] eighteenth of last month, giving an account of the inroads of the Indians in that quarter, which had so distressed them that numbers of the inhabitants had fled from their habitations. Account [that] seventeen thousand blankets are arrived in Virginia.

4. After dinner I carried a few lines written to the Speaker of the House of Assembly, signifying my intentions of resigning my seat in the Committee of Safety. Now the doing [of] this arose from an information R. Whitehill gave me at dinner, that the House in his absence this forenoon had passed a Resolve that they would desire the President and Council immediately to dissolve the Council of Safety. This was what induced me to take the start of them, and decline in time.

5. Baron De Holtzendorff's Aide-de-camp; come from camp, but brought no news except that he thought that our troops were to go soon into winter quarters. ...... The beginning of this week, three Delegates, viz: [Elbridge] Gerry, Jones and Robert Morris, set out by order of Congress to head-quarters, in order to consult only with Gen. Washington, on the present critical affairs of the army, the commissaries and other officers, &c.

6. Visited early by Col. Roberdeau. Stayed in solid conversation till past ten. Gave him Seventeen hundred and five Dollars, left me by my sons Christopher and Charles, in order to get them changed by Congress, if suitable and convenient, for the same number of Dollars, these having been defaced by lying in a damp place, which entirely took away all the names and numbers that were done with red ink.

7. News of the day, it's said, is that an express passed through this town to Congress with despatches that Gen. Howe left Philadelphia [on the] Fourth instant at eleven at night, with his army, consisting of ten thousand men, marched towards Germantown, attacked and drove [in] our picket guard, which being reinforced, returned, drove their advanced guard back, killed near twenty, amongst which, a Brigadier General, Captain, &c.; took sixteen prisoners; that we lost Gen. Irvin, who was wounded and taken prisoner, one Colonel, one Captain, twelve or fourteen privates killed, and maintained our post that night; that next day a general engagement, it was thought, was unavoidable, as the two armies lay in sight of each other; and that the enemy had burnt Beggar's town in their front.

8. Then came Norton Pryor, who brought a letter from son Charles, giving account ...... that both armies were in sight of each other, Howe's occupying Germantown, and Washington's Chestnut Hill, Whitemarsh, &c. (He and horse stayed all night, as he, after trial, could find no entertainment in the town.) Spent the evening in conversation respecting the difficulties attending our friends in and about Philadelphia, till near ten.

10. Yesterday, about noon, came into town, from the Northward, about four hundred soldiers of the regiment of Col. ——, in order to be innoculated for the small pox; went into barracks. They brought with them, it's said, about one hundred English prisoners that had been taken at different times.

11. News of the day, it's said, is that Gen. Howe, after giving out in Philada., that he was going with his army to drive Gen. Washington and his army over the Blue Mountains, after marching his whole army up to Chestnut Hill and staying there some days, last First Day night decamped and returned to Philada. on the Second Day, leaving behind him about two hundred of his men, in slain and taken prisoners. It's said they

have pillaged and carried with them everything that came in their way that was portable and of any value, besides burning [and] destroying many houses and effects, also taking with them, by force, all the boys they could lay their hands on, above the age of ten years. Thus, this time, has the great boaster succeeded in this vain-glorious expedition, to the eternal shame of him and of all his boasting Tory friends. It's said that last week, Joseph Galloway was proclaimed in Philada. Governor of this Province, by the knot of Tories there; that John Hall, cooper, is to be tried for his life for cursing George the Third, as is Robert Riché for writing to Gen. Washington (some say it was to Riché's wife) giving them an account of the fortifying of the City, &c. By some letters intercepted, there appears to be a combination between the Friends sent into Virginia by the President and Council and some inhabitants of Lancaster, in order to depreciate the Continental currency. Some of the letters are from Owen Jones, Jr., to John Mercer, Matthias Slough and Matthias Graeff. This discovery has obliged the Board of War to send all the Quaker prisoners to Staunton in Augusta County, and Owen Jones to close confinement, without the use of pen, ink and paper, except in presence of the Lieutenant of the County or his deputy, and the other Friends to the same restriction, unless they take an affirmation that they will neither act, speak, nor write anything that is against the Independency of the United States of America.

12. News of the day is that Gen. Howe is come out again from Philadelphia, with his army; crossed [the] Schuylkill at Middle Ferry, marched up Lancaster Road to the Sorrel Horse, thirteen miles from the City, and there rested yesterday.

13. Some people pretended to have heard a firing of cannon this morning. ...... This is a strange age and place, in which I now dwell, because nothing can be had cheap but lies, falsehood, and slanderous accusation.

Love and Charity, the badge of Christianity, is not so much as named amongst them.

14. Near twelve, came to pay me a visit the French Engineer, Baraset De Kermorvan, who came by my son Christopher's from camp, and is going to York Town. He brought me a letter from him of the twelfth instant, that gave us an agreeable account that all their family were in good health, but to counterbalance, mentioned that they had met with fearful alarms since the enemy left town, it's said with their whole army, in order to attack Washington's army at Chestnut Hill, but are now returned to town, finding his army too strong in that situation to engage him. This, Howe was informed of by a deserter from Col. Proctor's Regiment of Artillery; that they had taken in with them some cattle, and it's reported, a quantity of forage, although our people pursued them; and, by a person since come out of town, who says that twenty-five wagons, with killed and wounded, were brought in.

15. Upon the rumor yesterday of Gen. Howe's army's being on the Lancaster Road, it's said that the papers and records belonging to the Executive Council were packed up and sent by wagons to York Town; it's said that the English army is returned into Philadelphia and that our army is on this side of [the] Schuylkill. Our Assembly continues sitting here. It's said that a spirited letter is penned by them to send to Congress to-morrow, respecting the report of our troops' going into winter quarters, as the enemy are attempting to, and does, ravage the country for a number of miles' extent around Philada.

16. The circumstances of affairs of [a] public nature make a very gloomy appearance. Our City, with its virtuous inhabitants that could not escape, in the hands of cruel taskmasters; the country around ravaged, stripped and destroyed, with houses, barns, &c., burnt and levelled with the ground by the same band of ban-

ditti worse than savages; no priests nor prophets, but such as are delineated by Jeremiah in his Lamentations. The thoughts of these things, and having my children with their lovely offspring in the very jaws of these enemies, afflict me sorely, break my peace and disturb my est, but here I must stop, because the Lord is good and does not afflict willingly. The cause is of our side; we have grossly offended; yet spare us, O Lord my God Spare thy people and bless thine inheritance, for Jesus Christ's sake.

20. Also came James Davidson, who brought me from Gen. Roberdeau the Continental Bills of Exchange for what he took from me of said specie, being defaced with the damp.

21. No news of any moment to be depended upon, except General orders from head quarters, encouraging the army to build huts and to content themselves where they are now.

22. In [the] afternoon, returned the three men and two wagons from York Town, as went last. They called to get some sustenance, as they could get none on the road from York Town till here. After refreshing themselves, they set out for home just at dusk.

25. Yesterday came to this town from York, Gen. Conway, on his way down to head quarters, and also to propose two Brigadier Generals in the room of Gen. Potter [and] Gen. Armstrong, who propose to go from the army unto their own homes. No company dined with us to-day, except Dr. Phyle, one of our standing family. We had a good roast turkey, plain pudding, and minced pies.

26. This evening Col. Proctor called, drank tea, stayed some time, giving a relation of the sufferings of the back inhabitants, through the inroads now making by the Indians and the soldiery from Fort Detroit.

27. I spent the evening at home examining part of [the] History of Ephrata, brought me by Peter Miller

for my inspection and correction. There appears to be no kind of news to be depended upon, but as for lies, this place is really pregnant and brings forth abundance daily, I might safely say, hourly. Caleb Johnston, that was sent to prison for aiding and assisting [James] Brooks to get out of our prison, as it's said, is just released from confinement.

28. Our affairs wear a very gloomy aspect. Great part of our army gone into winter quarters; those in camp wanting breeches, shoes, stockings, [and] blankets, and by accounts brought yesterday, were in want of flour, yet being in the land of plenty; our farmers having their barns and barracks full of grain; hundreds of barrels of flour lying on the banks of the Susquehannah perishing for want of care in securing it from the weather, and from the danger of being carried away, if a freshet should happen in the river; fifty wagon loads of cloths and ready made clothes for the soldiery in the Clothier General's store in Lancaster (this I say from the demand made by John Mease to the President a few days past, when the enemy was expected to be coming this way, for this number of wagons to take away these stores); our enemies revelling in balls, attended with every degree of luxury and excess in the City; rioting and wantonly using our houses, utensils and furniture; all this [and] a numberless number of other abuses we endure from that handful of banditti, to the amount of six or seven thousand men, headed by that monster of rapine, Gen. Howe. Add to this their frequent excursions round about for twenty miles together, destroying and burning what they please, pillaging, plundering men and women, stealing boys above ten years old, deflowering virgins, driving into the City for their use, droves of cattle, sheep [and] hogs; poultry, butter, meal, meat, cider, furniture and clothing of all kinds, loaded upon our own horses. All this is done in the view of our Generals and our army, who are careless of us, but care-

fully consulting where they shall go to spend the winter in jollity, gaming and carousing. O tell not this in France or Spain! Publish it not in the streets of London, Liverpool or Bristol, lest the uncircumcised there should rejoice, and shouting for joy, say "America is ours, for the rebels are dismayed and afraid to fight us any longer! O Americans, where is now your virtue? O Washington, where is your courage?" ...... News to-day is that Col. Bull, on the twenty-fifth instant, made an excursion into Fourth street in Philadelphia, with two thousand militia [and] alarmed the City by firing off some pieces of cannon into the air, whereby some of the balls fell about Christ Church. He then made a good retreat back to his station, without the loss of one man. It's further said that it alarmed Gen. Howe, who was then at Darby, so that he and his army posted immediately with all speed back to the City. It's further added that Gen. Howe has ordered all the fire buckets that can be found in the City to be put aboard his fleet.

29. It's said that Gen. Sullivan, on the retreat of Gen. Howe's army on Christmas Day from Darby, on the alarm given by Cols. Bull, Antis and ——— (in three divisions, instead of one under Col. Bull as above, but all militia), took thirteen provision wagons loaded from the enemy. ...... Visited in the evening by Dr. Yeardwell, who told me they had made a hospital at Ephrata, in which were near two hundred and forty-seven sick and wounded men.

31. Visited by Jedediah Snowden and Benja. Harbeson, for me to sign a petition they were carrying about, for the purpose of requesting the Assembly to call out the whole force of this State, immediately, while there is a prospect of this severe cold weather's lasting, in order to attack Gen. Howe in and out of our City, and thereby entirely ruin his army, and rid the Colonies of such cruel monsters. I then went to writing or, more properly, correcting the Annals of Ephrata, and so continued till bed time, near eleven o'clock.

1778.

January 1. Fine clear sunshine morning, and pleasant for the season, and still continues to freeze hard. Wind but little at southerly. Thus has the morning of our new year been ushered in. God grant that this serenity may be a happy presage of that longed for peace and tranquility that is promised in the scriptures, that " nation shall not arise against nation, neither shall they learn war any more."..... Finished correcting the Annals of Ephrata.

2. Our Assembly, since they received the petition of the thirty-first,[1] are busily employed in conjunction with the Executive Council, in taking proper steps in order to grant the prayer of such petition. It's said that two Committees are appointed, one to prepare a Bill adequate to the Prayer, the other to draw up a spirited Remonstrance to send to Congress with the Petition and their Resolve; these to be sent by express. It's said that fifteen wagon-loads of ready-made clothes for the Virginia troops came and stay in town to-night. To-morrow they proceed for our camp. It's further said that ten other wagons loaded with [the] same commodity are come in here, going for our camp, but I could not learn from what port they came. It's said that our camp[2] looks as large as Philadelphia, most of their huts being built, laid out in streets and are very warm, and it's said they seem quite contented to rest there and let Howe keep the city for this winter, but I am in hopes they will be mistaken, as our Assembly and Executive Council are determined to call out the strength of this State, and therewith make a bold push, and their resolutions, I hope,

---

[1] The prayer of this petition was that the Assembly should "call out the whole force of this State [Pennsylvania] immediately, while there is a prospect of this severe weather's lasting, in order to attack Gen. Howe in and out of our City [Philadelphia] and thereby entirely ruin his army, and rid the colonies of such cruel monsters." Diary for December 31, 1777.

[2] At Valley Forge.

will be attended with the blessings of Heaven, the consent and approbation of Congress, joined with the zeal, fortitude and courage of Gen. Washington and his brave army.

3. Before breakfast fed the horse, bridled and saddled [it] to lend to Mr. McLean, Speaker, who was setting out for home, as the Assembly had adjourned to the Eighteenth of next month (Feb^y). His horse, he said, was about a mile from town. So he took a little boy with him to bring the horse back. Then came ——Vanchamp, who was also setting out for his home. ...... News that a brig from New York, driven ashore with the ice above Wilmington Creek, was boarded by Col. Smallwood and his men. She mounted twelve guns, but lay upon one side. The Colonel brought two pieces of cannon with him. It's said, before he boarded, a boat full of men and officers put off for the Jersey shore and got away. After our people's firing a few shots, the vessel struck her colors. It's said they found and brought from aboard her between fifty and sixty men, forty ladies, complete suits of clothes for four regiments, eight thousand seven hundred and fifty stand of arms in three hundred and fifty chests, twenty-five in each chest, the baggage for the officers of four regiments, a great quantity of clothes not made up, twelve pieces of cannon with carriages, some hogsheads of spirits, sugar, raisins, currants, oranges, several casks of wine, a quantity of baggage for different officers, ladies, &c., &c., &c., &c.; that a number of the goods were landed at Wilmington.

4. Soon after came Wm. Atlee's son and daughter, enquiring for the doctor. He was just gone out. The request was that he would go to our neighbor's house to take care of an English prisoner (but he turns out to be one of the new raised levies in [New] Jersey) that they had sent there to be nursed, he being very poorly, and his name was Mrs. Atlee's maiden name, and this had induced her to take so much care of him. A poor ex-

cuse when at this same time there are near upon two or three hundred of our State's soldiers in the greatest distress and extremity for real want of common necessaries, even the want of a little straw to lie upon. O poor Pennsylvania! how art thou fallen, so that thy very sons, who are daily maintained and nourished by thy posts of profit, are the very men that prey upon thy bowels, and who, under the show of friendship, are making deeper and ghastlier wounds than either Gen. Howe, the head of monsters and brutes, was, is, or ever will be able to make: for this reason [that] they come, as an army of banditti and savages, to steal, kill and murder, but you false, base and atrocious enemies, wound, steal [from] and murder your best friends, supporters and benefactors, even those who have raised and lifted many of you up from poverty and contempt. Yet this is now your reward to them, acting the cruelest of deceit and hypocrisy, in the same strain and in the same line, actuated by the same spirit as Judas of old, " and forthwith he came to Jesus and said Hail Master, and kissed him." Matthew, 26:49. Mark, 14:45. O ye false sons of Pennsylvania, be ye alarmed and look and behold the dreadful precipice over which you are standing! Cease now while mercy is yet stretched out to you by the Almighty hand of Love, who sees and marks out all your hidden works of darkness. Now is your appointed time, now is your day of salvation, the which if overlooked your master in iniquity, whom you now so zealously and fervently serve, will, in the end, leave and forsake you, as he did your forerunner in hypocrisy and deceit, in which you have greatly exceeded him. Read his destiny as it stands upon record, as an example to all the betrayers of God and their country. Matthew, 27: 3, 4, 5.

5. Various thoughts ran through my mind during this engagement, as being entirely alone, and as the times bear such a melancholy aspect and as the expectation of the poor inhabitants of the City returning to their habit-

ations is now quite over, as our army is now gone into winter quarters, this makes their schemes to be all abortive, therefore blessed shall all those be who have their minds retired and fixed upon God alone, for these will have peace in the most violent commotions that nature can be agitated with, as their wills are subjected to the will of our heavenly Father. This is the state my soul longs to be an inhabitant of.[1]

6. Spent some time in conversation with Capt. Markoe, John Hubley and some others on the affairs of the times, which appear very gloomy. By accounts from the City, Howe lives there in great plenty. None of our people attempt to molest them. By two women who left the City [it is reported that] they have a great concourse of market folks from Bucks County, who attend the markets constantly; that this day week fifty or sixty men went inside of their works at Kensington, and after some time returned back without any interruption from the sentinels, they appearing to be very careless and not under any apprehension from our army; they further said that three topsail vessels were set ashore by the ice between Gloucester and Cooper's Ferry, that it is said the Jersey people had pillaged what they could and then set them on fire; that during this time there was a constant fire from the City and Kensington upon the people, but had not heard whether they had killed any or not.

As I have, in this Memorandum, taken scarcely any notice of my wife's employment, it might appear as if her engagements were very trifling, the which is not the case but the reverse, and to do her that justice which her services deserve by entering them minutely would take up most of my time, for this genuine reason how that, from early in the morning till late at night, she is constantly employed in the affairs of the family, which

---

[1] On Monday, January 5th, 1778, the celebrated "Battle of the Kegs" was fought.

for some months has been very large, for besides the addition to our family in the house [is] a constant resort of comers and goers who seldom go away with dry lips and hungry bellies. This calls for her constant attendance not only to provide, but also to attend at getting prepared in the kitchen, baking our own bread and pies, meat, &c., but also on the table. Her cleanliness about the house, her attendance in the orchard, cutting and drying apples, of which several bushels have been procured, add to which her making of cider without tools, for the constant drink of the family, her seeing all our washing done, and her fine clothes and my shirts, the which are all smoothed by her, add to this her making of twenty large cheeses, and that from one cow, and daily using milk and cream, besides her sewing, knitting, &c. Thus she looketh well to the ways of her household, and eateth not the bread of idleness, yea, she also stretcheth out her hand and she reacheth out her hand to her needy friends and neighbors. I think she has not been above four times, since her residence has been here, to visit her neighbors, nor through mercy has she been sick for any time, but has at all times been ready, in any affliction to me or my family, as a faithful nurse and attendant, both day and night, so that I can in great truth take the words of the wise man and apply them truly to my case, "Who can find a virtuous woman? for her price is far above rubies. The heart of her husband doth safely trust in her. She will do him good and not evil all the days of her life. Many daughters have done virtuously, but thou excellest them all." Proverbs 31 : 10, 11, 12, 29. ...... Dr. Phyle and I then finished correcting the Annals of Ephrata. ...... News of the day is various and whether true or not is uncertain. From South Carolina, it's said that a sloop is arrived there which had been bound from Granada to New York with seventy puncheons of rum and six hogsheads of sugar brought in by the mate and crew who had confined the captain; that [by] Messrs. Otis and Andrews of Boston, agents for purchasing clothing for continental troops, upwards of five thousand suits with shoes, stockings, shirts, &c., have been procured and are now on their way to camp. This with the other supplies from Virginia and other quarters, gives a pleasing prospect of seeing our whole army completely clothed in a small time.

7. After tea, came George Bryan and Dr. Rush; spent the evening; near nine they went away. ...... Dr. Phyle gave my wife to-day twelve pounds of powdered loaf sugar of the Barbadoes kind. He sent, some days past, by William Bell, to deliver to my son Charles for him to convey to the Doctor's wife in Philadelphia, if practicable, four half Joes. He purchased them in Lancaster. He said he paid twelve Pounds apiece for them.

By the conversation with those gentlemen to night, there appears to be a general murmur in the people, about the City and Country, against the weak conduct of Gen. Washington. His slackness and remissness in the army are so conspicuous that a general langor must ensue, except that some heroic action takes place speedily, but it's thought by me that G. W. must be the man to put such a scheme into practice. Notwithstanding, a cry begins to be raised for a Gates, a Conway, a De Kalb, a Lee, but those men can't attain it. Such is the present concern of fluctuating minds.

8. While alone, the care of our Heavenly Father presented itself to my view in this that notwithstanding his judgments are visibly over this land and that although we the inhabitants do not learn righteousness, yet he is daily guarding and blessing us, an instance of which appeared to the view of my mind, respecting the capture of the brig run ashore near Wilmington, related in Dunlap's newspaper of yesterday, wherein amongst the many things enumerated are three hundred and fifty chests of

arms, with twenty-five stands in each (is eighty-seven hundred and fifty), clothing for four regiments with the baggage belonging to the officers of four regiments, &c., &c. These appeared to me to have been ordered by Gen. Howe, in order to be ready for the troops of Gen. Burgoyne, for which, transports, it's said, are sent, under the pretense of carrying those troops for England, but instead thereof to fetch them into Philadelphia, as, by our enemy's behavior, it seems that no faith, respecting the law of nations, is to be kept with rebels. Thus has Providence again assisted us in a wonderful manner and defeated this deep laid scheme of our inveterate enemy, for which merciful favor my soul bless the Lord our God. Amen.

9. I was visited by Dr. Newman, who arrived in town last night from Pittsburgh. He brings an account that the Indians in that quarter are pretty still during this cold weather, but are expected to be troublesome when the spring approaches. He says it's [a] fine country for provisions of all kinds, wild fowls, beasts and fish in great plenty, vast quantities of what's called sea coals for firing to be had with very little labor, but for all those blessings a monstrous spirit of infidelity and profaneness reigns through every department of men in those parts; for which reasons, the blessings intended by Providence for our good, we prostitute to base purposes, so as to make them to be a curse. ...... This evening wrote a few lines to James Davidson to desire him to come and attend Council [the] beginning of next week. ...... One hundred and fifty Virginia Continental troops, it's said, went through here for the camp, this day.

10. Soon after came Capt. Markoe, who said that John Benezet was just come to town, who had left Gen. Gates yesterday at Nazareth, who informed him that the Canadians had risen and taken all Gen. Burgoyne's baggage and the officers with theirs amounting, it's said, to one hundred and fifty thousand pounds; the officers kept

prisoners. By letter to ——— Young from his wife's relations up [the] North River, it appears that an English twenty-eight gun frigate (it's thought the Mercury) going up the said river ran upon the cheveaux de frise there and [in] about five minutes she sank and every soul perished that was aboard.

11. This day arrived here from camp Col. Hartly and his battalion ordered for Yorktown.

12. After dinner received letter from Paul Fooks, dated twenty-fourth December, giving an account of the hardships he sustained during the space of ten weeks he was as a prisoner in his own house [in] Philadelphia; that he had been but about three days out, was poorly and weak at Thomas Reese's house.

14. News is that Gen. Gates went to Congress yesterday.

15. This day came to town Col. Morgan of the Rifle Battalion, going home to see his family. Many Continental troops in town, getting sundry clothes in order to go to the camp. ...... Just thereupon came Joseph Robins, French starch-maker, from Philadelphia. We then drank tea, while he gave a wretched description of poor Philadelphia, the destruction that has attended the different interests there, as well as some account of the havoc made of some of mine that he knew of. He had brought some of Humphreys's newspapers[1] with him. I set to peruse some of them which are so replete with lies and falsehoods that I am really astonished.

17. My mind seems anxiously concerned on account of our distressed friends and acquaintance, with our brave Gen. Washington, as he and his army are now obliged to encounter all the inclemency of this cold weather, as they with him are living out in the woods with slender covering; our poor friends in town, many of them in want of fuel and other necessaries, while our

---

[1] The *Public Ledger*. It expired May 28, 1778.

internal enemies, under the protection of that savage monster Howe, are revelling in luxury, dissipation and drunkenness, without any feelings for the distress of their (once happy) bleeding country. Here I must stop, as the theme is too melancholy and distressing. ...... Yesterday was sent to prison by order of President and Council —— Dingee, of Chester county, for refusing to take the oath of allegiance, nor would he give security for his upright walking and good conduct.

18. News is that the Jersey people have destroyed thirteen sail of English vessels that were put on shore in different places in our river by the ice, and plundered as many of them as they could before they burned them.

19. News to-day that a vessel is arrived at Carolina from France. The captain brought the letters, but upon the letters to Congress from Franklin being opened, they were all a blank. In his to his son-in-law, Bache, he refers him for news to the members of Congress, as there he was very particular. This makes it to be presumed that the messenger in France had suffered the letters to be taken away and those substituted in the room of them. Time will disclose this fraud and by whom it was transacted. It's said that Thomas Willing, with some others in town, had purchased a parcel of blankets for our prisoners there, but before they would deliver them applied to Gen. Howe, acquainting him of their intention. He sent them for answer not to send them any, as they should receive no such donations but what were sent directly from Gen. Washington to them for their use. This message and answer, I understand, are transmitted to Gen. Washington. What his judgment on this singular affair is, has not yet transpired, as I have heard.

21. News to-day is that the plan formed by Assembly and President, sent to Congress for their concurrence, is adopted; sent by them to Gen. Washington, is approved of and to be carried into execution as fast as possible.

22. This is a wonderful place for variety of sentiments and behavior. You may speak and converse with some, whose sweet countenances will tell you that you are highly agreeable to them while you talk to them in their way, but change the discourse by asking them to spare you some hay, oats for horse, wheat, rye, wood, butter, cider for yourselves, &c., &c., to be paid for in Congress money; or that the English army is likely to be defeated and our people to get the victory, oh! then, their serene countenances are all overcast, a lowering cloud spreads all over their horizon; they have nothing to say, nay scarcely to bid you farewell. I went into town to Wm. Henry's. While there [arrived] Hugh Hughes, wagoner from Philadelphia, who came with ten other wagons and three officers, as commissioners, with clothing for the English prisoners. These are permitted to travel where they please without any control, and to pay for what they purchase with Congress money, but our poor wagoners must not enter with provisions into Philadelphia without a guard and that at night, and brought back directly [the] same way; our Commissary with twenty-five head of cattle, taken in with a guard and not suffered to have a receipt for them, nor suffered even to shake hands with some of his acquaintances, nor to purchase anything but with hard money. The wagoner was John Moyer; the Commissary with the cattle, John Chandler. O poor Pennsylvania, how you are imposed upon and suffer your children to be made dupes. Hugh Hughes, as above, was detected in passing forty-five shilling bills counterfeited, sundry being found on him, and was sent to our prison by Wm. Henry. No doubt some of the officers have of the same money.

25. After dinner came back into town the eleven wagons with baggage that, it's said, was sent a few days post by Gen. Howe from Philadelphia, for the use of his people who are prisoners in this state, and which arrived here a few days ago and left it the day before, but

by order from [the] Board of War they were sent after, the goods put into our stores, the wagons and horses sent to [the] Continental stables, the officers under restrictions at Jordan's, the wagoners and some prisoners sent to prison and the women to ramble about the town. ...... It's said that John Brown is now discharged from prison, but not to go five miles from Manheim, and £500 security for his good behavior.[1]

26. Just passed by near a dozen light horse, who had been at York, going to head quarters. Yesterday one hundred and fifty Virginians came into town.

28. News is that the December mail was arrived at Philadelphia, but that Howe would not suffer any of the letters to be delivered. It's said Lord Chatham is at [the] head of affairs at London and that Gen. Howe has ordered all the shipping in [the] Delaware to be got ready for sea; that flour in Philadelphia was £5 per hundred in hard money, beef two shillings and six pence per lb.: fire wood [oak] £4 per cord, and other necessaries such as eatables, in proportion; great quantities of dry goods, but all to be paid for in hard money, but none to be taken out after being bought except by stealth.

29. After dinner went down to John Dunlap's for the Supplement to the *Pennsylvania Packet*, it containing the Resolves of Congress relating to the acts of retaliation upon Gen. Howe's prisoners agreeably to the usage that our people who are prisoners with Howe receive. ...... Passed through this town from camp to Yorktown this day, Gen. Conway and the Marquis de la Fayette.

30. A person from York brought sundry letters from, I apprehend, some of our Tory Friends there and [in] Virginia to be forwarded, but upon conversation, he took them to some more suitable person to have them sent. By him was learned that John Parish and Isaac

---

[1] John Brown was an emissary from General Howe. See the *Colonial Records*, vol. 11, pages 344 to 348 and the *Pennsylvania Archives*, vol. 6, pages 25, 30, 36 and 45.

Zane the Elder with two or three other Friends were then at York with the Congress, soliciting the discharge of the Friends that were sent away by the President and Council of Safety into Virginia, but their request was not complied with when he came away, but they were politely received.

31. Last night was a grand ball or entertainment, kept at the house [of] William Ross, the tavern keeper, which [it] is said was very brilliant, at which, it's said, were above one hundred men and women assembled, dressed in all their gaiety: cold collation with wine, punch, sweet cakes, &c., music, dancing, singing, &c., held till four this morning. Who were the principals in the promoting or in the expenses I did not learn, but [neither] the President nor any of his family was there, but Gen. Mifflin was. Account is brought that Monsieur Pliarne was drowned a few days ago, attempting to cross the River Potomac. He was a pleasant agreeable young gentleman. He visited our family here about three weeks ago.

FEBRUARY 1. My wife with me is much concerned respecting son Benja. as he was so poorly by the accounts the twenty-third, since which we [have] heard nothing from that quarter. This makes it more difficult for us, and the more especially as last night near ten o'clock, my wife went up stairs to a closet in [the] front room. When she came down she says, I believe Benny is dead. I asked why? She said that she was shuddered when she went into [the] room respecting him, and had not been thinking of him but saw nothing. Now it is to be noted that she is not of a timorous disposition, so that she can go any way or stay in the house all night alone, being under no fear of apparitions. Just as we sat down to dinner, came Jacob Baker. When I saw him I was struck. I asked him no questions, but to sit down and dine. I wanted none. My heart was full. After dinner he gave me two letters from my two sons, which gave me an account of his illness and of his departure; that without sighs or groan [he] departed this life about six o'clock on the evening of the twenty-ninth of last month. Thus I have lived to hear of the departure of my first born in the   year of his age, and who will be much lamented not only by his own connections to whom he was near and dear, but also by his acquaintances, which were very numerous, occasioned by his kindness and hospitality, which was very large.

5. My wife said at breakfast that before she came to bed last night, coming from [the] kitchen, she heard a most hard and uncommon noise in the elements, which appeared like the ice when [it] breaks up in the river. ...... My mind keeps thoughtful on the death of my son. Sometimes, I'm, as it were, satisfied; then a damp comes over and carries it away; so that I find nothing can settle or secure peace but an entire resignation to the divine will without any reserve.

6. Yesterday morning went from here, who came [the] evening before from York, the Marquis de La Fayette, who was going forward for Canada.

8. Some time past an Address was sent from the prisoners who were sent by [the] Committee of Safety into Virginia, to the Congress and also to the President and Council, the which was brought and presented by Alexander White, the lawyer of Winchester. He delivered one to the Congress at Yorktown, the other he came with to Lancaster. They prayed that they might not only be kept from being sent farther into Virginia to a place called Staunton, but that they might be permitted to return home to enjoy that liberty [of] which they are unjustly deprived. It was set forth in the said memorials that they were willing to engage not to give any information of any kind that came to their knowledge. The Council referred the matter wholly to Congress. They, after many debates, had not determined, so that after some days waiting Alexander White returned without

an answer. Whether any has yet been obtained, I've not learned. Account brought yesterday, that Wm. Coates and two other officers were taken prisoners near Abington by some of Howe's parties.

9. The roads [are] almost impassible, so that I'm afraid I shan't hear from my family at this distance, nor how our friends in and near Philadelphia fare. These thoughts give us much uneasiness upon their accounts. .....
News to-day is that Dr. Franklin was assassinated in France by a person who had concealed himself in his lodging room, but not wounded so as to be mortal, but was thought to be so by the perpetrator.

10. It's said that last night was a ball kept at Ross's, as before, carousing, music, &c., till near five this morning, then [they] went a sleighing, &c. This ball, it's said, was at the expenses of Henry Kepler Jr. .... Two companies of militia from Cumberland County passed through this town to-day for head quarters.

14. My tender wife keeps diligently engaged and looks upon every Philadelphian that comes to see us as a person suffering in a righteous cause and entitled to partake in some degree of our hospitality, the which she administers with her labor and attendance with great freedom and alacrity. This is a great encouragement to me.

15. Sat down to reading and writing. Upon opening the Bible, the twenty-third [chapter] of Jeremiah presented. Upon reading I could not help taking notice of the similarity of that day with ours, the nearness of connexion between the behavior of their called Priests and Prophets with all those called Ministers, Preachers, Prophets in this our day. Visited by Thos Urie, one of the Council. He brought me a book written by Thomas Blackwell entitled *Schema Sacra*, printed by Francis Bailey, Lancaster, 1776, the tenor of which is for erecting and establishing the doctrine of absolute predestination. By my promise I was necessitated to read part of it, the which small doing soon convinced me that it would be time unprofitably spent to read the whole, so I laid it by.

16. It's said that accounts from Philadelphia are that the enemy has unpaved the streets, and that the Hessians were embarked on board the ships; that sundry of our soldiers who had deserted and come into the city, Howe had ordered ropes round their necks, whipped them round the city and then turned them out; that John Allen is dead, also that two hearty whigs had died in prison, viz., Robert Eastburn and John Hall, the cooper.

18. An account of a fray at Pequea between some Virginia officers and our militia officers, in which a Virginian was killed, upon which Col. Boyd came to town this day and surrendered himself up. Several Assemblymen came to town this day.

19. I have often had to remember what David said that blessed is he whose God is the Lord and whose hope is in the Lord his God. Children can easily forget their parents, but the Lord never forgets his children (all men).

21. In conversation with R. Whitehill, sympathising and lamenting the distressed state of this province, through the ill conduct and mismanagement of our chief officers in public stations, the indelicate and profane conduct of the inferiors in every other department, the atrociousness of their public and private behavior, with the total neglect of religion, discipline and good order. These are the sappings that will undermine, and without a speedy return to the opposites in the course of virtues and heroic actions, we shall soon fall into irretrievable ruin and desolation. ...... It's said that eleven prisoners were brought to town yesterday from head quarters; that many of our soldiers die in the different hospitals and also at camp. ...... Last night was a grand ball, this being the third held in town lately, notwithstanding the grievous sufferings that this state lies under and labors with. Last night, I understand, there was in Lancaster what is called a brilliant ball, to which assembled a great number of fops, fools, &c., of both sexes, old and young.

It was kept at the house of Major Wertz, formerly a tailor who, some time past, and many others there met, made a pretense to religion and to be the followers of a crucified Jesus, but are declaring now by their wanton behavior that they will not have him to reign.

23. News, it's said, is brought that Gen. Howe gives from Forty to Sixty hard Dollars for every Committee-man or officer in the state brought to him. Thus are we insulted by a parcel of poltroons, whom we are able either to take or to drive out of the country, would we but play the part of honest, upright men unto our country and our families. O Pennsylvania, where is your zeal, integrity, honor and heroism?

24. Eleven prisoners brought into town.

25. I set about sorting some books that Paul Fooks brought up with his. ...... Paul Fooks gives us many affecting accounts of the inhabitants of Philadelphia. Account brought that the Tories had taken from Newtown in Bucks County, in conjunction with Howe's Light Horse, the clothes and the workmen making them of Stewart's and carried them to Philadelphia. It's said by some come from Philadelphia that one hundred guineas, some say one hundred and fifty, were proffered for apprehending me and bringing me into the city. This account is sent me in order to prevent me from going any way within the enemy's reach, as they are much enraged against me through my friends, the Tory class.

26. Sundry Friends visited the Assembly yesterday and to-day.

27. News is that there are now in Philadelphia one hundred and twenty-one new stores, amongst which is one kept by an Englishman, one by an Irishman, one by an American, the remainder, being one hundred and eighteen, by Scotchmen or Tories from Virginia; Gen. Wayne is gone with his brigade and four pieces of cannon into Billingsport, and that Gen. Greene has taken

between the lines on [the] Schuylkill and Chester County four hundred horses and taken them to camp.

MARCH 1. Visited by Thomas Urie, Councillor; stayed some time in conversation. It's to be remembered that those gentlemen who visit my apartment are worthy of double honor, because they generally deliver the sentiments of the department they belong unto, and sometimes listen to the sage advice given to them, which, I presume, often proves of singular advantage to them in their future conduct, as words of truth convey knowledge to the honest-hearted, and I have known sundry persons cried up as great wits in public affairs and councils, yet they themselves have been governed and ruled by foolish servants, and some men who have been applauded for their cunning, yet have been perpetually cheated. Few are qualified for Statesmen and Councillors, notwithstanding they may be called to that station. For this reason some men under the notions of weeding out prejudices, eradicate religion, virtue and common honesty.

4. Last Sixth Day another Ball or Assembly in Lancaster, where, it's said, cards were played at a hundred dollars a game. President[1] there. O poor Pennsylvania!

6. It's said that the people who keep the ball in Lancaster allow the Hessian band of music Fifteen Pounds for each night's attendance. This, James Davidson told me he was able to prove and make good, if called upon.

7. Accounts to-day are that Gen. Wayne, in the Jerseys, attacked a foraging party of Gen. Howe's there, killed several, took a number of prisoners, two hundred and fifty head of cattle, which, with three hundred head he had collected, he sent unto Head Quarters; that our General, Washington, had ordered one Worrall, a spy, condemned by Court Martial, to be hanged, which was done.

---
[1] Thomas Wharton.

8. Arose early in order to serve the horse, as Robert Whitehill was going to ride him to Tobias Miller's, where his own horse was, in order to ride him to Yorktown, he being appointed with John McClean to wait upon Congress in order to confer and lay some matters before them from the Assembly and the Executive Council.

9. Breakfasted with us Fooks, Thorne [and] Payne. Came Hermon Husbands with a plan of his projection, respecting the sinking of our paper currency by a general tax, which, after his reading and considering, we advised him to lay aside for the present. ...... A French spy from Philadelphia brought under a file of musqueteers by Capt. Lang to be examined by Paul Fooks.

10. My wife's pain in [the] face much better. This gives me fresh spirits as her constant assiduity and pains are very extraordinary, and her tender regard and care of me are beyond description. To which may be added [that] her kind, humane and Christian behavior, unto all that fall under her notice, is worthy of remembrance particularly; her daily and painful labor in the kitchen, providing necessaries for the hungry, her care for their sweet and comfortable lodging, her tender and compassionate hand in procuring and applying suitable medicines, such as she can procure for inward or outward maladies. So that the afflicted of every kind that come under her notice meet with all the ease, relief, and comfort that's in her power or her reach to administer, for which I hope and am sure the great Lord of the Household will fully reward her in due time.

11. It's said that Susannah Lightfoot and Valentine, two women Friends, sent word yesterday to our Assembly, sitting in Lancaster, that they had a message to them from Heaven. This day near eleven in [the] forenoon, the House adjourned and attended in [the] Court Room to hear her, but I'm informed [it] had but little effect and weight with them.

12. Hermon Husbands said news came to Assembly yesterday that the inhabitants on the sides of our river Delaware had, within [a] few days past, taken three ships bound up to Philadelphia. One of them mounted ten guns. They were loaded with rum, sugar, dry goods, ammunition, some soldiers and wheat flour. It's said those boats were commanded by Capt. Barry. ...... Several Committees of Assembly out on various bills this day. Great assortment of sundry goods brought into this place a few days past from several places, the persons paying no regard to the law requiring them to take out permits for selling, &c.

13. Yesterday a Court Martial was held here, where four persons for being concerned in purchasing and stealing horses for the enemy were tried; one of them acquitted, one to be imprisoned during the war, two to be hanged on the sixteenth instant (this as I am informed).

16. This day about one, the two persons condemned at Court Martial last week were executed agreeably to their sentence.

18. It's said that Henry Marson and Wendal Myer, the two men executed here this week, confessed at the gallows that they were guilty of stealing and procuring horses for Howe's army. Last night, it's said, forty of the sailors taken by Capt. Barry in the vessels taken by him near Reedy Island, came to this town under guard. See the particular account of the affair in the *Pennsylvania Packet* of this day. There is an account that a party of riflemen has taken four wagon loads of sundry goods, in which are four dozen silver table spoons, silver handled knives and forks, fifteen hundred weight of hams, butter, cheese, flour, with household furniture, &c., &c., [and] sixteen fine horses within one mile of the Middle Ferry. It's thought they were loaded in York and Lancaster Counties. Our people in the fray lost two men. It's said that Wm. Todd, the chairmaker of Philadelphia, was brought to Lancaster this day by an officer of the

Light Horse, on suspicion of passing counterfeit money, but upon examination before [the] Town Major, he proved of whom he had received it, upon which he was discharged.

19. Yesterday, it's said, news came that Howe had sent away, in a parcel of his transports, near upon seven thousand of his men. This I could not credit, yet that piercing grief thus to be so long banished from my children, city friends and relations caused some secret wishes that it might prove true, because my still dwelling so far from my connexions makes it a kind of banishment, which I do wish was happily removed by Howe's being obliged to abandon with his fugitives, either by flying for their lives, or by their being happily made our prisoners.

20. Drank tea with us, Fooks, Whitehill, Thorne [and] Ramsay. This last brought me [a] letter from son Charles [dated the] nineteenth instant, letting me know that the different branches of the families were tolerably well; that daughter Sally was safely delivered of a fine boy on the seventeenth instant near twenty minutes past five o'clock in the morning. [They] have called his name Benjamin after his poor father who was the first fruit of mine and his dear mother's social happiness, whose memory ever will be sweet, pleasing and agreeable to me, and whose sweet company I have deplored since she has been taken away, and although her departure and loss has been wonderfully supplied and made up to me by the present happy blessing sent me by a kind Providence, yet I love and do revere her memory which is still and will be to me precious.

22. Davidson bought and read the fifth *Crisis* just published this day.

24. Near two hundred soldiers left our barracks for camp. ...... News is to-day that the British have burnt down great part of Germantown and that a number of trading vessels are arrived to the Southward, with several large ships with goods from France. Our house con-

tinues still to be much frequented by sundry persons from different parts and many from Philada.

25. Granted permit to Alexander Nelson to sell by vendue twenty-two hundred and eighty pounds of Bohea tea, being part of the estate of Wm. Leidiel, deceased. ...... I set about sundry jobs, at one of which [I] broke the blade of a pocket knife, which at this time is a great loss, as none are to be bought but at a monstrous price in this place. ...... Yesterday and to-day, it's said, came through here on their way home to Cumberland County, where they belong, thirteen companies of militia, their time being completed at camp. The night before last and last night balls for the gentlemen and ladies of Lancaster.

26. Visited by John Scotten, John Wigdon, Capt. Price, Col. Clarke, Capt. Lang, James McLean [and] William Duffield. Disputes ran high respecting the supplement to the Test Act. Agreed to have a meeting this evening in Lancaster, to reconsider it. Took a walk towards Lancaster Court House to view the New England troops who were to march for head quarters, but were obliged to postpone till to-morrow for want of wagons. After I returned, came Capt. Markoe, Benja Harbison [and] Capt. Lang. Settled some preliminaries they went to execute, in warning sundries to meet this evening. ...... We went to Wm. Rose's Tavern, where we met some others to the number of thirteen. Spent the time in free conversation till near ten.

28. Afterwards came R. Taggert [and] B. Harbeson, who brought the Petition from the Country to the Assembly respecting the supplement to the Test Act, for me to sign, but upon consideration, it was thought most convenient to write another on the same subject to be signed by sundries in this borough, to be presented with the other, upon which one was written, which I concluded to show to sundry persons to-morrow morning and take their judgments thereon.

29. Chrisr. Ludwick from Yorktown brought news

from there that a gentleman of veracity declared that the accounts from France were that the French, the Spanish, the Prussian, and Polish Courts had all declared for the Independency of America by declaring and acknowledging them, and that a Treaty of Commerce was concluded by Dr. Franklin with the French Court for thirty years, upon which the Doctor was received and acknowledged at that Court as Ambassador from the Free and Independent States of America, and that the ministry in England was changed and Lord Chatham fixed in the place of Lord North; that a forty gun ship was arrived at New Haven loaded with woolens, linens, &c. I then went into Lancaster and got the Petition signed by many.

APRIL 1. News to-day that the Jersey militia had surrounded fifteen hundred English troops near Salem Creek, who had gone on shore to plunder, and that Capt. Barry near Reedy Island had taken twelve boats belonging to the English and some prisoners.

2. Went to Lottery Office, took out three Lottery Tickets, one for Paul Fooks, two for the four children of Sally Marshall. These three were a present from Blair McClenachan, for which he gave me the cash and requested me to carry them through the different Classes, with assurance that should they come out all blanks, he would pay me the cash for renewing them. ...... Assembly adjourned this afternoon till the thirteenth of May.

4. About eight o'clock waited upon Gen. Read at Wm. Atlee's. He there wrote a polite letter to Gen. Washington on my application, in order to procure a pass for daughter Patience to go into Philadelphia, to secure sundries belonging to my three sons. ...... Then came Capt. Lang. Went with him to Wm. Henry's; was qualified to serve as one of the Commissioners on the Forestalling Act. I then qualified Capt. Lang to act as Commissioner in procuring sundry clothing for the

Army. ...... Some troops from Virginia came to town, it's said, this day going for camp.

5. Came to town, it's said, Gen. Gates, Mifflin and another officer, and it's said that Gen. Lee[1] on his parole is come to camp.

6. It's said that thirty-five prisoners were brought to town this day, one, the Lieutenant of the Roebuck, a Captain, with sailors and marines.

7. About noon came into town Thos. McKean, Chief Judge, attended by Sheriff and sundry other gentlemen. We then came home. Dined with us those that breakfasted. Afterwards went to town, spent some time in conversation with sundry persons. When Court opened, went to Court. Stayed while the Commissions of Thos. McKean as Chief Judge [and] William Augustus Atlee as Second Judge were read, Magistrates [and] Constables called [and the] Grand Jury qualified. Then McKean delivered an elegant and spirited charge on the nature of our government, suitable to the circumstances of the times.

8. I went into Court, where John Evans, Third Judge had his commission read.

9. Went into town with Fooks; visited Gen. Lee, going to Yorktown. Then went into Court, where —— was burnt in the hand for manslaughter.

10. To-day and yesterday passed through this place near upon five hundred men from Virginia going to the camp.

12. This day Gen. Greene came to town from headquarters.

15. Breakfasted with us Fooks [and] Thorne. I then paid the latter on account of the Council of Safety, as per receipt in book, four hundred and five Pounds, twelve shillings. I then went down to [the] barber's, got shaved by his wife, thence to [the] Court House,

---

[1] General Charles Lee, " The Englishman."

where I was qualified as Grand Juryman for Philadelphia and Chester Counties.

17. Marched through this town, with drums, fifes, colors, wagons, &c., on their way to camp (without stopping here) above four hundred Virginians under Col. Smith.

18. I went, got shaved by the barber's wife, from there to Court, hearing the trial of [the] Boyds, &c. It's said that thirteen English deserters came to town this day; left Philadelphia last Second Day.

19. Paul [Fooks] set about packing sundry of his things to go by the wagon to-morrow to Yorktown with the Lottery wheels from Reading, which stop here to-day.

20. Paul Fooks set off this morning for Yorktown. ...... The prisoners tried last Seventh day and night, viz. Col. and Capt. Boyd, James Wilson, Archibald Henderson and Charles Caldwell, for the murder of Capt. Hammond at Capt. Wallace's the Seventeenth of February last, after a long trial, were acquitted, and Skyles and Hastings were run away; so not to be had this time. ...... A great many counterfeit Continental bills passing of the Eight, Six and Five Dollars Bills, neatly imitated.

21. This forenoon a company of soldiers that had been sick here marched out of town for the camp.

25. Most of the Friends from Virginia came to town this day. I gave some of them an invitation to my house.

26. Our good friend in town, Grace Hastings, sent my wife by daughter Patience one pound [of] fine Green Tea and would not take any pay for it. Charles Darragh brought it here yesterday which was very acceptable to us, and this particular mark of esteem will not be readily forgotten, it being the only present made to us by friend or foe, relations or strangers. Thanks be to His blessed name, He has not left us without His daily blessings, administered to us in this our exile, though with difficulty sometimes in procuring, yet there has been and is a visible hand of help continually stretched out, so that we

have never wanted. May our souls ever reverently bless and adore this glorous Deity.

27. Dull sunshine morning, yet warm. The cooing doves in pleasing strain, to soothe their mates in plaintive strain. The blackbird and the mockbird sing, to welcome in the pleasing spring. They chirrup, hop, from tree to tree. This raises thankfulness in me, to pay my God in hymns of praise, with cheerful heart through humble lays. Amen. ...... Then came Gen. De Kalb. He took his leave, being ordered to camp. ...... By the packet to Philadelphia, there is account of Lord North's Proposal to Parliament for passing an act to qualify sundry commissioners to come to America to treat with them upon conciliatory terms. ...... This evening the friends who were brought to town from Virginia last Seventh Day got a pass from [the] Executive Council to pass unmolested to Pottsgrove, and then to act agreeably to their own choice, for the present, in taking the test or to go into Philadelphia at their risk.

30. News is brought that great part of New York is burnt down, and that Gen. Amherst is arrived there; that our army increases fast, being joined by six hundred New England troops [a] few days past.

May 1. News from Yorktown that Gen. Lee is exchanged[1] and ordered to camp.

2. Yesterday afternoon arrived here Simeon Deane, brother to Silas Deane, with expresses from the Court of France, containing their declaration and acknowledgment of our Independency, and ratifying a treaty of alliance and friendship, acceding to us all the territories in America that were claimed and enjoyed by the English, unto which the king of Spain has acceded, &c. He left France, it's said, the Eighth of March in a Twenty-eight twelve-pounder-gun frigate [of] three hundred men, landed at Casco Bay, called at camp, had eight lighthorsemen to attend him, left Lancaster in two hours for

---

[1] For Gen. Prescott. This General Lee was Charles Lee.

Yorktown. ...... About half after one, died the negro woman Dinah, without sigh or groan; she had lain very quiet for a day or two; scarcely any pain, as she, I heard say, told her mistress. She was between fifty and sixty years of age. I was engaged part of this day in [the] orchard and likewise in hunting out a proper person to lay out the negro woman, as all the poor women here are rich in imagination, so that it was with difficulty one could be procured at any rate.

3. Some trouble to get persons to put [the] negro woman into her coffin. Oh! what a wretched place is here! full of religious profession, but not a grain of love or charity, except in words, in the generality of the German inhabitants. ......: Buried Dinah, having yesterday invited the negroes in Lancaster to attend the funeral. ...... Then came Capt. Lang and Col. Gurney; said that Generals Gates and Mifflin were come from York to Lancaster [and] had brought a copy of the preliminaries settled with France to be published.

6. By accounts received, about seven days before Simeon Deane sailed from France for this continent there sailed from Quiberon Bay in France for America, four sixty-four and four thirty-six gun ships, French, three American frigates with eight large deep-loaded transports for this continent, having, it's said, forty thousand suits of clothes complete for our army. The other parts of their loading are a variety of goods for the use of the public, for sale.

10. Received a letter from son Charles giving account that all the different families were well. In [the] letter, is mention made that Lydia Darrah came out on the Sixth from Philadelphia. Little news, but that Howe was there then; that the English troops were cutting down very fast the wood in the Jerseys opposite Philadelphia for the transports, as also for fear that the Americans might come there and have the advantage of the woods to cover them. ...... Accounts are, as brought

yesterday, that, a few days past, about three or four hundred of our militia, under General Lacey, near the Crooked Billet were surprised by seven or eight hundred English Light Horse and Foot, when after a close and sharp engagement our people gave way. [They] lost, killed, wounded and taken prisoners to the number of thirty. It's said that some of the wounded had eight or ten stabs with [the] bayonet and [were] badly cut with broadswords, and, what is worse, that the English threw some of those wounded into a parcel of buckwheat straw and then set it on fire. Oh the monsters! Oh the human shapes worse than brutes!

11. Past eleven, by invitation to Thomas Cuthbert's (hatter) to eat gammon [and] drink punch, his wife being delivered of a fine boy a few days past. Returned home by twelve. News is that four thousand troops from Virginia are actually on the road, going for camp. Nine wagon-loads are arrived at Lancaster, loaded with linens of different kinds. By letter it's said that sugars are fallen at Baltimore from fifty to twenty-five per hundred weight, spirits from three pounds to twenty-five shillings per gallon and coffee to five shillings per pound ; that a fine vessel mounting twenty-six guns with men in proportion was fitted out at Antigua to cruise and take the Philadelphia Rattlesnake. They met and engaged each other for seven glasses, when the ship struck and was carried in with a brig taken by the Rattlesnake ; carried into Martinico. Visited by Timothy Matlack to enquire for news, but as he never communicates or tells me any, I am grown as saucy, for I never ask him for any, he being too great a man. News just brought that the English in thirty-six flat bottomed boats went up the river near Trenton and burnt all our vessels that were lying there. Some say that the whole of our fleet was sunk by our people so that they could not burn then.[1] A number of men marched from here

---

[1] The whole *continental* fleet was burnt. The *state* fleet, having been sunk, was saved.

this day for camp. ...... This evening the Court House was illuminated and some pieces of brass cannon fired a loyal salute of thirteen guns besides small arms, bonfires, &c., on account of the alliance concluded with France.

13. News came this day from head quarters that war [is] declared by England against France. This was told in Lancaster by Capt. Jackson of Philadelphia, who left head quarters yesterday about noon. ...... Several of our Assemblymen came to town this afternoon.

16. I must say that the little that I do really tires and fatigues me. What formerly was scarcely a play is now a burden. However, I and my wife, who has a large share of labor in and about the house, have our choice: that is, either to do the necessaries or to leave them undone, as there is no person, white or black, male or female, old or young, to be had at any price, as we can find, and I have taken a good deal of pains on that head. ...... A parcel of English prisoners sent off this morning into Virginia. ...... The officers that ran away and some privates [were] retaken and brought into the borough and closely confined ...... By account from George Schlosser, in a letter from his daughter at Bustleton, it was seven of our wounded prisoners that the English burnt some days past near the Crooked Billet.

17.[1] Beautiful, pleasant morning, [a] little cloudy there having fallen in the night a refreshing shower. Our orchard and garden refreshed, the trees luxurious, the vegetables green, the sprightly birds skipping, chirping and singing praises to the Giver. ...... With thanks to God for his kind favor in thus refreshing nature and blessing us, I retired to my little room as usual. I then received the York-town paper brought by Mr. Bullock, sent me by my old friend Paul Fooks. ...... I and wife took [a] walk, spent some time in [the] orchard and garden. They were both pleasant after last night's rain.

---

[1] Sunday.

We were alone, as our Poll directly after dinner took her walk and was not returned. So we served [the] creatures, milked, made tea and drank it by ourselves. Spent the evening alone. I went to bed by ten. My wife sat up till near twelve, waiting for Poll, but no Poll.

19. News this morning is that the French fleet, consisting of six men of war, three of our frigates and eight merchant vessels were safely arrived at Boston some days past. ...... News just brought me by Col. Davis, then came James Reed who confirmed it, that [the] express just come says that the English at Philadelphia had embarked,[1] and that our army was gone down to take possession yesterday. We eagerly wait for the confirmation.

22. The news is a confirmation of the French fleet with some American frigates and eight or ten sail of merchantmen having arrived at Boston; that the Marquis de La Fayette with three thousand men marched towards Chestnut Hill, that six or seven thousand of the English came out in order to take the whole; that our people made a retreat without the loss of one man; that twelve English Light Horse came over to them; six more were taken by our people, and it's said, that our Indians killed and scalped the last parcel, and further that whilst the English army marched after the Marquis de la Fayette, the remainder marched into the Jerseys in order to be ready when the army returned to cross [the] Delaware also and make a forced march for New York. ...... In the evening had some conversation with several of our Assembly respecting petitions being sent to them to take the Abjuration out of the Test of Allegiance and Fidelity. One of them was from the Moravian [minister], one from Tho[s] Barton, minister of the Church of England in this borough, both of which were rejected.

23. Visited by George Schlosser; brought account

---

[1] This report was premature.

that Thomas Wharton, our President, died last night of an inflammation, it's said, in his head; been complaining for eight or ten days past. Breakfasted by ourselves; then to conversation with the Moravian minister from Bethlehem on the abjuration of George the Third, but he seemed to be fixed that he could not, nor would not, do it, let the consequence be as it may.

24. Preparations making, it's said, at [the] Court House for a grand interment of President Wharton this afternoon at the Lutheran Church. It's said the vestry of that church gave an invitation and permission to be buried there, which the vestry of the English Church neglected, and the Friends were not applied unto for leave to be buried in their ground.[1] ...... In the afternoon, went to the burial of President Thomas Wharton, attended with military honors to the Lutheran church.

25. Came to town and encamped this side [of the] ferry, between four and five hundred troops from Virginia.

28. Visited by Thoˢ. Smith, who [had] received [a] letter from Col. Cox that left camp last night. The purport was that Gen. Howe had put all his cannon, artillery, baggage, women and children on board his fleet, except four wagons for each regiment, as it was thought the army intended to make a push across the Jerseys for Amboy. Further accounts [are] hourly expected. It's further said by an officer from Wilmington that a sixty-gun ship came down, sent ashore to Gen. Smallwood an officer requesting him to surrender the place or else [he] would demolish it. Gen. Smallwood returned for answer, he would defend it to the last man. [He] immediately dispatched [a] messenger to Gen. Washington who immediately ordered him and all his forces to come to camp, and he was apprised of Gen. Howe's manœuvre, upon which they marched for camp immediately. It's further said, by undoubted authority, that Spain has acceded and

---

[1] Mr. Wharton's family were Quakers; his father was one of the persons sent from Philadelphia into Virginia.

declared us independent. ...... Drank tea with us Christopher Ludwick;[1] left camp this morning; said the army was almost ready to march, which was expected in a few days, as they were waiting upon the movements of Gen. Howe's army; that old Christopher Sower[2] was prisoner at camp. Those who took him had shaved and painted him.

29. C. Ludwick told me that our Indians at camp had killed three officers by mistake owing to their being dressed in the English officers' uniform. (So much for fashion.)

JUNE 1. Visited by Topham, the potter, who has got released from a nineteen months' imprisonment in New York and Long Island. ...... It's said that two vessels are arrived at Baltimore from Martinico, in twenty-one days; that they have an account that war was actually declared at Port Royal in Jamaica, against France. It's to be remembered that the above news was freely communicated to me by Timothy Matlack, which being so contrary to his constant practice, I make this memorandum in order that I may not forget this singular act of his friendship.

2. Spent some time with Councillor James Adgar. He informed me that Parson Barton had petitioned Council for leave to sell his estate and leave the State agreeably to the Act in that case made and provided, which, he presumed, would be granted him. ...... Visited by Chrisley Musselman; stayed some time in conversation respecting the Test required to be taken by all the male white inhabitants of this State above the age of eighteen years. Dr. Neff and son John took it last evening.

3. News just come to Tho⁵. Smith from Col. Cox [at]

---

[1] Ludwick was baker to the American army. In his will, he made provision for founding charity schools.

[2] Sower or Sauer was a German printer in Germantown. He was attainted for treason to the American government.

head quarters that the army of Britain were strengthening their lines in Philadelphia; yet, nevertheless, that a great number of vessels had fallen down the river, and that three of their regiments actually crossed into the Jerseys yesterday at Cooper's ferry.

4. A very heavy fog. I arose by four, as my wife had been up some time at work, cleaning house, and as she could not rest upon account of Poll's not being yet returned. This girl's frolics always afflict her mistress, so that to me it's plain, if she does not mend or her mistress grieve less for her, that it will shorten Mrs. Marshall's life considerably; besides, our house wears a quite different face when Miss Poll is in it (although all the good she does is not worth half the salt she eats). As her presence gives pleasure to her mistress, this gives joy to all in the house, so that, in fact, she is the cause of peace or uneasiness in our house. I received a letter by James Searles from Paul Fooks, letting me know that since he wrote his of the second instant, Congress had sent for him and appointed him their interpreter with a salary of One Hundred Dollars per month. ...... A day or two past, Thomas Barton, Missionary, petitioned Council for leave to sell his estate and to remove out of this state, which was granted under the limitations contained in the said Act. ...... Twenty-five prisoners, brought from camp, came here, it's said, to-day.

5. Just going past nine wagons loaded with provisions for camp from Carlisle. ...... In the evening came Paul Fooks and his boy in [the] wagon from Yorktown.

6. Arose early. Sent Paul's boy to G. Schlosser's, who was to buy us [a] quarter [of] meat of [the] Philadelphia butcher, and as the market is soon over and G. S. an early riser, he did it to oblige us, and he purchased a lovely hind quarter of veal, weight seventeen pounds at two shillings, for which we were highly obliged to him. ...... P. F. breakfasted with us. He then went to [the] Lottery Office, where the managers attend, settling

the Prize list for the press. ...... News of this day by
William Cox of Philadelphia and letter from Dr. Shippen
to the President,[1] is, it's said that Col. Loring[2] came out
with flag on the fifth to Col. Morgan of the Riflemen
and let them know that Gen. Clinton intended to evacuate the city ; that therefore an exchange of prisoners
should be immediately made. Upon this Mr. Boudinot
was sent into town, and, by his letter out, it appeared
they intended for New York, and that the city might
be clear of the enemy by First day next.

8. After [I had] gone to bed, came [an] express with
a letter requesting I would send to the President of Congress, Henry Laurens, the particulars I had relating to
the surrender of Gen. Burgoyne, with the list of prisoners,
stores &c., the which I complied with, sending [a] copy
of what I had on that subject back by the said express.

9. It's said that the Commissioners from England are
arrived at Philadelphia. This, it's said, has retarded the
English troops from evacuating Philadelphia, but that
there is a large detachment with their flat bottomed boats
at Cooper's Point in the Jerseys.

10. I arose pretty early, as my wife is much engaged,
having no person to assist her, nor will she agree to have
any body, except her beloved Poll is sent for to camp
and brought back. This I cannot agree to, so as to be
the acting person. If she does it herself, I don't forbid
her, but for me to offer a reward for a common w....
to be brought to my house I cannot consent, so as to be
the active person. Here wife and I differ widely in
sentiments.

12. Wife and I set about our little concerns in our
little family ; as to the human species none but ourselves.
So that with this and the other little concerns we seem
to be fully employed for some time in several parts of

[1] Upon the death of Thomas Wharton, George Bryan succeeded to the
Presidency of the Executive Council of Pennsylvania.

[2] The husband of Gen. Howe's mistress, mentioned in the Battle of the
Kegs.

the day, but my poor wife almost constantly, and thus she verifies that old saying that "woman's work is never done." ...... Dined with us Peter Swart and his wife; had a good deal of conversation respecting taking the test. A day or two past, it's said, that ten of the Menonists were brought from [the] back part of this county to this jail, refusing to take the test; committed by Curtis Grieb.

13. Visited by John Carryle, a Menonist; spent some considerable time in religious and political conversation respecting the test required to be taken throughout this state. He went away seemingly pleased and satisfied.

14. Took a walk to view the Eighth Pennsylvania Regiment marching through the town with their baggage wagons, women, &c., for the back counties in order to protect them from the incursions of the Indians there.

15. A good number of horses went through this place for camp to-day.

16. Dined, Jane Cannon, Mrs. Callison, James Davidson and wife, several children. Came also Robert Whitehill. All but [the] last mentioned set off after dinner with two wagons with their goods for South Carolina. My dear wife was extremely hurried, having nobody to assist her, yet she provided nobly for them and dispatched them with great alacrity and satisfaction.

17. Got this week's newspapers; then I returned home, read the news. News from Dr. Shippen from Moor Hall of yesterday that the enemy might be expected to leave Philadelphia. ...... I sat for some time in [the] orchard, reading Hartley on the Millenium.

18. Then to some other jobs; then into my room. I seem now soon tired; "the grasshopper seems to be a burden." ...... Timothy Matlack called, said the Congress to a man had rejected the proposals made by those conciliators from Britain, viz. the Earl of Carlisle (with his three doxies), William Eden, Esq., Capt. Johnstone Esq., formerly Governor of West Florida,

Lord Howe and Gen. Clinton, who, it is said, are arrived at Philadelphia, as, it's said, that Lord Cornwallis is also, without any troops. A number of Hessian prisoners marched from here this day to the number of four hundred in order to be exchanged. Part of Col. Hartley's regiment from Yorktown marched through here for head quarters to day, past eleven. News just brought that eleven deserters came in from [the] city the sixteenth instant; that the enemy's baggage, they say, was principally gone on board ships, that an evacuation of the city was hourly expected, and that the city was very sickly.

19. Past seven [A. M.] Timothy Matlack, just come, says accounts are arrived that Capt. John McLane,[1] with about fifty light horse [and] one hundred of the foot troops, took possession of Philadelphia yesterday morning [at] three o'clock. Further confirmation hourly expected. ...... Past twelve, the morning news [is] confirmed by letter to [the] President of Council from Gen. Washington, letter from Col. Cox to Thomas Smith, by expresses, &c. Benja. Harbison, Thomas Smith, John Dunlap with several others set off for Philadelphia. ...... Signed some permits in order for my setting out for Philadelphia. Dr. Phyle[2] waited upon me, proferred his company in driving me in my chair to Philadelphia. Agreed to set off as soon as convenient.

20. Visited by Capt. Lang and Commissioner Craig. We went together to see Capt. Markoe, who came from Philada. He, being upon the lines, entered the city, on the notice of the enemy's being gone from there. He confirms the account of McLane's taking possession of it, as it was said, with this addition that the aforesaid captain kept so close on their rear that he took sundry prisoners[3] and some wagons, but as to the route the

---

[1] A mistake for Capt. *Allen* McLane, who commanded the American advanced guard.

[2] Originally a German Redemptioner; the father of the late wealthy Mrs. Stott of Philadelphia.

[3] Col. Allen McLane stated that these prisoners were taken at the corner of Ninth and South Streets.

enemy intended to take, any further than the Jerseys, was not known.

21. Accounts just come that the Indians to the westward are making sad havoc of the inhabitants.

22. Breakfasted with us G. Schlosser and Dr. Phyle. We then set out for Philada., Dr. Phyle riding with me in the chair; George Schlosser and his son-in-law in a chair; Timothy Matlack and daughter in another; Daniel Wistar by himself in a four-wheeled carriage. Baited at [the] sign of [the] hat; then proceeded to the sign of [the] wagon; dined there; from there they went to [the] sign of the white horse; the Doctor with me to John Jacobs's (where was David Rittenhouse); drank tea and soon went to bed.

23. Got up soon, but so likely for rain, we stayed breakfast; then set off for town near eight. Stopped at [the] Union, at [the] Black Horse, baited. ...... Set off for the city. Within a mile or two was presented a poor prospect, houses ruined and destroyed, fields of fine corn without fences, &c. We crossed the bridge at the middle ferry.[1] I put up [the] chair at Charles's stable, horse at Stephen Collins's (whose little son attended him while I stayed in town), drank tea and slept at Capt. Timmon's.

24. Rose early; sauntered about; breakfasted at Stephen Collins's; dined at John Lynn's; attended at Coffee House; then viewing the desolation, with the dirt, filth, stench and flies in and about town, scarcely credible. There was a large quantity, but some very ordinary meat in market, great quantities of vegetables and some fish.

25. Took a walk by myself to our once rural, beautiful place (near barracks) now nothing but wanton desolation and destruction, that struck me with horror and detestation of the promoters and executors of such horrid deeds. My mind was so pained I soon returned into the city.

---

[1] At Market street, where there was a floating bridge.

26. Breakfasted and dined at Stephen Collins's with my children. In the interval, engaged in viewing some of our and others' houses with wonder and amazement on the scenes of malice and wanton cruelty, yet my late dwelling house was not so bad as many others, yet grief seized me in beholding the ruins, viz., houses quite demolished, of which ours near [the] Bettering House [was] quite gone with the brick-walls, chimneys, &c., the doors, cases, windows and cases, etc., either destroyed or carried away entirely.

27. Set out for the country near eight, in company with son Charles, his wife, Nancy Parrish, Daughter Sally and her daughter Hannah, Dr. Phyle, etc., in different chairs. Stopped at Levering's;[1] at Plymouth[2] burial-ground, viewed the grave of my dear Benny; stopped a few miles farther by the side of [a] house, for the horses to rest, it was so melting hot. (It's said that some horses died on the road with the heat.) Got to Sally's past four, drank tea and the Doctor and I supped and slept there.

JULY 1. Near nine returned Thomas Rees from town; said he had been twelve hours coming, occasioned by the heat; that near four hundred Hessian deserters with English prisoners were just brought into the city.

2. Wm. Henry and wife called; showed [a] copy of [a] letter from Gen. Washington to Gen. Arnold giving an account that an engagement was last Monday near Monmouth Court House in Jersey, where our army beat the English grand army off their ground and encamped upon it that night, in which time the English made so silent and forced [a] march that they were six miles ahead next morning. Many killed on both sides and many perished with the heat.

4. It's said that seventy deserters came to Philadelphia this day.

---

[1] In Roxborough Township, Philadelphia County, still existing.
[2] In Montgomery County, Philadelphia.

7. After dinner Charles and wife went home with Sally in order to see whether proper or no for Sally to move her family to town, as they had made an hospital of the Presbyterian meeting-house facing her.

8. It's said that thirty-nine English grenadiers came in a body to Gen. Washington's camp.

15. I arose early. We breakfasted. My horse in chair; son Christopher on his horse, with his overseer on another (Joseph Thomas). After my taking a very solemn and affectionate farewell of my dear children, and their sweet lovely offspring, we set out. The overseer accompanied us over the Schuylkill and then returned home. We proceeded on (through several miles. [of] badly cut roads by the wagons last winter and spring). Near eleven reached John Jacobs's, who kindly received and entertained us. After dinner (David Rittenhouse dined with us. He was going with a wagon load of his goods from Lancaster to Philadelphia), about two, we set out; stopped at [the] sign of [the] ship (met with Jacob Deitrick and his wife, going from Philadelphia to his house at Lancaster, with whom we kept company till we got home very agreeably). Near thirty-eight mile stone, waited till some wagons that were behind came up with us, as we were creditably informed that sundry persons had been stopped and robbed thereabouts, but we were preserved. We reached [the] sign of the wagon, where we rested and stayed all night. Fine starlight, here we slept with our great coats on top of the bed clothes.

16. We arose early, geared our horses, with the friend and his wife and proceeded to Hopkins's Tavern (sixteen miles from Lancaster); breakfasted plentifully, being both clean and good (the people having some complacency attending them); set off for Lancaster, where we arrived safe (but I was really tired, though I had rode Kitty's horse from the wagon to Hopkins's) and was very heartily and kindly received by my dear and most

affectionate wife. Yesterday we met with many persons and their families moving into Philadelphia; the same to-day, with a great number of women, children, cattle and horses (but few men) who, they said, were driven away from their settlements on the North East branch of the Susquehannah by the Indians, supported by the garrisons of Detroit [and] Niagara, and who are joined by numbers of the Tories and disaffected party in those parts. The sight was truly affecting and distressing to me (and I have great cause to praise and to adore Infinite Wisdom who has been so graciously pleased to preserve me and my tender families in so wonderful a manner. May the solid sense of such gracious mercies never leave me but live and remain with thankful praises in my soul forever and forevermore! Amen).

17. We arose early, being a fine morning. Mamma got breakfast for son Christopher, who set off for home by five o'clock, after taking an affectionate leave of us, and our recommending him to the kind and providential care of our great Lord and Master, Jesus Christ.

18. Some Continental troops came into the borough this day. People from the back woods come down and coming in great numbers so that the county of Northumberland[1] will be laid quite waste by the English and savage barbarians, except the Almighty in his goodness prevent. ..... We then sat down, my wife and I very comfortably; drank a dish of tea with great satisfaction. John and wife with their child came [and] received their portion, as did a poor little girl, who, with her father, mother and two more children, fled for their lives and brought little else with them from [the] back woods. [To] these we gave the key of [the] house [which] Thomas Smith moved from, in order to cover them for a while from the inclemency of the weather, and to partake of some small hospitality.

---

[1] This county at that time extended to the northern boundary of Pennsylvania, embracing territory now divided into sixteen counties.

19. Col. Hartley's Regiment marched through here on their route for the back woods. Accounts of heavy firing last Sixth Day near New York. No particulars.

21. My dear wife meets with but little respite all day, that proverb being verified that " woman's work is never done." ...... It seems a little discouraging to have no help about us, besides living in a neighborhood of lumps of mortality, formed in shape of men and women, but so unpolished, so hoggish and selfish, that no good, kind sociability makes any impression upon their boorish nature. ...... News that fourteen sail of large and small prizes are sent into Egg Harbor [and] Morris River[1] by the French fleet off Sandy Hook.

22. Visited by James Farran [a] poor man and family, fled from [the] back woods. ...... Visited by William Bonham, who, with his wife, brother and family, was driven away from their homes in the back woods. ...... Then dined, my wife, as usual, sending some portion to the afflicted and distressed. I then, after dinner, visited Mrs. Bonham and children at Robt. Taggert's.

24. This morning, it's said, there passed through here near two hundred head of cattle; and about one hundred and fifty horses stopped here, for the use of the Light Horse. These came from Virginia.

26. Fine sunshine; clear, pleasant morning. I arose past seven; wind eastwardly. I took my walk in [the] orchard and observed the little concerns on our rural plantation. A general stillness now from the noise of drums, fifes, &c.[2] The little birds, with their mates, chirping from tree to tree; the fruits and vegetables, plenty and gay; the harvest got in, having been blest with fine crops of grass and grain, and fine weather. Thus has kind Heaven blest and [is] blessing us! Oh! saith my soul, that a universal hymn of praise and thanksgiving may arise and spread in and over our soul to our

---

[1] Maurice River in the southern part of New Jersey was probably meant.
[2] This was Sunday, and the soldiers had removed from Lancaster.

great and blessed Benefactor! Amen. In [the] afternoon I went to the Dutch Presbyterian Meeting House, where a suitable and good discourse was delivered on this text, Cor. ii, Chap. 4: 17, by one —— Fifer, minister of the Church of England living at Frederickstown or Fredericksburgh, I did not learn [which]. Returned with Ed. Shippen, who pressed me to stop at his house, and drank [a] glass of beer of his own brewing. ...... After drinking tea, past seven, took [a] walk to Robert Taggert's, from there to the above mentioned meeting house, where the aforesaid parson preached to [a] large collection of people on this text, Eccles., 12:1, which held till past nine.

27. Account brought that our Poll was living in Yorktown at a tavern kept by Rob. Dunn. ...... Drank tea; half after seven, went to the aforementioned meeting. The said person that officiated last night preached on this text, Deut. 32:29.

28. I went into town; spent some time in conversation with sundry persons at Wm. Henry's store on the news of the day, that is, that another French fleet of seventeen sail of the line is arrived off Sandy Hook; have taken a number of prizes; that provisions at New York were exceeding scarce; at Philada. very plenty and the prices moderate.

30. Passed forward to Wm. Henry's store, met sundry Lancasterians there, where was read the Third Day's Philada. newspaper, in which is said under the Boston head that the French fleet under Admiral d'Estaing was gone to Rhode Island; had taken twenty-seven sail of English vessels; whether part of the Cork provision fleet or not, was not told. ...... I went and borrowed Capt. Hervey's horse for Charles to ride with my wife to-morrow to Yorktown in order to find her Poll, as she was informed that she lived at one Robt. Dunn's, who kept tavern there.

31. Fine pleasant morning. My wife rose near four; I near five; sent for Capt. Hervey's horse. Charles

fed them, saddled them; eat his own breakfast as my wife could not eat anything (as indeed her daily fatigue is quite too much and, at present, no help, as I can find, is to be had, which gives me great uneasiness, yet I have some hopes that the Good Hand will open some way to relieve us, though at present I see none). They got equipped and set off from here about six o'clock.

AUGUST 1. Visited this morning by Adam Zantzinger, but brought no new news. ...... Near three, afternoon, my wife returned with Charles and Poll, that she found at Yorktown. ...... Afterwards came R. Taggert and B. Harbison, who by a person just come into town, brought account of an engagement between our army and the English, on the thirtieth, at the White Plains, when the latter left three thousand killed and wounded on the field of battle, but no further particulars. Many people in and around Lancaster speak of a very heavy firing of cannon being heard the same day by them and others.

6. Spent some time in conversation with some of the Justices and Assemblymen respecting the Menonists in prison in order for their enlargement and respecting the signing of two petitions that were intended to be presented to the Assembly.

9. Soon after came Ed. Milne from Philad., brought me a letter (and newspapers from son Christopher with six papers of the patent snuff) giving me an account of the health of their families, &c. He also brought a letter (and two newspapers) from Father Paul,[1] requesting I would send him his clothes, books and sundries that he had left here. ...... We drank tea; then Ed. Milne went away into town to enquire after the wagon to carry away a large trunk of plate he had sent here in the spring for security, with P. Fooks's goods.

12. News of the day is that there has been, last week, a great fire at New York, in which, it's said, one hund-

---

[1] Fooks.

red and thirty houses were consumed with two of the principal King's stores, with all their contents. It's further said that many of the inhabitants, engaged in endeavoring to save the dwelling houses, were by the English and Tories cursed as damned rebels and many of them cast into the flames and there perished; it's further said that a large English magazine-ship, near New York, was blown up about the same time. The same officer who tells this says he left the city of Philada. yesterday; saw an officer from head quarters just arrived there, who said, an express arrived as he came away, with the account of the surrender of Rhode Island to the French Admiral, who had landed four thousand of his troops on the island, to coöperate with our army. Thus stands the report for the present. It's said that a Dutch and Spanish ship is arrived at Baltimore, loaded with merchant's goods.

16. Arose early, eat breakfast; then went in our chair to Dr. Kennedy's. Sent Charles back with [the] chair; stayed till the Dr.'s carriage was ready, in which with his negro man (past nine) we set out for Philada. Stopped at the sign of the Hart; served horses; then proceeded; stopped on [the] road; eat some gammon, drank some toddy; so went forward through a heavy rain to the sign of [the] Wagon, not much wet, as the carriage had a very good covering. I slept here, or, I would say, lodged.

17. Got up early, fed horses and set off in company with Capt. Nicholas Brown Seabrook of Richmond Town, of Henrico County in Virginia (in a sulky without any covering. So he traveled yesterday with us). I paid for Dr. and self twenty-five shillings and ten pence (the Dr. brought oats with him). Near where Capt. Fitz[1] the robber infested, we were joined by one man and two women on horseback, who seeing us coming, waited in

---

[1] See an interesting account of this celebrated freebooter in Mr. Lewis's History of Chester County.

order to have our company over those hills. Hereabouts the rain abated. We rode on to Capt. Weed's at Downing Town, where we fed ourselves and horses. Afterwards set off and stopped at Ed. Jacobs's tavern near [the] White Horse, where we dined; from there to the tavern near [the Sixteen Miles stone, where we lodged. In the night Dr. Kennedy was taken violently ill with purging and vomiting. Capt. Seabrook, self and negro man assisted, as the people of the house gave themselves no concern.

18. In the morning early the Capt. set off for town. I waited till near ten (he, the Dr. being so poorly). We rode to the Widow Miller's; there we dined and fed horses (here I paid for Dr. and self twenty-seven shillings, at Ed. Jacobs's twenty-eight shillings). Then set off and arrived at Philad[a] near five. The Dr. put up at the Indian Queen.[1] I lodged at son Charles's house (the Dr. so tired that he could not walk down there). Drank tea at Timothy Matlack's; went to see Paul Fooks; not to be found; so I went to bed early.

24. Rose early. Went to D. Rittenhouse to get him to change some old money for a poor honest man. Breakfasted there. Weather cold; wind northwardly. From there to J[s]. Jones, whom we had left in our house, to search for sundry goods taken away, viz., fine iron grate, Scotch stove, corner cupboard with glass doors, all the iron backs, cranes, etc., etc., etc. Visited at Blair M[c]Clenachan's [and] Dr. Chovet's. I was then waited upon by the aforementioned Spanish gentleman[2] and the chaplain to him and the French Ambassador,[3] with whom I went and dined.

26. Received [a] letter from James Cannon, with account of his wife and James Davidson's family's arrival at Charleston, South Carolina, the twenty-sixth [of] July, all well.

---

[1] At or near the south east corner of Fourth and Market Streets.
[2] Don Juan de Meralles, the Spanish Ambassador.
[3] M. Gerard.

27. Sent son's cart and horse to Dr. Chovet's and brought what books he had saved of mine at two trips to son's shop; left them up stairs there. ...... Went and drank tea with Parson Duché, his father, mother and wife; then to son's, where Jona^t Sergeant came [and] requested [leave] to give up our house he had taken, to which I consented (as it was not grand enough for him). Went to Grace Hastings's, who had spoken before and wanted it for a gentleman named Tim^y Pickering.

28. I got up early. Walked to Campingtown in quest of my cupboard, but found none; to Wm. Rush's for my cranes, but none there. Breakfasted at Grace Hastings's; let the gentleman have my house on the same conditions [on which] Sergeant had taken it, viz: at Fifty Pounds per year, and to repair it fit and tenantable.

SEPTEMBER 2. Then to Coffee House; waited till Lieutenants Lyons, Ford and Wilson and John Wilson, gunner, were brought on board two government vessels off Market Street wharf, where the two first suffered the law and the other two [were] reprieved.[1] The number of spectators was very great; from [the] end of the market house, where I stood upon a bench.

5. Near nine set off; reached Levering's; fed horse and [had] some drink for John F. and self; paid eight shillings and three pence; then proceeded to Charles's, where we got safe near four.

11. Just after came Major Loxley; brought [a] letter from town to my sons in which was mentioned that a gentleman from Lancaster had called at their house to look for me, who said that my wife was very ill; had kept her bed for three days. This gave me great concern and I immediately concluded for home.

12. I got up at four [in the] morning. Cloudy with small rain. We got breakfast, the horses served, the

---

[1] They had deserted to the enemy during the attack upon Fort Mifflin. See the Colonial Records and Pennsylvania Archives.

phæton made ready. Kitty went with me and took John Darragh to be as company on his return. We set off near six. Rained pretty smartly till after we had passed [the] Schuylkill, then moderated. Proceeded over [the] bridge at French Creek; came to Potts's; fed our horses; then proceeded and reached Jones's tavern, where we dined [and] fed our horses (cost twenty-five shillings); then set forward; reached Capt. Reese's tavern at [the] Blue Ball by dusk. Here we took up our residence for the night. Upon the whole, we had middling good weather, yet both we and horses were tired as the roads were so exceedingly hilly and stony, I think longer and worse than the great road is over the Valley Hills. We scarcely met any travelers on this road, but saw plenty of squirrels. We drank coffee for supper and slept in our great coats, stockings, &c., for fear of fleas and bugs.

13. We rose early, fed our horses; I paid [the] reckoning, thirty-eight shillings and ten pence. Set off for Lancaster, passed through New Holland, in which were many but indifferent and some good houses, built in the Dutch fashion, on both sides of one long continued street. The men, women and children seemed to be plenty, mostly Germans and of the middling sort. The roads here were in general good, fine woodland and many fine plantations, with a great quantity of wild pigeons and squirrels, regaling themselves in the fields and in the woods, with some flocks of partridges. We reached Lancaster past ten; found my wife abed and very poorly, yet nevertheless she arose. Polly got us breakfast of good coffee, gammon, &c., of which we partook cheerfully, as we had by that time got a good appetite. ......
Just at dinner time came John McLean, Robert Whitehill and William Duffield on their way home from the Assembly at Philad^a., which had broke up on the eleventh. They stayed and dined; then set off for their respective houses. After dinner my son Kitty prepared and set off for home with John Darragh, taking the

candles that I had bought for him. In the chair-box by him I put P. Fooks's warming-pan and Cunningham's book on Bills of Exchange and the Deeds, Mortgage, Bond and Judgment of Robt. Taylor, as the man had requested me to send them in order that he might discharge the debt.

16. I paid unto Daniel Stricker, Collector of [the] Continental Tax, Ten Pounds fifteen shillings and nine pence.

18. Mamma seems quite cheerful and will be industrious, for all that I can say or do; the reason is her girl Poll is a very ordinary lazy hussey.

19. Spoke to a person just come from Philadelphia, who said the news there was that war was actually declared between the French and English.

22. I received [a] letter from P. F. dated [the] nineteenth. The news is that war against Great Britain was declared at Martinique the fourteenth of August; that the courts of Spain and Portugal had ordered all British ships out of their ports in the space of six days or to be seized; that the British fleet that was cruising off Boston is returned to Sandy Hook; that the Packet was arrived and brought orders for the Commissioners to return home, and to the fleet and army to evacuate New York, but [it] was not said where they were to go [as it] was not known, but some think, and it's probable, they will go to Halifax and the West Indies. Ten regiments, it's said, will go to Jamaica. It's further said that a large ship mounting twenty-two guns has been allotted to the Tories and is now full of men, women and children of that tribe bound to Halifax.

24. News to-day is that the English fleet has left New York and Sandy Hook.

OCTOBER 3. This morning, I presume, Parson Barton moved off the last of his effects, in two covered wagons. This morning and last night came to town, it's said, about ——— Scotch, English [and] Hessian prisoners, who stayed to recruit themselves on their march to the Eastward from Virginia to be exchanged. They had not the appearance of our poor emaciated countrymen, discharged by the English tyrants. Ours were reduced to the utmost extremity; those, hearty, plump and fat, with wagons to carry their baggage, women and children; ours so stripped as hardly [to have] rags to cover them. So disproportionate are those circumstances, but Heaven, I hope, will protect us from their future cruelty and barbarity.

5. It's said by private hand that there are fifteen or sixteen sail of vessels with salt in [the] Delaware river, some of them from France, &c.; that John Roberts, miller, was tried for High Treason and convicted, as was Abraham Carlisle, carpenter.

6. Past one, the English, Irish and Dutch prisoners marched out of town to go where they are to be exchanged.

9. Accounts from Philadelphia are that the Friends took up the body of Molesworth in the night time [and] transported it somewhere, but the public are not satisfied and say it should have been done in the day in a public manner.[1] It's said they have taken him out of one hole and put him into another in the same ground. It's thought to have been the greatest and largest yearly meeting for a long time past.

13. Accounts from town are that a number of English landed at Morris[2] river and Egg harbor last week and destroyed several vessels, rigging, cargoes, &c., with a good deal of other mischief and then decamped; that Abraham Carlisle was put into the dungeon.

14. It's said that John Roberts, miller, is condemned and confined in the dungeon.

---

[1] James Molesworth was hung for High Treason. His offence consisted in endeavoring to hire men to pilot the British fleet up the Delaware. See the Life of General Joseph Reed, *Pennsylvania Archives*, vol. 5, pages 270 to 282, *Colonial Records of Pa.*, vol. 11, page 197, and Dunlap's newspaper.

[2] Maurice?

15. Paid Shaffer Five Dollars for bringing a barrel of sugar from Philadelphia some time past. Paid seven shillings and six pence to [the] stageman for sundry pamphlets from Stephen Collins entitled *A Serious Address to the Quakers.*

17. We arose early; breakfasted. Wife got ready against the wagon came, in which went Wm. Bonham's wife, three children and servant girl, with some of his furniture, my wife and Wertz's sister-in-law for Philad^a. Set off about half after ten [in the] forenoon. Bonham rode on horseback, as he had three cattle to drive, and another horse led at the tail of the wagon.

20. Just heard that on First Day, about twelve o'clock noon, my wife and her companions were all safe and brisk at "the Wagon." This, Robt. Taggert said, he had from Judge Atlee who saw and conversed with them.

21. Fine delightful morning. I got up early, yet our Poll was gone. This is her trade, morning, noon and night, or any time of the day for hours together. I talk and advise her but all to no purpose. It would not be a small sum that would induce me to encounter with the difficulty, but my desire of keeping her until her mistress returns keeps up my care and attention.

22. (Poll behaves herself exceeding well this morning.) Charles sent every morning since Mrs. went away to the baker's for three sixpenny loaves of bread. ...... Had fire made in [the] lodging room. There I supped and Charles and I spent the evening till near nine. Miss Poll out all this time. I sent Charles to hunt for her and also to enquire of the neighbors, but no intelligence to be got; so we fastened house, kitchen, &c., [and] went to bed.

23. Cloudy. I roused Charles up by day light. Found Miss Poll in the straw-house. She came into the kitchen; talked away that she could not go out at night, but that she must be locked out. If that's the

case, she told them that she would pick up her clothes and go quite away; that she would not be so served, as her Mistress did not hinder her staying out when she pleased, and the kitchen door to be opened for her when she came home and knocked. The negro woman told me, as well as she could, what she said. I then went and picked up her clothes that I could find. I asked her how she could behave herself so towards me when I had conducted myself so easy towards her, even so as to suffer her to sit at table and eat with me. This had no effect upon her. She rather inclined to think that she had not offended and had done nothing but what her mistress indulged her in. I told her before Betty it was not worth my while to lick her, though she really deserved it for her present impudence, but to remember I had taken all her clothes I could find except what she had on, which I intended to keep; that if she went away, Charles with the horse should follow her and bring her back and that I would send the bellman round the borough of Lancaster to cry her as a runaway servant wicked girl, with a reward for apprehending her.

24. I arose early to send to B. Landiss's for butter; got [the] horse fed; just them came Catty; brought two pounds [of] butter. I kept her to breakfast; paid her twenty-four shillings for this time and the last. I also sent by her to give her master one Moyadore, one English guinea and one English shilling to pay him for the load of first crop hay that he sent me while [I was] in Philadelphia.

27. Charles arose near daybreak and I soon after, in order to find my nightly and daily plague, as she took her walk again last evening. Charles found her. We turned her up stairs to refresh herself with sleep.

29. After breakfast let our Poll down stairs, where she has been kept since her last frolic.

30. Fastened Poll up stairs last night; let her be about [the] house this morning, pretty handy.

31. I arose early as I have done for some time. Did I not, they would lie till nine o'clock, as some of them have done.

NOVEMBER 2. I think that my old enemy Satan is much concerned in the conduct and behavior of that poor unfortunate girl, in the first place to bewitch her so after the men that she seems to have no rest when away from them, the which must in the end, except grace prevent, prove her utter ruin : in the second place he knows that her actions give me much anxiety and indeed at times raise my anger so that I have said what should have been avoided, but I for the future hope to be more upon my guard and thereby frustrate him in his attempts

5. Breakfasted ; then to picking some apples left in [the] orchard, as the wind blew so fresh and I had turned [the] cow into the orchard, for as she was in such fine order I was apprehensive some of our ordinary butchers might make too free and take her to their homes. I presume that yesterday while I was [at the] burial, some persons got into the orchard and took away most of my pears though not fully ripe and I had kept them there to ripen.

6. News brought last night that John Roberts and Abraham Carlisle were executed [on the] fourth instant.

8. Spent part of [the] forenoon in conversation with Levy Marks, who called to see me and kindly invited me to come and dine with him, and this I should remark that none of my friends in Lancaster have paid me that compliment since my wife went to Philadelphia but himself, and with whom I dined the day after she went from here. ...... Our house has been pretty quiet these two or three days that I have kept Poll up stairs.

10. About eight my wife came home in [the] wagon to the door.

19. Little to be done but to eat, drink, make fires and sit by them, except my wife who keeps constantly employed in providing, directing and doing for self and

family, so that she is both the first and the last where there is any thing to be done of labor and care.

20. I saw yesterday's paper just come from Philadelphia, that gave an account in a letter from Boston that in a late storm on the third instant the Somerset man-of-war of sixty-four guns was lost to the southward of Cape Cod, forty men drowned and five hundred made prisoners and then on the road to Boston; further that for ten days before fifteen English men of war had been cruising in that latitude, supposed to be Commodore Byron's fleet looking out for the French fleet at Boston, [which] expected to sail but did not till the fourth, the day after the storm. Another letter from Elizabethtown, of the eleventh, says that one seventy-four gun and two other large men-of-war were seen going up to New York, having lost all their masts, &c.

21. After dinner took [a] walk to the barracks to see part of Col. Bland's regiment of light-horse going to their homes in Virginia.

24. To Wm. Henry's store; stayed some time hearing that Sebastian Graff and John Whitemore had assaulted the sentry at Henry's store, taken away his gun from him and beat him.

29. Sundry recruits enlisted here marched for camp this morning.

DECEMBER 1. This day, going down town I saw Wm. Henry and —— ——, Commissary, go into a slaughter-house. I followed. They were killing, by order of [the] Commissary. The cattle were so young, little and poor that Squire Henry with me concluded that if the Commissary would sell them to farmers, or give them away, it would be a saving to the country [of] the butchers' wages, the salt, the packer, and the casks, besides the hauling, because after all that was done, the meat was not good or fit to be eaten. Thus is our state imposed upon, for the want of conscientious, upright men's being put into offices of such moment.

2. Visited by Francis Bailey, [who] came to borrow Saturday's Dunlap's paper to transcribe some articles into his paper.

8. Visited by Capt. Pedro, who told us [the] news from Philadelphia, that the French fleet under Count D'Estaing had taken Halifax and released three thousand of our people who were prisoners there; that Joseph Reed, Esq., was elected President, and George Byron Vice President of this state.

A great number of wagons have been about this borough from different parts of this county. Nothing for them to do, after waiting many days, so [they] returned back. Some of those wagons came from thirty to forty miles. Such fine work our Commissaries make, being both ignorant and careless of their duty.

9. To Anthony Weltze [the] butcher's; there agreed with Jacob Snyder, miller, for a fat hog to be delivered some time in a month at four pence per pound hard money. Borrowed two silver dollars from friend Weltze and gave [them to] him for earnest. Coming here met Esquires Hogg and Harrison, Assemblymen, going home, the Assembly being adjourned on the fifth to the first day of second month, February. Spent some time with them. ...... [A] large drove of cattle went through here this day for the camp.

11. I had a restless, painful night with my old disorder, head ache, noise in my head, &c. These exercises are like the sounding of the trumpet, in order to alarm us by letting us know that this is not our rest or place of abode, but no other but as different stages or removes to pass through in order to reach that happy resting place where the wicked one shall cease to trouble and where the soul that's longing for Redemption will find that blessed port and haven of rest that's situate in the presence of its beloved Jesus.

13. I went before dinner down town, it being reported that Burgoyne's army taken prisoners had crossed Con-

nestoga Creek, but it was a mistake. Returned home, wrote [a] letter to Paul Fooks, sent it and his floor-cloth by Frederick Shaffer, who was going to Philada. with his wagon, by whom my wife sent one barrel of cider and one barrel of apples to Grace Hastings, she being so exceedingly kind to my wife when she was last in Philada. Spent [the] evening by ourselves. Our Poll goes and comes where and when she pleases.

14. Went to the barracks. One division of Burgoyne's troops, said to be seven hundred and eighty-one, came to town. ...... James McLean, from Philada. going home, called; stayed [and] drank tea; said [that] flour in town [was] Nine Pounds per hundred weight, beef, prime pieces, five shillings per pound, salt got down to five pounds per bushel, but no news of any moment stirring.

15. The division of the artillery, grenadiers and light infantry, including Lieut. Col. Nulling's detachment and the Ninth Regiment, all British prisoners, amount to seven hundred and eighty-one; came to town yesterday, marched out this morning. In [the] afternoon, came to town the Second Division of British, consisting of the Twentieth and Twenty-First Regiments, amounting to Eight hundred and seventy-three with their women and children. Came home to dinner; then walked to barracks to see the troops come in.

16. Visited by an inhabitant of Lancaster, a tin man, [who] brought home the things he had mended. Paid him fifteen shillings. He stayed some time in religious conversation.

17. Notwithstanding such heavy weather over head and exceeding dirty under foot, Poll after breakfast went to see the soldiers that came as prisoners belonging to Burgoyne's [army]; returned by two o'clock (fine and dirty trull) ...... Yesterday came to town, the Third Division of the British, consisting of the Twenty-fourth, Forty-seventh and Sixty-second Regiments, amounting to Nine hundred and twenty-three prisoners.

19. Kept Charles digging, he being very careful not to work too hard nor too long at a time. ...... The three divisions of English prisoners left the barracks this morning to proceed on their journey. In [the] afternoon came to the barracks the First Division of Germans, consisting of the Dragoons, Battalion of the Grenadiers, Regiment of Rhite and Regiment of Rush^{rs}, amounting to Nine hundred and forty-seven, besides women and children. ...... A great many of the Dutch round Lancaster came in to-day, I presume to wait upon the German prisoners.

20. The second division of Germans consists of the Regiment of Speehts, Battalion of Hanoverians and Hessian Artillery, amounting to Nine hundred and thirty-five, besides women and children.

21. This morning the First Division of Germans here marched away.

22. The divisions of Hessians or Germans set off from our borough.

24. After breakfast went down town to Wm. Henry's; got qualified by him to act as Commissioner. I also qualified Wm. Henry agreeably to the Act of [the] General Assembly of this State, passed [the] Fifth instant. From there by invitation to Bush's house to drink [a] glass of wine [and] eat sundries that were provided to regale the principal inhabitants of the borough, occasioned by his daughter's being married last night to Simon Solomon, shopkeeper.

26. Our trull returned this morning before I arose. Her mistress gave her a good sound whipping. This latter was a rarity. ...... A number of Col. White's Light Horse (said [to be] two hundred and fifty) came to-day, it's said, to be quartered this winter. A parcel of the German prisoners returned back, as they could not cross the Susquehannah for ice floating, etc.

28. This morning, one of the Light Horsemen received forty-eight lashes, it's said, in the barrack-yard, for insulting one of the inhabitants. ...... James Farran

came and spent part of [the] evening in his Astronomical strain.

29. The Germans that returned back set out as the river was frozen hard.

30. After dinner, my wife, James Farran and wife with Charles [being] in my room, I read to them a Thanksgiving Sermon, formerly preached by Dr. Sherlock before Queen Anne. Paid two shillings and six pence[1] for twopence worth of yeast.

1779.

JANUARY 1. The Dutch kept firing guns last night and to-day, it being, it's said, customary.

2. I had all our little jobs to do, as our man Charles without any notice, was, he said, for setting out for Baltimore. I accordingly paid him his wages for five months at Four Pounds per month, which amounted to Twenty Pounds. Paid him the balance due to make up that sum. He then took his clothes [and] walked off without bidding me or any one about [the] house farewell.

6. Visited by Major Count Montford; drank tea with [us]; just come from Philada; brought several letters and newspapers from Paul Fooks, dated Dec. 20, 24: Jan. 3; one from James Cannon dated November 22d; one from Thomas Hale.

7. About ten, our Miss Trull appeared in the kitchen. I had been engaged serving creatures and mending [the] front fence where she and the dog had broken to come in and go out at, at times.

8. Gave [a] sharp charge to our Poll for her monstrous behavior.

9. Visited by Major Montford. Lent [the] first and second volumes of the *History of Sumatra* during the sieges of Amurath 1st, 2d & 3d, and a volume entitled *Gentleman's Calling by the Author of the Whole Duty of Man*. ...... Our Poll stayed at home all this day. I can't remember when it was so before.

---

[1] In Continental money.

10. One of my neighbors, James Farran, told me his girl had been for flour, the price Eight Pounds, and at [the] same time, most or all of last year's crop not yet threshed. It appears to me that our rulers are only engaged about matters of public dispute respecting themselves and some few individuals, at [the] same time neglecting the public utility, and prosperity of the State in general; thus are we now situated. ...... As Poll had behaved tolerably yesterday, she had, upon asking her mistress, her best clothes to go to church, as she said. While we were eating part of [a] good roast turkey for dinner, and had given her a good portion, she dressed herself and packed up all her clothes, new and old, clean and dirty, took them with her and away she went and [we] have seen no more of her, as yet.

13. Yesterday afternoon Dr. K...... rode up to my door, asked in his polite way how I and my family did? was there anything he could serve me with he had? I thanked him, told him when I wanted, I might call upon him; invited him in, but he was in a hurry with his man. So I got shut of his blarney.

21. Wheat, ten dollars per bushel; Flour from eight pounds to nine pounds per bushel. ...... [Paid] half a crown for fourpence worth of yeast; two shillings and sixpence for a sixpenny broom.[1]

23. It's said that about seven this morning there was an exceeding great redness in the sky; then appeared a large rainbow, that seemingly reached from north to south and remained for some time. Last night came Robert Whitehill; stayed some time in political conversation; said "that the people in Cumberland and York counties were generally displeased with our Assembly for their taking upon them to call a Convention at this time, and are preparing a Memorial that will be signed by some one thousand, to be sent down against their next meeting in opposition to their proceedings on that

---

[1] These payments were in Continental money.

and some other of their actions." He further said "that the feast or entertainment given by the House on the election of Gen. Reed for President of this state cost Two Thousand Three Hundred and Five Pounds and fifteen shillings, Seventy Pounds of which was spent by the three members, viz, Robert Morris, Gen. Mifflin and Jonathan Potts who were appointed to get the same prepared and met two nights for that purpose at the City tavern."

24. Last week was brought here President Reed's Proclamation for the discharge of all those persons throughout the State confined in prison (they first paying all prison fees incurred by their confinement) for their pertinaciously refusing to take the several oaths or affirmations required by the laws of this State, dated Philada. 29th Decr. 1778, Signed Joseph Reed, President. Spent this day at home. In the afternoon, visited by James Farran, my poor neighbor, yet a sensible man, but talks abundance on the affairs of England, his native country, where he made some figure in astronomy, of which he has a complete knowledge, as appears from letters and some pieces he published in the Leicester newspapers on that subject.

26. Gen. Phillips, second in command to Burgoyne, in town, going after his fellow prisoners to Virginia.

FEBRUARY 4. A report just come, [it is] said, from Philada., that the enemy had landed near Elizabeth Town and that Gen. Washington had left Philadelphia last Third Day in order to join the army and had ordered all his officers immediately to repair to their different posts.

5. Two men stood in [the] pillory this morning (horse stealing).

8. News of the day is that Gen. Arnold has left Philada., and gone over to the English.[1]

---

[1] This rumor is very remarkable. Arnold went over in September, 1780, nineteen months afterwards.

9. News that Capt. Lang carried [a] parcel of shirts, as Commissary to our camp, but they proved to be so little (it's said but two and a half yards in [a] shirt) that they returned him the shirts and all, to return back as a cheat to the public.

11. Took a walk with R. Taggert to see Col. White's regiment of Light Horse exercise.

13. News from Philada. is, by report, that Col. Bannister of Virginia is detected in Virginia with a large sum of counterfeit money concealed, and those [whose] names [are] here following are said to be concerned with him in that affair; that he (Bannister) is in jail there in irons. Whether this be founded in fact, I can't say: (viz.) Col. Edward Walker, Charles Williamson, Capt. Ephraim Leipels, Churchill, Anderson, Sterling, Harris, Thomas Woodford, Samuel Morgan, Henry Wright, Joseph Bond, Horvlet Williamson, Drewry Bordge, [and] Benj. Alfrund.[1] Account just brought that a Spanish vessel with dispatches from the Havanna is arrived at Philada.

14. To Righteousness my spirits raise
And quicken with thy life and love,
That I may walk here to Thy praise
And after live with Thee above.
Grant I in glory may appear
Clad with our Resurrection vest,
When thou shalt lead thy flock most dear
Up to the mansions of the blest.

15. Heard Seventh Day's paper read. No news, but disputes between Gen. Arnold and proceedings of Council and a second letter in support [of the] resolve of Congress respecting taking the sense of the people to have a new Convention. ..... It's said that one hundred Continental Dollars are given for one half-Joe. ...... Delivered James Lang One Thousand Dollars remitted me some time past for public services.

20. It's said that half-joes within these few days have fallen from Twenty-Four to Eighteen and sundry goods lowered fifty per cent in Philad^a.

---

[1] This was a British story. See the *Bland Papers*.

22. After encountering with violent headache, towards morning I got a little sleep; took [a] pinch of Patent snuff which purged my head greatly. ...... Visited by Col. Clark, going home from Philada., he could not stay, as he had heard his family were poorly. Scarcely any news stirring, but a spirit of dissension amongst the people, blaming and traducing, he said, [the] President, Speaker of the House, &c.

26. Last evening a drove of several hundred head of fine cattle went through here towards our camp. Just received [a] letter from daughter Sally, with some garden seeds, Thursday's newspaper and [a] pamphlet entitled "Consideration on the mode and terms of a Treaty of Peace with America. London, printed 1778. Philadelphia, reprinted by Hall and Sellers, 1779;" also [a] letter from P. Barker, mentioning part of [the] news said to be come from Congress, viz: that the Spaniards have acceded to the Independency of America and [are] to assist France with thirty sail of [the] line of battle ships and to lend the United States of America Thirty Millions of silver dollars, and that the Dutch have agreed to supply the Americans with a considerable loan to be guaranteed by France, &c., &c.

March 1. Yesterday came Pame Palasky's[1] Regiment of Light Horse and Yager Infantry. Last night a quarrel ensued between some of them and Col. White's Light Horsemen, but was soon quelled, yet some of the men were wounded, but not dangerously.

3. No news stirring that I heard. except [that] Palasky's Regiment of Light Horse and Yagers went out of town for the southward — a parcel of thieving fellows.

7. Be it remembered that my good wife constantly milks the cow night and morning, and, besides her daily house work, makes us cheeses, besides supplying our family with plenty of good cream and two poor families with milk. Here is prudence and industry.

---

[1] Pulasky?

11. Yesterday nine of Col. White's Light Horsemen were whipped at [the] Continental stable and barracks, it's said for mutiny, because their provisions were not good, and their pay detained for some months.

27. It's said, by packet to New York, "the States of Holland have agreed to lend the Independent States of America One Million of Money." ...... Yesterday and to-day, it's said that a number of ship carpenters came here on their march to Middletown, Pittsburgh, &c., in order to build some kind of vessels on the lakes for the ready transportation of troops into the Indian country, Detroit, &c.

APRIL 8. Some Assemblymen passed through here to-day on their way home, as the Assembly broke up [on] the Fifth; adjourned to the Thirteenth [of] August.

10. Visited by Capt. Joy, going to Virginia. With him saw the Act of Assembly dated April, 1779, crying down the use of hard money in the purchasing of any kind of commodities in this State.

11. News brought to-day by one Berry, who, he said, left Philadelphia [on] Fifth day last, that Proclamation was made by order of Gen. Washington, for such of the inhabitants as would not assist in defending the city, immediately to leave it, as the English army was expected to be there; that numbers, upon that, were moving their effects out of the city, and he among the rest was come away. ...... Antony,[1] with John Jones, went to Quaker's meeting to day, where Antony preached, as he called it, although he was requested to desist, but would not, so they by consent broke up the meeting sooner than they would have done, as he would not obey James Webb, who ordered or desired him to be silent and not to disturb them.

17. Visited by Dr. Newman who said a number of

---

[1] Antony Taborro, a new servant who came to Mr. Marshall on the tenth of April from his son's.

April 1779] *of the American Revolution.* 215

pistols from Philadelphia were carried through here yesterday for Col. Hartley's regiment at Shamokin, and that the honest inhabitants in Philadelphia were much displeased at the acquittal of G...... and S...... as their behavior had been so atrocious while the enemy were in the city.

20. News from Philadelphia that eight or ten vessels were arrived from [the] West Indies with sundry kinds of dry goods, &c.

21. Gen. Lee,[1] it's said, with his dogs and doxey went through here for Virginia [on] Second Day. Gen. McIntosh passed through here [on the] same day for [the] back woods. News to-day that sugar was fallen in Philadelphia to fifteen shillings per pound, coffee to thirteen shillings within these few days. ...... I'm told half a Joe sold for Sixty Pounds to-day.

23. Fine clover, now black; peaches, cherries, many of the garden vegetables all killed. We cut off the tops of our peas to see whether they will put forth afresh. I fear our apples have suffered greatly: their beauty is exceedingly marred. O Lord, thou givest and at thy pleasure takest away. Blessed be thy name. Visited by Charles Hall, to whom I gave papers relating to the Constitutional Society, to take to a meeting of many of the inhabitants of this county, who are to meet this day.

24. Visited by Philip Thomas (carpenter in this borough), I think the most sensible, resigned Christian I have conversed with in this place; stayed some time. Lent [him a] book called *The Everlasting Gospel*.

25. Visited by Charles Hall, who has just received [a] letter from Squires Thorne and Masterlett, acknowledging the receipt of our Constitutional Letter and their approbation of the proposal made them of calling a meeting in their neighborhood this week, the result of which they would communicate as soon as possible afterwards.

May 1. News that the Indians have killed twenty-

[1] General Charles Lee.

three persons and taken one of our Assemblymen prisoner above Sunbury. —— Delaware Indians came here this day on their way to visit Congress and the French Ambassador at Philad[a].

2. Just before breakfast received a letter of [the] twenty-sixth with two newspapers from Paul Fooks. ...... Paul's letter says " This morning [the] French Ambassador and Mr. Moralez,[1] escorted with our Light Horse, set off to pay a visit to our worthy Gen. Washington at camp. A French frigate is arrived at Boston. The express arrived this morning after the ambassador's departure with the packets and is gone after him. It's said that this vessel has had only eighteen days' passage.

3. News is that [a] very large ship [bound] from Jamaica to London came to Philada. [on] Seventh Day morning, prize to Capt. Douglass. After dinner took [a] walk by myself and attended upon the exercise performed by the Light Horsemen. There were a great number of spectators.

4. News came yesterday confirming the account of the seven prizes being arrived at Boston. [They] found, it's said, on board the Jason, one cask of sundries and in specie forty thousand English guineas.

6. After dinner took [a] walk down the streets; very quiet, it being the fast day appointed by Congress. ...... In the evening came son Kitty with the carriage.

8. Arose early; breakfasted half after five; set off in Kitty's carriage with him. Reached Hopkins's tavern; baited [the] horses; proceeded from there to the sign of [the] Ship; (we eat some victuals we had with us on the road as we came along) baited the horses there. About four P.M. set off; crossed [the] Schuylkill about dusk, reached Kitty's soon after dark, pretty well tired.

10. Set off for town; reached there before night.

12. This day [a] prize brig arrived, taken by Capt

---

[1] Don Juan de Moralez, the Spanish envoy to the United States.

Collins with one hundred and sixty-three hogsheads of molasses [and] some sugar.

15. Went and visited Wilson Peale's pictures, a curious collection

17. Saw our Poll, but [she] flew away, so could not speak [to] her.

20. Col. Proctor's regiment marched out of [the] city for [the] back woods.

21. Signed [a] petition to Congress respecting our Continental money.

22. Went to B. Harbison's; went with him to the Constitutional Society. After they adjourned, a number of citizens being there voted me into the chair, where [upon] sundry proposals were moved respecting our present situation and a town meeting agreed to be called next Third Day [at] four o'clock at [the] State House Yard. Six persons were appointed to draw up an address to be delivered. Near eleven, broke up.

24. In the evening, went to Nancy Clark's, as the militia, after being reviewed, marched by her door and through part of the city to [the] Coffee House. Computed Horse, Fort 2nd Artillery [to] amount to three thousand.

25. Took [a] walk to our late beautiful place, now desolate; to my old place in Moyamensing, where I dined; returned; Town Meeting in the State House Yard; Daniel Roberdeau in the chair; all as peaceable as could be expected; drank tea at Charles's with some members of Congress. I omitted to mention my meeting [a] few days past with sundry of our magistrates and requesting them to be out of the way, if possible, on this day, on account of the meeting. The same I requested of our President, Joseph Reed, for reasons I mentioned, and they, I have good reason to think, complied with my desire, for a town meeting was greatly in my mind for some time, and I came from home with that intention, used all my influence to promote it and was happy

to see it completed so amicably. This paid me for all my trouble, and I am in great hopes that it will be of infinite advantage to the whole State. Amen.

27. Visited by Roberdeau, who went with me to some of the Committee, complaining of the illegal proceedings of —— Dean, who, being one of the Committee, had, nevertheless, joined with some others in purchasing a parcel of molasses just come, contrary to their own resolutions, for which transaction we requested he might be expelled their board, in order to pacify the minds of the public, who were irritated.

28. Accounts from Germantown that one thousand bushels of wheat [were] seized in a mill near there, concealed. Four or five wagons [were] stopped [and] brought back to the city last night, loaded with rum, sugar, tea, coffee, salt, &c., the invoices charged as rated by [the] Committee, but advanced on casks, boxes, &c., as Fifteen Pounds per hogshead, barrels at Ten Pounds. A schooner [was] brought back after gone from [the] wharf, [it is] said with three hundred barrels of flour covered over with street dirt. To such mean shifts are the disaffected driven since the Committee has been elected. Many suspected persons [have been] taken up and sent to prison, in which number are Richard W......Thomas S......y, —— M......, B. H......, Levi H......, &c., &c. Peter K......n, had three and a half hogshead, of rum seized this morning by the Collector, not being entered. Flag of truce from Santa Cruz. Sundry persons and goods came this day from Baltimore [for] fear of the English.

29. Visited, as I have been, I think, since in town every day, by Paul Fooks, who shows me the utmost kindness and respect in his power. Dr. Phyle came to us at Charles's; says accounts from Charleston are that the enemy were repulsed by our people so as to fly before them, leaving fourteen hundred on the field killed and wounded. This is great news, when fully authenticated.

30. Butter yesterday in market sold for Two to Three Dollars per pound, meat of different kinds from four shillings and six pence to ten shillings per pound, flour (little in market) Twenty Pounds a hundred, green peas from twenty shillings to twenty-five shillings the half peck, radishes from two shillings and six pence to three shillings and nine pence [a] bunch, good best spirits Seven Pounds five shillings [the] single gallon, molasses, sold by [the] hogshead, from Four Pounds to Four Pounds ten shillings per gallon, oak wood at the wharf Sixteen Pounds per cord, Hickory up to Twenty Pounds, house rent risen from Fifty Pounds per year to Five Hundred Pounds, from Eighty Pounds to One Thousand Pounds, Twelve Hundred Pounds, &c.[1]

JUNE 1. Went and paid Fox for two pairs of shoes, one for self, one for negro woman, Fifty Dollars.

2. Paid Grace Hastings Eighty Dollars for two silk handkerchiefs.

3. Paid Polly Garrigues Five Pounds five shillings for wrist banding eight shirts and thread; paid Betsey Halloway Five Pounds two shillings and six pence for hemming six neck-cloths.

6. Having taken leave of my children, grand-children, friends, &c., set off with Kitty in his carriage with granddaughter Hannah about six in [the] morning. We reached Levering's tavern, baited horses, proceeded for Kitty's, which we reached safely past twelve, thanks to our Great Benefactor and Preserver. Found the family well. When Providence meeting was over several Friends came and dined; spent [the] afternoon; after tea went away. They were pleasant and cheerful.

7. Just out of bed, received [a] letter from Dr. Phyle, giving account of six French ships (four of them with goods, two armed ships) arrived at Baltimore. Spent this day walking, reading, &c., at Kitty's. In [the] evening came negro Moses from town; brought further account

---

[1] See *Hazard's Register*, vol. 3, p 201.

of the defeat of the English at Charleston, with this circumstance that the English were repulsed, returned to the charge, such as to push bayonets, then beat off leaving seven hundred on the field. It's hoped this would prove another Burgoyne, &c.

11. After dinner had horses and my things put into Kitty's carriage and past three Charles and I, after taking leave, set off for Lancaster. Reached John Jacobs's near sunset, where we stayed, supped and lodged, they receiving us exceedingly kind and friendly.

12. Arose early, breakfasted, put on great coats, being cool, wind northwardly, set off about six, reached the sign [of the] Wagon, baited our horses, then proceeded to the sign of the Hat, baited our horses, got a gill of best spirits at both places with some water. Victuals we brought with us; stopped and eat on the road. We then set off, reached my home in Lancaster near six.

14. Visited by sundry of my Lancaster neighbors; informed me of a town meeting they held the eleventh instant, at which I was elected a member, requesting me to act and to attend at the Court House this afternoon. ...... At dinner, [came a] messenger requesting my attendance at [the] Court House. ...... Eleven members besides myself attended out of the fifteen chosen; proceeded to the first business; chose a chairman, which unanimously fell to my share. We next proceeded to settle [the] prices of eatables (excepting flesh and vegetables) on a similar plan with Philad^a and as [there were] some complaints respecting hard money, it was thought proper to refer that and the prices affixed to a Town Meeting to be held next Fourth Day.

16. To the Court House; took the chair by appointment at four, addressed the people, read the prices affixed by [the] Committee, who then entered into sundry resolves (as printed in the Lancaster newspaper, June 19th). After the meeting was over, met in committee; report made by the chairman of the proceedings to the com-

mittee, who sent to the printer in order to have them published. They adjourned to Second Day morning, ten o'clock.

18. After dinner met the Committee; broke up, after directing circular letters to be written to the ten Colonels in this county enclosing the proceedings of the Town meeting agreeably to the resolve. ...... Wrote [a] few lines for Circular Letter, carried it to two of the gentlemen appointed who approved of it and ordered it to be copied [and] when the letters [were] completed [to] bring them to me to be signed. While I had been at home, they told me that Lady Washington, accompanied by sundry light horsemen and her menials, passed through the borough on her return home. Returned home with me Ed. Shippen, who for this week past has been pretty closely engaged in reading Wm. Law's works [with] which I have furnished him (he says, to his great satisfaction).

20. I wrote a few lines enclosing two German papers [containing the] proceedings of the Committee in Philadelphia, received last night, requesting some of our committee, if they thought proper, to fix them up under the care of [a] sentry on Mr. Henry's store door this morning.

26. We have long waited but yet have no official accounts of the repulse of the enemy in their attack upon Charleston, yet the accounts coming so many different ways leaves no doubt of their defeat, with me, which is related thus, that the enemy lost near one thousand men in killed and wounded before the town; this happened the eleventh of May, commanded by Gen. Provost, the troops in the town commanded by Gen. Moultrie. The enemy retreated up the neck, between Ashley and Cooper rivers. It's said that Gen. Pulaski, at the head of his legion had reached Charleston a few days before the enemy, and that, sallying briskly out of the lines, [he] took one hundred and eighty of their advanced

guard, forty of whom, being Tories, were hanged for attempting to rise during the attack upon the town, so that by all information received, it's expected the main body must surrender themselves prisoners, though perhaps the troops that retired to James Island might escape away in their boats.

27. After breakfast, I planted a number of coxcombs (although there is a number [of] two footed ones in and about this borough).

28. After dinner went and met committee at their room in [the] Court House. Sundry affairs were brought before them, amongst the rest, a poor man complained that John Hopson, a committee man, chosen but [who] never attended, charged two shillings and six pence per pound [more] for coffee than was stipulated. He, being sent for, attended, confessed the fact and [said] that he would sell no more without he was suffered to sell at his price. The behavior of Hopson satisfied the whole committee that he was no more a friend to the country than his interest led him, that being his ruling passion, it's said.

JULY 4. Mamma went to meeting, where Antony spoke and was forbid, but [it] had no effect. He appeared to be most consumately bold and ignorant in his way of speaking there, and about [the] house I'm obliged in a stern manner to order him at times not to say one word more, which kind of resolution, though disagreeable, I am obliged to make use of in order to silence him.

5. After breakfast went into town, where preparation was making for Col. Jacob Glotz's regiment to march about a mile out of town this afternoon, to celebrate the nniversary of our Independence.[1] Notice of this was sent me by billet this morning and [I was] afterwards waited on by the aforesaid Col. and George Hoffs with a polite invitation to accompany them. Near two o'clock went down to the Court House, where, after some little time,

---

[1] The Fourth of July fell on Sunday this year

having joined Col. Jacob Glotz's battalion of militia, placing me at the head of [the] Committee who walked two by two, then the corporation, the Colonels, one and two, with their battalion, colors flying, drums, fifes and band of music, [we] went in procession down Queen street to a spacious piece of woodland, adjoining Conestoga Creek, with [a] fine spring, where, after some time spent in sociable cheerfulness, the men having grounded their arms, they then formed in order, whereupon the following healths were drank, I being Toast Master, viz:

1st. The true Independent and Sovereign States of America.

2d. The Great Council of America.

3d. His most Christian Majesty, Louis 16th.

4th. His Excellency, Gen. Washington.

5th. The American Army and Navy, may they be victorious and invincible.

6th. The Nations in Friendshlp and Alliance with America.

7th. The American Ambassadors at Sovereign Courts.

8th. The Memory of the Officers and Soldiers who have fallen in defense of Ameriea.

9th. Pennsylvania.

10th. May only those Americans enjoy freedom who are ready to die for its defense.

11th. Liberty Triumphant.

12th. Confusion, Shame and Disgrace to our Enemies: May the foes of America, slaves to tyranny, humble and fall down before her.

13th. May the Rising states of America reach the summit of human power and grandeur by enjoying every blessing.

Each of these toasts was attended by a discharge of the musketry that would have done honor to old veterans. After which, they all returned under the same regularity, walked through some of the principal streets and drew up in front of [the] Court House where they discharged three regular volleys of musketry [and] received every man some cool drink. I then went into the front, thanked the officers and privates, in the name of the Committee, for their great zeal shown in the support of the Freedom of Independency in general and for their manly prudence, good conduct and sobriety on this memorable occasion, for which they returned me their hearty thanks. The Col. then dismissed them and they deparated in great good humor, peace and harmony. The Committee broke up and I returned home completely tired, yet pleased with our conduct.

6. Last night, or rather this morning, I was awakened by the sound of music. I got up, went to [the] front door, found our band of music, [who] made an excuse for their coming by saying they did it purely to show their regard and respect they owed for my prudent and good conduct shown to the Borough of Lancaster. I thanked them very kindly, told them I had nothing else at this unseasonable time. They answered it was all they required, played a few more tunes, then retired, exceedingly well pleased. I then went to bed, it being about one o'clock.

In the morning, visited by Sundry of our Committee men; informed me that the other company came in about half an hour after ours broke up, behaved themselves as drunken madmen, cursed the Committee, called them rebels and all the Whigs that took their parts, paraded round the Court House, many of them, and went to Reigart's, such as the G...... s, H......, S......, Z......, B......, P......, P...... and many others. Some of our people got angry, by the repeated abuse and kept as quiet as could be expected, though as some of them were struck at, they returned the compliment, so that a few blows passed and our people passed it by for the time. What may ensue, I know not. Wrote a few lines to be published respecting our proceedings on yesterday.

7. Simon Levy, I heard, called upon B......, [to desire him] to ask his pardon for his ill behavior, which Barton said he would not to the best man in the country, upon which Levy down with [and] gave him what he thought sufficient with promise to serve him so whenever he met him till he asks his pardon. Most of them that offended Col. Glotz have acknowledged that they were drunk and asked his pardon publicly.

8. Visited by ——, harnessmaker, who put [a] few stitches in our chair-harness, &c. Paid him two shillings and six pence. He stayed some time and spoke feelingly of the inward work of Christ in the soul in order to be the true Christian in deed and in truth. He departed in a sweet frame of spirit.

9. Before breakfast, engaged in [the] garden with our nonsuch gardener. Mammy weighed her cheese that she has made this season, weighed eighty-eight pounds, besides two that have been used in the family; twenty-four pounds of butter. John's family have their milk every day, besides some others who have a share and our own cream twice a day, besides our cow, except at her first calving, don't give but between three quarts and a gallon at milking, so that I can say no woman in point of industry in these parts can equal her in the dairy.

13. Gave a certificate to Josiah Lockart, as Chairman of [the] Committee of Lancaster to Wm. Henry, Chairman of [the] Committee in Philadelphia, in order to permit him to bring up such goods as he may purchase in Philadelphia. This afternoon, a negro man from Cecil County, Maryland, preached in [the] orchard opposite to ours. There were sundry people. They said he spoke well for near an hour. Afterwards Antony spoke, but the people left him and the boys were like to be rude.

15. Visited this morning by Major Wertz and Simon Snyder [who] brought Dunlap's newspapers [of] June 29th and July 13th, containing the regulating resolves

of our army, of [the] Boston and Philadelphia county Committees, highly spirited and comprehensive. Account of three valuable prizes [brought] last week to Philadelphia, one a vessel of one hundred and ninety hogsheads of Jamaica spirits [and] six pipes of Madeira, another of three hundred tons burden loaded with three hundred hogsheads of molasses and sugar, the third with rum, sugar, salt, &c. After dinner visited by Ludwick Laughman, just come from Philadelphia. Brought a letter from son Charles of [the] thirteenth instant, informing they were all well, with some newspapers and some papers from [the] Committee in Philadelphia. Stayed some time in conversation. I distributed some of the Philadelphia papers in order to inform our country folks of their proceedings. ...... Gave certificate to John Messencope, as Chairman of the Committee in the borough to deliver to Wm. Henry, Chairman of the Committee in Philadelphia, in order to permit him to bring out such goods as he may purchase there in order to sell here.

16. John Jones brought me word from Peter Musselman that he could supply me with all my winter's fire wood. This, I think, is a favor from heaven, as he is so upright a man, and will prevent my applying to sundry self-righteous persons for that commodity, who will take every advantage in ordinary wood and short measure, besides looking that I am greatly indebted to them for supplying me.

17 Visited by Wm. Henry; brought me [a] letter, enclosing two or three newspapers from Paul Fooks, dated the sixteenth; stayed some time. He said that it was said in Philada. that the French king had made a present to the States of [a] forty-gun frigate which B. Franklin called Poor Richard.[1]

---

[1] The name " Le Bonhomme Richard," was given by Paul Jones, he having obtained the vessel by following a piece of advice in Poor Richard's Almanac; " If you wish your business done, go; if not, send."

20. Account this day of Gen. Wayne's taking the English fortress at Stony Point, last Friday morning [at] day-break by surprise, without firing a gun, with the loss of four men only; he himself wounded in the cheek. The garrison consisted of five hundred men, Sixteen pieces of cannon and a large quantity of baggage and stores [were taken].

21. Visited by Col. Glotz and Wilton Atkinson, Esq., of Sunberry, to whom I gave sundry papers of the proceedings of [the] Committees of Philada. and Lancaster in order for their government in forming Committees in Northumberland County. News of yesterday confirmed through another channel with this circumstance that it was three o'clock in the morning. Our people after securing [the] prisoners, turned the guns of [the] fort upon the English shipping, which obliged them to fall down the river.

23. News brought of the enemy's burning the towns of Fairfield, Bedford and East Haven.[1]

AUGUST 1. [For] returns of the prisoners, baggage, stores, ordinance, &c., at Stony Point, taken by Gen. Wayne, see *Pennsylvania Gazette*, No. 2563.

2. Came John Garrigues, Jr., said he ran away from the British army near Charleston; had a pass from Gen. Moultrie; supped and stayed all night.

3. After dinner, met [the] Committee at [the] Court [House]; elected Chairman of the Committee by an unanimous vote.

4. The officers, prisoners taken at Stoney Point, came into the borough this morning.

6. Just going to bed, favored with Thursday's newspaper, sent by Major Wertz, by his son in the rain, giving account of D'Estaing's taking [Grenada], beating the English fleet so that they were obliged to go to different ports to refit. [The] French took in the fort

---

[1] In Connecticut.

seven hundred men, [six] Colonels, [thirty-four] Captains, [three pairs of] Colors, [one hundred and two] Cannons [sixteen] Mortars: obliged them to surrender at discretion as they took [Grenada] by storm. This paper contained [an] account that our friends carried the election in Philad^a for the Committee.

7. Wrote the rough draught of an Address to the Inhabitants of this County.

9. It's told me that two fellows from New York were detected at Small, the tavern-keeper's, with large quantities of counterfeit money, [it's] said, Fifteen Thousand Dollars, and committed to jail. There was a third, but he escaped.

11. The two persons taken for passing counterfeit bills, being pursued from the Jerseys, were taken away in irons.

13. I was favored with four American Magazines, [for] April, May, June [and] July from Robert Taggert; took the pains and time to go through them.

14. News of the day is that Spain has declared these States independent; that a fleet of twenty-six men-of-war had sailed from ——— to Corunna; joined there by twenty-four ships of the line; had taken on board twenty-five thousand land forces; had sailed for Ireland; that Ireland had revolted and the French had retaken Pondicherry in the East Indies; that a fleet had sailed from ——— for America, in which was a new Ambassador coming in order to replace the one here, who was to return home.

20. Roused out of bed by [a] person at [the] door, with [a] letter from Paul Fooks, dated the seventeenth with newspaper of that date, giving account of the [arrival of the] new French Ambassador, Chevalier de Luzerne, with his Secretary and John Adams Esq., late Commissioner from the United States, in a French frigate of thirty-two guns.

22. News is that Spain has declared us independent;

that war was declared at Porto Rico against England [on] the fifteenth [of] July. [For] particulars of several interesting pieces of intelligences, see Dunlap's *Advertiser*, Tuesday, August 17th instant.

23. Past five met [the] Committee, where John Moor appeared, acknowledged that he acted impudently in not coming when sent for in the morning and promised to behave more prudently in future. This acknowledgment was accepted and ordered to be published.

26. Buried my poor cat this morning, that was sick sometime past. I set great store by her. ...... To Major Wertz's; heard Tuesday's Dunlap's paper, August 24th, read, giving account of Major Lee's surprising the garrison at Paulus Hook with four hundred men, and taking the whole garrison, that were not killed or wounded, prisoners, with the loss of about four or five, after a march of eighty miles.

28. Visited by two English officers, prisoners, to know if I would let them part of my house. I received them politely yet let them know my sentiments so fully that they will not make a fresh enquiry, I think.

SEPTEMBER 4. To writing, after I had shaved myself, which I had not done, I think, for twenty or thirty years past, but our barber was got so impertinent and extortionate it was time to try. Received [a] letter and newspapers with [the] King of Spain's Declaration against England, from son Charles.

6. Near noon our Poll returned; came in [a] carriage with some of Saml Morris's family, two brothers who, she said, were going to York Town. It was that Morris who had married Amos Strettle's daughter (and Samuel his brother). She was going with him.

7. Account just come from Gen. Sullivan of his giving the Indians a defeat, that were under Butters and Brant, near Chemung or Newtown, on the thirty-first of last month.

8. Near nine, went to [the] Committee room; came

away about twelve; came home, wrote [a] copy of [a] circular letter to the ten Colonels; took it down; approved of; copies ordered to be written to send to them by some of [the] members; finished and broke up the County Committee by adjourning to the first Tuesday in October next.

10. Walked to the Continental stable to view a parcel of old wagon and cart wheels perishing there.

13. Gave mammy going to Philada. ninety dollars to near her expenses and John and Debby's to Kitty's.

16. Miss Poll arose with calling, past eight; eat breakfast; dressed her head in tip-top fashion; went down town to look out for passage; came back while I was [at] Committee, took her things [and] was gone before I returned from Committee past twelve.

19. In the evening came Dr. Neff, Ed. Shippen and Robt Taggert; brought account of the French fleet under Count D'Estaing being off Sandy Hook.

26. Antony went to meeting. ...... I kept engaged, helping to cook [the] pot against master came home. I may in some sense say so, as he gives himself no trouble about the place. He comes and goes as he pleases. If he is spoken to, it breaks his peace. He loves quietness and stillness, yet he is all the while a talking, so that I'm obliged to command him to be silent, and, with great reluctance sometimes he will obey.

27. Letter from Charles of the twenty-fifth. ...... He adds, "I am just informed an express is arrived from Georgia with account of the French fleet's [having] arrived there and that they were to make an attack on Savannah. It is also reported that the Experiment of fifty guns, commanded by Sir James Wallace, and several other vessels were taken.

30. John Jones, just come, brought [a] letter of [the] twenty-eighth, informing that Mammy was hearty and all their families well, with deal of love.

OCTOBER 1. Antony keeps still pottering. While quiet its bearable.

3. Lent Robert Thornburgh a book entitled *The Marrow of Divinity* by Thomas Boston. ...... Visited by Robert Taggert; brought yesterday's paper, where under the Boston head there was an account of the English fleet's being blockaded in Torbay by a fleet of fifty-four ships of the line, French and Spaniards.

7. Letter from son Charles, with two newspapers. His family poorly with colds; Mammy brave and hearty; no news of her return but that there had been a great disturbance in the city [on] Second Day afternoon, at which several lives were lost. No further particulars.

9. Came Jacob Seachrist Jr.; paid him One Hundred Dollars for three cords [of] oak wood, he brought me.

16. Four Dollars for two loaves of bread.

17. I arose past seven; had our gentleman to call down stairs. I spoke to him for not serving the cow; ...... He began in his way of all's being right, &c., &c. I set about serving our family and let him, as in common, do as he pleases. I think I have hired a plague to my spirit, for, after all my resolutions to bear with his pride and impertinence, I am overtaken and though I scold or talk sharp to him, it answers no end. He is still the same Antony; as he says, complaisant, careful, industrious, thoughtful, &c., so that, in his conceit, no person can exceed him. In the evening came my wife in [the] chair and son Charles [on] horseback.

22. Kept pottering about sundries; Antony grunting and stowing away a few potatoes.

26. After dinner, visited by Ludwick Lauman; brought me the news of Count D'Estaing's seizing most of the English vessels in Carolina and Georgia, both men-of-war and transports, with two Generals and a large body of troops, and that Gen. Lincoln was gone to the Savannah after the remainder, account of which [is] daily expected. It's said this engagement was obstinate for two hours and forty minutes; great numbers killed on both sides.

November 6. Paid Captain Pedree, Collector of Tax, Fifty-seven Pounds, eight shillings, being State, County and old man's taxes.

11. Lent Judge Atlee, *Belisarius;* received Churchill's volume of Poems I had lent him some time ago.

24. To Wm. Henry's, who was writing [a] letter to the President of the State, acquainting him that he was informed that John Mercer had purchased part of the manor in this county that belongs to the Delaware Indians for the sum of —— Hundreds, hard money, of the late Governor, Penn, who had obtained their Reserve Deeds from the Sheriff of Lancaster in and about the year ——, who had the remainder of that tribe then in prison, from whom he received those Deeds.

25. Two letters from Paul Fooks. One of them of [the] twenty-second says, "I have just heard from [a] member of Congress by advice from Martinique of the combined fleet's beating the English under Sir Charles Hardy in the channel; took one ninety, two seventy-four gun ships; that twenty sail of French and Spanish[1] men-of-war with one hundred transports had an engagement with the English under Peter Parker in the West Indies; sunk four, took two men-of-war with them to Martinique; that Count D'Estaing was going home to France in [a] frigate to be cured of his wound; had left five of his frigates for the protection of Charleston, with the Experiment of fifty guns, three sloops of war [with] copper bottoms [and a] twenty gun ship that came from Liverpool, with one of thirty-six guns from Glasgow. These were his prizes. Some of his ships are come to Chesapeake Bay to land some sick and wounded, take in provisions and proceed after the rest of the fleet to the Islands. News of yesterday, that government had taken up at New York more than twenty-eight thousand tons of transports, which are more than necessary to carry every thing from there."

---

[1] *English* in the original; a slip of the pen.

DECEMBER 23. Gen. Gates went through here, going home to his family in Virginia.

24. Came Robert Whitehill, stayed and dined. He was going to Philadelphia. I requested him to use his influence with the Trustees of [the] College, newly chosen, to send an invitation to James Cannon [and] James Davidson to return and become again tutors in the College.

29. Sent [a] letter to the Rev. Dr. Ewing, under cover to Paul Fooks, to whom I wrote respecting the same subject of getting J. Davidson and J. Cannon places in the college of Philadelphia.

31. We went to bed ...... but not before we had a fresh encounter with Antony, who had taken upon him (although I had before charged him not to concern himself with her, but if any thing was amiss to acquaint her mistress therewith) to abuse the negro woman as she had not made his bed, as he said, fit for him to lie in. I interfered and desired him to go to bed and not disturb the house. This rather inflamed him so that I took him by the arm to put him up stairs. He started from me, went out in the yard, said he would not be thus abused; he would not be insulted. I accordingly shut the door. After a considerable space of time, he came and requested I would let him in. I did so and spoke to him to this purpose, Antony, thy behavior is such that I cannot have thee about house, except thou wilt behave thyself in another manner, and thou must remember that a good while since I ordered thee away upon such an occasion, but thou, as now, promised to behave better and saidst that thou wouldst be contented to stay if I paid thee no wages, but would give thee some necessary clothes and what else I thought proper, as thou didst not desire to go away from here. To this he readily assented and said he was still of the same mind, and he hoped he would in future be more still and quiet, as that was the state he loved to live in and it was in

hopes to live so retired that he left my son Christopher's to come tnd live here. He said abundance in his way on this topic. Upon the whole he went to bed still and quiet, as we did to ours [it] being near twelve o'clock, we being so disturbed and detained by him.

1780.

JANUARY 2. Near six, came Dr. John Morgan, in order to get my testimony respecting Dr. William Shippen Jr.'s conduct in Philad^a when I with others had the care of the sick soldiers, that had been prisoners at New York, the flying camp, &c. Drank tea ; stayed all night.

3. The Doctor went down town; came back with Charles Hall Esq. who qualified me respecting some transactions of our Committee in Philad^a for sick soldiers, some time past.

4. Came to town this day, a number of English prisoners under guard from Philadelphia. Most desperate traveling through the snow.

5 Heard in Lancaster that Richard Penn's fine house in Market Street was burnt, where John Holker lived, the second instant.

6. Favored with two newspapers sent me by Ludwick Lauman ...... giving account of the Spaniards' actually beseiging Gibraltar and having taken Pensacola and that a fleet was sailed from Sandy Hook the twenty-third of December of one hundred and forty sail, with six thousand English troops, said to be for South Carolina ; that Gen. Washington had detached from the grand army a body of three thousand Virginia and North Carolina troops for the better defense of that important place, and that a body of twenty-five hundred North Carolina militia were preparing and a body of militia from Virginia, both going to [South] Carolina ; and that the English were completely routed, lost four thousand, and six thousand surrendered prisoners at discretion in the

JAN. 1780] *of the American Revolution.* 235

East Indies between Bengal and Poonah to an army of the natives (*Penna. Packet*, Dec. 30th, and Jan. 1st).

8. It's said that the prisoners that came the other day were sent away this morning.

10. Visited by Esq. Shippen; stayed some time in conversation; informed me that he just heard it reported in Lancaster that [a] ship, it's thought [the] Roebuck,[1] and a twenty-gun frigate in the last storm there was, [were] lost off Middletown Point, near Shrewsbury, and the crews of which mostly escaped in boats to New York. The forty-gun ship was driven ashore near Egg Harbor; one hundred of the crew found dead on board, the remainder, sixty in number, were happily relieved by the generous Americans. *P. Journal*, Num. 1321.

12. It's said that part of two regiments of Virginians, five hundred men with ten wagons, came to town this day on their route to Carolina. Excessively bad roads with snow, and cold with wind fresh [from the] North West.

16. It's said the five hundred troops of Col. Ball or Hall that come the other day, marched this morning; would have gone yesterday but for [a] Court Martial's being held on three soldiers for robbing a man here, for which they were whipped. To-day arrived Col. Nevil's regiment of five hundred men, on the same route as the others for Virginia and South Carolina. ...... We requested Antony, if he went to meeting, not to attempt to preach; if he should, I expected they would pull him out and probably duck him in the creek. He said that he was not afraid of man, if his father bid him, but they were blockheads. He did not go, but told [the] negro woman, that they were wicked, bad people and he would pray no more for them.

18. Oak wood, [it is] said [sells for] Sixty Dollars per load, and hickory, Eighty [Dollars], notwithstanding

---

[1] It was the Mermaid.— Ed.

G. R. employs the Continental teams to haul it, for which he don't pay one single penny, either for the driver, horses or wagons. O poor State of Pennsylvania.

21. Learned that there was a splendid Assembly last night at [the] Court House, Lancaster; twenty-one ladies, double quantity of men, band of music, dancing, singing, gaming, drinking, carousing, &c., &c. It's said, every subscriber is to pay Three Hundred Dollars, any interloper of assembly nights admitted upon paying Thirty Dollars, each night. Gen. Woodward with his attendants left Lancaster yesterday on his journey to Virginia.

22. I went down to Wm. Henry's store; stayed till past twelve, in which time marched out of town Col. Nevil's regiment for Virginia, with six fine brass cannons and a number of wagons. ...... Butter, one shilling per pound hard money. ..... A set of Lancastrians sleighing about; went about three miles from town. A few days past, it's said, a company numbering thirteen, had a collation, afternoon and evening. Their expenses amounted to Four hundred and fifty Pounds. Jovial Times!

25. It's said that yesterday came into town, the Third Division of the Virginia troops, five hundred men, Col. Guest, on their route for S Carolina.

28. Came Gasper Singer; brought a hog which weighed one hundred and twenty-four pounds; paid him Three Pounds in gold; three bushels of Indian Corn; paid him Thirty-six Pounds, paper money. He stayed, dined with us. He tells that five of our soldiers that went last week from here for Virginia died of cold on the road.

FEBRUARY 2. Dined with us, William Bispham; bought of him three and a half yards [of] yard-wide tow linen; Paid him thirty-eight continental dollars; lent him the second volume in folio of Bishop Burnet's History of his own time.

11. Waited upon by——Myner and——Mercer, collecting for repairing the engines and ladders. Gave them

three Pounds. ...... Fine assembly and collation last night.·

14. After breakfast, I took [a] walk to [the] vendue of Cornelius Land's household goods, where they were sold extravagantly, as per a specimen here annexed to show that the people here in general set no store by our Continental paper money ; viz. : A frying pan, Twenty-five Pounds ; A wood saw, Thirty-seven pounds, ten shillings ; Three split bone handled knives, three ditto forks, rusty, Twenty-two pounds, ten shillings ; An old mare of eleven years old for Eight hundred and five pounds ; One gallon stone bottle of the bead sort, Seven Pounds, ten shillings ; one common razor without a case, with hone for setting, Twenty Pounds ; one pair of common spectacles in case, Eighteen Pounds ; small Dutch looking-glass, six inches by four, no ornaments, but worse by age, Eight Pounds, ten shillings ; fifty sheaves of oats for Eighty Pounds ; an old eleven inch square face eight-day clock, walnut case, Two hundred and ten Pounds ; an old straw-cutting knife, box, &c., Fifty Pounds ; and so, in general, throughout the sale, the which so amazed me that I told them it was high time for a Bedlam to be built in Lancaster.

15. Last night, it's said, there was a great entertainment for the English officers (prisoners) at Peter Hofnager's ; grand supper, with music, dancing, &c.

MARCH 1. Last night much disturbed by Antony, who had got into one of his crazy fits, differing with the negro woman. At these times he is very violent in his complaints to us, in order that I might punish the poor creature, but, as latterly I've kept quiet in myself, he rages terribly, uttering a number of the most out of the way wicked expressions, yet not downright swearing, but mammy says it [is] cursing in the Popish way. ...... A. in tantrums all day. I lighted him to bed at night.

3. Antony cleaned [the] stables ; seemed disordered in his mind ; talked a good deal ; I gave him no answer.

Mammy thinks he was calling for vengeance upon some persons, but in the Popish dialect, being at [the] same time, he thought, very devout and very holy.

6. News to-day, it's said, is that the Irish have [beaten] three thousand English soldiers in Ireland and all the tories.

10. Past ten came into town two companies of light horse, commanded by Capt^s Shaffner and Markom. ...... It's said there have been two balls this week for the youth here, one at Slough's, the other at Peter Hoffnager's and one for the elders at the Court House [on] Fifth day night.

12. Accounts that the sick prisoners of Burgoyne's [army], above one hundred, were moved towards Virginia yesterday. ...... The light horse that came here a few days past marched away this morning for S. Carolina.

13 [For] a remarkable piece of cruelty in the English, see Dunlap's *Pennsylvania Packet*, Thursday March 9th, 1780. Quite [the] reverse treatment of the French, see *Pennsylvania Gazette*, March 8th, Numb. 2593.

17. Hamilton, Purdies, Capt. Doyle and Thomas Cuthbert bound over for assaulting a German that would not acknowledge St. Patrick.

29. Visited by Ludwick Lauman; brought the resolves of Congress [and] the resolution of our Assembly, respecting the depreciation of our money. ...... In [the] evening came Robert Whitehill, Esq. ...... He informed me [that] Dr. Cooper, —— Carter, and Wm. Story were proscribed and banished the state; that James Davidson and James Cannon were appointed to their former tutorships in college and invited to return as speedily as convenient.

31. News of the day that a French fleet, eight men-of-war with convoy, was arrived at [the] Capes, with [a] large quantity of goods for the states; that two English frigates were off our Capes, who put out to sea and were chased by two French men of war. Confirmation

expected. Gave One Hundred Dollars to Sus. Thornberry to pay Caleb Johnson for writing [the] Deed of [the] house on paper and Ten Dollars to pay Charles Hall for his trouble [in] going three miles to have the Deed acknowledged.

APRIL 12. After breakfast, went by my wife's desire to the drum-maker, to try to get two rims for cheesevats without bottoms. Returned without them, as he had no stuff to make them of, nor would the farmers, he said, sell him any timber without hard money, so must remain idle in his business.

13. Visited by Ed. Shippen and Ludwick Lauman; spent some time in discourse on affairs of government; near dusk, took [a] walk to the barracks; a company of artillery just come from Philada., going to Fort Pitt.

15. It's remarkable that two Whigs, namely Wm. Henry and Ludwick Lauman, both brought up lately gold from Philada. for the English officers, prisoners here, and delivered it safe, gratis: the first one hundred and fifty guineas, the latter, one hundred and seventeen guineas.

22. It's said that Congress passed [a] resolve on the eighteenth that the holders of Loan Office certificates shall sustain no loss thereon by any depreciation of the bills loaned subsequent to the respective dates of the said certificates; further, that last week was brought into Philada. Port, the Letter of marque ship Needham of fourteen guns from Jamaica, bound to New York. [The] cargo consists of four hundred and fifty hogsheads and thirty tierces of rum, taken by the sloop Active, Capt. Day, belonging to Philada. This day the first tree in blossom, I've seen this season, was in Mercer's garden facing us, an apricot.

25. Visited by George Inglis, to whom I paid four pounds, ten shillings for the hatchet and chisel, I bought at his vendue.

27. It's said that the Assembly usually held here every

Fifth night is dissolved last week. The excuse for it was, that the weather was grown too warm for the ladies to dance.

28. Just going to bed, past ten, came Dr. John Morgan and the Under Sheriff, who had been after him to Ephrata, having a writ against him in the suit of Dr. Houston for slander of him, it's said, in the time of the flying camp. I proposed that if the officer would leave him here, I would deliver him up in the morning, but the Doctor chose to go down to Adam Reigart's. So they went away before eleven.

29. Returned to dinner. In the interim Dr. Morgan called; said he had been bailed for ten thousand [dollars] by Col. Atlee; thanked my wife for our civilities with his compliments to me, he being just going to pursue the cross-examination with Dr. Shippen in the sundry different places. At dinner, came Dr. Houston. By his coming and conversation, I thought he was conscious that his conduct with Morgan was censurable, which, in conversation, I let him know was mine and many others' judgment on this occasion, it appearing to them as a scheme of Dr. Shippen to prevent his proceedings and therefore altered the minds of sundry of Dr. Shippen's friends, who were in his favor and interest before this action, being so glaring and fraught with malice and ill will.

May 3. Came Col. Lowry and L. Lauman to advise about forming [a] petition to our Assembly respecting the resolve of Congress relating to the Congress money of forty for one; having settled some preliminaries, returned into town to consult some of the principal men.

4. [A] great holiday with the Dutch, called Ascension Day. Near noon visited by Col. Lowry and L. Lauman; got me to draw a petition to be signed by the people at large in this county to the Assembly at their next sitting, praying them to rescind the vote of Congress for suffering one silver dollar to be equal in paying taxes to forty

Continental, and also [praying for] their enacting to strike the sum of one hundred thousand pounds in paper currency and that one dollar of that be equal in value to the silver dollar. I dined, then wrote [a] rough draught which they soon called for and took with them to copy.

5. Served the creatures with scanty allowance and poor cut straw scalded for the cow. Mammy milked her; gets but little. A. cleaned [the] stable, but little dung to what used to be. This gives me great concern at present and uneasiness of mind on the poor creature's account. To this added A.'s impudent behavior would be too much for me were it not sweetened by my dear wife's moderation and consolation upon those occasions; as to the scarcity, we can't prevent, and his folly and insolence are not to be prevented except by turning him out of doors, and this I a'n't free to do, as the poor creature has no place to resort to. I bear with his imperious conduct for the present. Whether he takes the advantage of the scarcity of hands and thinks we will bear with him sooner than turn him away and have nobody, I can't say, but I think he is afraid to try the experiment by going away when I have ordered and desired him to go and never to return.

6. Yesterday, it's said, three men were whipped and pilloried [and] one of them cropped; this day, two whipped and pilloried; all of them, it's said, for horse stealing.

8. Took a walk near [the] magazine, our militia companies being out to be reviewed; near four hundred; no fire arms.

10. Went down to court; spent some time; a trial of a person for [passing counterfeit money; brought in guilty; three others from Virginia tried and acquitted, and one —— Leech, who keeps tavern near the Gap, also acquitted by the jury, though, it's said, proof was strong against him. Numbers of people are displeased with this last verdict, as they say this is not the first time he has been concerned in such base practices.

11. News to-day that our people in the Jerseys lay in ambush for a party that came down from the English, of which they had information, killed several and took eighty prisoners; that the Marquis de La Fayette in the frigate ———, a thirty gun ship, was arrived at Boston from old France. In the afternoon, we were visited by the three Judges, McKean, Atlee and Bryan with John Smith, lawyer of Yorktown; stayed in conversation, viewed our garden and drank tea.

12. Thomas Cuthbert, just come from [the] lower counties,[1] said an express went through Wilmington last Tuesday who informed that before he left Charleston a sixty-four gun ship and two or three transports, in attempting to go over the bar, struck ground, the tide failed them, on which our people from some of the batteries or fort beat them to pieces.

13. This was a remarkable day for the German men and women bleeding at Chrisley Neff's. So many came that I presume he must work hard to bleed the whole. Strange infatuation!

15. I went nowhere from home this day although it's a very high holiday in this place, and as it was a most pleasant, agreeable, fine day, numbers were diverting themselves abroad, some riding, some walking, others playing long bullets, &c.

16. In the evening received [a] letter from my sons, of the thirteenth, with three newspapers up to that time. Under the Boston head, April 27th, saith "Last Tuesday, arrived at Salem a large letter of marque ship of about twenty guns, having on board one thousand barrels [of] pork and beef, seven hundred and fifty barrels of flour, eight hundred firkins [of] butter and a quantity of dry goods to the amount of fifteen thousand Pounds, bound from London to New York. She is prize to the ships Franklin and Jack." Under the same head is said "Tuesday last arrived here Capt. Brown in twenty-four

---

[1] Now the state of Delaware.

days from Guadaloupe, who brings advice that five sail of the line had gone from Martinico to join eight Spanish ships of equal rate at St. Domingo, whence, it is said, they were going to Georgia.

18. It's said that the Marquis de La Fayette arrived at Philadelphia from Boston [on] the fifteenth. He left France, the twentieth of March. Capt. Paul Jones, with his squadron, was to sail in fifteen days after.

20. Pretty long conversation with Councillor Hambright on the different and, as I apprehend, the impolitic movements of our rulers in the affairs of government and especially on the account of the depreciation.

27. Arose early; breakfasted near six; took leave of wife and set out; stopped at Wm. Bispham's, fed our horses; from thence to the sign of the Wagon, fed horses there; proceeded to Downingstown, drank tea there, fed horses; from thence to the widow of John Jacobs's; supped and stayed all night.

28. Breakfasted; set out past six; rode to [the] sign of [the] Buck; fed our horses; thence proceeded to Philada., where we arrived near three. Roads very dusty, weather very warm.

June 1. Visited by G. Schlosser, with whom I went to wait on the Commissioners at [the] Court House respecting my taxes. ...... News that the ship Aurora from this port [was] taken just as she was out of [the] Capes by a frigate from, and carried into New York; a vessel retaken by our people, the prisoners brought to town.

2. To [the] Loan Office: received bills on France for interest due, Four hundred and fourteen Dollars.

5. To [the] Loan Office; received certificates for interest due Two Thousand Dollars, in cash Nineteen and a half Dollars and two shillings and six pence, as they complained they had no cash to pay off the interest due on the former certificates. Poor encouragement to us Whigs who had confided and trusted our all in the

public funds! ...... Paid R. Fleming, [for] cutting my hair, shaving three times and setting two razors on the hone, Sixteen Dollars. Five vessels arrived yesterday from Port au Prince with sugars, coffee, molasses, cotton, &c.

6. News that Charleston was in our possession [on] the eighteenth [of] May, brought by James Gray, the rider, who came [from] but a few miles from there. There came ten or eleven vessels, chiefly from St. Eustatia, to-day. News in the afternoon that Charleston surrendered [on] the twelfth [of] May; this again contradicted.

8. News brought by a delegate, its said, *via* Baltimore that Charleston was safe [on] the nineteenth [at] four P.M. ...... A report just spread that the ship Iris was taken by the ship Hermione and the privateer Trumbellon.

9. News by express that the enemy landed in the Jerseys near Springfield [on] the night of the seventh; some horse, the others, foot; it's said their numbers from five to ten thousand. Skirmishing began with loss on both sides. News again for certain, it's said, that Carolina was safe [on] the nineteenth of May; that the English had made no impression on the garrison of Charleston.

10. Drums beating to call the militia; Major Lee's corps of light horse left this city for the camp last evening. ...... Dined with P. Fooks, Town Major[1] and J*s*. Davidson at Col. Timothy Pickering's. This morning, by proclamation of the President and Council, martial law was declared, in consequence of which a number of horses were pressed for the use of the army, from those, first, who had not taken the test, viz: for instance, Wm. A......'s two coach-horses, four from Jer. W......, three from Joshua H....., two from Sam*l*. E....., three from P......, two from Wm. G......, one from

---

[1] Col Lewis Nicola.

John P......, two from James P......, &c., &c. News again to-day that Charleston surrendered the eleventh of May, but not believed; great anxiety amongst the virtuous Whigs. A prize in the river to the Fair American, bound from London to New York.

11. This day arrived four French Ships, one of them said to mount twenty-eight guns, one Polacre, two other brigs, our own, with a prize brig and schooner. It's said that there are on board these ships seventeen hundred hogsheads of sugar, besides rum, coffee, salt, cotton, &c.; and that the English under Gen. Knyphausen are fortifying themselves at Elizabeth Town. A number of horses [were] sent off to-day for Gen. Washington's camp. It's further said that account is that the French have taken Barbadoes, beaten the English fleet [and] killed Admiral Rodney, and that the Spaniards have taken Gibralter.

12. Some prisoners, brought from aboard the prize, sent to prison. ...... Drank tea at G. Hastings's; paid her Three hundred and thirty-four Dollars for stuff for petticoat and [a] small piece [of] blue worsted binding. ...... To [the] Coffee House, where was reading Rivington's newspaper, containing the capitulation of Charleston, but, as this came through the Tory line and [was] by force extorted from John Mercer, who, when taxed about this paper, absolutely denied it until by confronting him with Daniel Wistar and Owen Jones Jr., and by threats [they] recovered it from him, as was related to me by Paul Fooks, who was one of them that attended him till delivered, numbers did not believe the authenticity of it.

The tax-gatherer having taken a pair of choice andirons that Charles or his wife had lent to Wm. Brewer, I had to attend the having them restored. At first the tax-gatherer behaved, I apprehended, a little insolently, but he, perceiving that I intended to interest myself, relinquished them, went and picked out a time-piece to supply their place. As that was really Brewer's property and seemed to be almost his all, as he has, through his persisting not to pay taxes, suffered most of his goods and furniture to be taken from him and sold, and this, he apprehends, is suffering for the testimony of truth, &c., and as I had received some money I went in the evening, paid the collector the sum assessed, namely Ten Pounds, and saved him his time-piece for another opportunity.

13. Strong dispute about Charleston.

14. Six or eight vessels said to come up from St. Eustatia, St. Martins and Santa Cruz ...... Visited to-day, as I was once or twice before, by Samuel Huntington, President of Congress. ...... To [the] Coffee-House, where accounts are brought that Gen. Lincoln's first Aide-de-camp was arrived with a capitulation of Charleston on the twelfth [of] May, with sundry circumstances that attended that unfortunate transaction.[1] This unexpected account was to me and many others exceedingly painful and grating, but so it was and must be borne with. ...... It's said an embargo was laid on to-day.

15. Breakfasted at Charles's, but much chagrined with the accounts of yesterday, as it seems to appear that our General, Continental troops, ship's stores, &c., were given to Clinton in exchange for Charleston, in order to save their houses [and] effects, [the loss of] which in case of a storm and being overcome might be the consequence, but as they did not intend to dispute with Clinton any longer, the inhabitants and militia refused to fight, which so enraged the General, as it's said, that he almost came to the resolution to fire upon them and force his way with his troops, if practicable, but was overpersuaded from such a rash attempt, as he would have both them in the town and the English out to encounter with. Under these perplexing, interesting circumstances, they obliged him, the general, to capitulate, contrary to his

---

[1] It will be observed that he was a month and two days on the way.

judgment or intention, as his whole force of Continental troops, by accounts, did not exceed fifteen or sixteen hundred men; and by letter of confidence to Dr. Phyle from Gen. De Kalb, that came with the express from Fredericksburg, [he] says that he "can find no faith, dependence or virtue in the state of Virginia, but hope that the French fleet and army will relieve us. For my part, I expect a most fatiguing campaign, being now and having been detained for the want of wagons, &c."[1] It's said that the first four classes of the Philada., with four classes of Bucks and Chester county militia, are ordered to hold themselves in readiness to march. ...... Drank tea at Christopher's. Thomas Cuthbert [and] James Cannon, with Lieut. Col. Tennant, Aide-de-camp to Gen. Lincoln, came; spent some time in conversation respecting Charleston.

16. News from the Jerseys that our army was well, but wanted rum; that on the engagement, fourth day was a week, our people had nothing but water to drink, yet they had behaved well [having] taken sixteen prisoners [and] killed and wounded many. This I received from Dr. Glentworth, who said he left head quarters two days ago. Dined at Christopher's, took [a] walk to the wharf, as eight sail of small vessels, prizes to the sloop Comet, were then in sight.

17. It's said that three prizes and [the] retaken brig with load of tobacco came up last night; sent in by the Holker. ...... [To the] Loan Office, got some bills on

---

[1] Extract from a letter from Patrick Henry, Governor of Virginia, dated 1779, and to be found in the Memoir of Richard Henry Lee, volume 1, page 195. "Public spirit seems to have taken its flight from Virginia. It is too much the case; for the quota of our troops is not half made up, and no shame seems to remain for completing it. Great bounties are offered, but I fear the only effect will be to expose our State to contempt, for I believe no soldiers will enlist, especially in the Infantry. Can you credit it? No effort was made for supporting or restoring public credit! I pressed it warmly upon some, but in vain. This is the reason you get no soldiers. Let not Congress rely upon Virginia for soldiers. I tell you my opinion, they will not be got here until a different spirit prevails."

France for interest due. ...... Patience and Betsey bought fifty pounds of coffee [at] Eight Dollars per pound; sent it as their present to the collecting ladies for the army.

19. News that Cornwallis had put two men on each horse, a sufficient number who surprised a post of our people to the amount of four hundred, massacred the whole that fell into their hands without any mercy or compassion; that Col. Washington and one or two others made their escape. ...... Great murmurings amongst the people in general, occasioned by the ill conduct and management of ——— respecting the depreciation of the money, heavy taxes, militia fines, enlisting men, dearness of commodities, through the large quantities imported on which the greater prices are affixed. Dined at Christopher's. Charles went with me to see after spirits, wine, coffee, salt, &c., and bought none, as the great quantities just imported had raised the prices considerably. Wonder of wonders, never known before!

21. This day Lady Washington came to town from camp; met by our Light Horse and escorted by them.

22. Account that Col. Knox is at Trenton with orders to put the stores on board the flat-bottomed boats. Three flags of truce at Chester, arrived from Charleston with prisoners on their parole. Gen. Lincoln came up to town. No women but one, it's said, are come with those vessels.

23. One pound of Souchong Tea, sent by Daughter Sally as [a] present to Mammy cost two silver dollars. sold to Cornelius Barns four French certificates,

Dated June 17th Number 500 for 300 Dollars
" " 1st " 497 " 300 "
" " 1st " 2153 " 30 "
" " 1st " 2154 " 30 "

$660

at 46s for one, amounting to 30,360 Dollars.

This day forty English prisoners brought into town.

24. The City Light Horse set off for head quarters. ..... Arrived a vessel from Cales,[1] fifty days passage, said that the French fleet for America had sailed. Came up also a ship and brig, prizes to the Fair American, the ship from Charleston to New York with the rigging, anchors, guns, &c., of a sixty-four gun English ship that was lost.

26. News of a skirmish at Springfield in the Jerseys last Sixth Day. It's said our people under Gen. Macksfield withstood the British, came to push bayonets and kept the field. Accounts from Virginia say that the French fleet off Cape Hatterass fell in with the Russell man-of-war of seventy-four guns, two frigates and twelve transports with Hessian troops on board from Carolina for Halifax; took the whole of them. This news, whether true or not, has made many long faces.

29. Drums beating for the militia to go out on the commons. Yesterday our light horse returned to camp and, it's said, some of the Jersey militia, having been dismissed by Gen. Washington for the present and received his kind thanks, for that the English left the Jerseys on their repulse at Springfield, after burning most of the houses, and precipitately went off in the night with their cannon, and that our people leveled their works next morning. ·George Wallace, formerly a respectable inhabitant of Philadelphia, now of or near [New] Brunswick in the Jerseys, told me at the Coffee House that a reputable neighbor of his, and who had been in that affair, assured him that he counted nineteen wagons, loaded with wounded and dead, carrying off in their retreat, and many wounded got away as well as they could, as no more wagons could be got, so that many were left dead and wounded. Just brought in, fifteen prisoners and four or five deserters. This day Lady

---

[1] *Cadiz* was formerly so spelled by the English, but probably *Calais* is meant.

Washington, with many, gentlemen and ladies, was regaled in barges on our river, in viewing the wharves, shipping, &c., whose various colors [were] displayed and their decks and yards manned. Visited by Gen. Lincoln, who was very solid and polite. He is a plain, familiar man.

30. Thomas Pultney and wife came to town; said they had seen my wife. She was bravely, busy in the garden, &c. This was very agreeable for me to hear, as they brought me abundance of love verbally. ...... I took much pains to find pieces of green broad worsted binding and at last completed it by thirty-six yards; cost me one hundred and forty Dollars.

JULY 1. Breakfasted at Charles's; soon after came Joseph Warner the elder (boat builder) who gave the following relation, viz: "that this day week, in the afternoon, his son Joseph, coming to town for him in a horse chair, being near unto Coates's brick yard, Wissahicken road, there came on, he supposes what is called a whirlwind, which immediately took up horse, chair and him in it, so high, he thinks ten feet, as that the top of the chair being overturned with the horse came first to the ground with the bottom of [the] chair uppermost, and [they] were carried, he supposes, the space of one hundred feet. The fall broke the chair, hurt the horse badly, but the young man, his son, in the chair received very little damage, except the fright this accident occasioned." News of the day at ten o'clock A.M., " that West Point was taken by the English three days ago;[1] that Gen. Cornwallis had conquered South Carolina as far as Chatham [and] returned with great trophies to Charleston; that the French and Spanish fleets were met by the English in the Channel, which had destroyed both the French and Spanish, and in consequence of which the states of America would be fully subdued by the last days of next September," &c., &c.

---

[1] A false report.

2. It's said that Governor Rutledge and [the] late President Laurens, of Charleston, arrived here by land. They brought, it's said, letters to Congress that Gen. DeKalb, with seven thousand men, was on the march for South Carolina. ...... Arrived a vessel from Boston with continental sugar. From Baltimore by letter [dated] St. Eustatia of the thirteenth of June [we learn] that twelve Spanish ships of the line, with four of French and twelve thousand land forces, were arrived at Martinico.

3. Paid Benj. Betterton one hundred and thirty Dollars for [a] handsaw, drawing knife and some little coopering.

4. Commencement began at [the] Philadelphia College this forenoon, at which many attended. ...... This being the anniversary of our freedom from English bondage, sundry vessels saluted the town. ...... The company of Artillery and Invalids' Regiment marched to the State House, where the Congress, President of the State and Council with a number of officers attended; bell ringing, guns firing till the evening and until numbers were so drunk as to reel home. As my sons had declined paying their quota for the raising [of] two men in their districts, and Capt. McLane calling, I snatched up some money of theirs and paid him, being Four hundred and eighty Pounds.

I queried why the City Vendue was not farmed out, as it appears to be a valuable branch of business and, as I'm informed by John Cling, vendue-keeper formerly, would rent for near Five Hundred [Dollars] in specie per year, and by the sales there to-day which were exceedingly large and valuable, with household furniture and many damaged casks of nails, seemed to satisfy me of that truth. Nails sold from forty to fifty shillings per pound, &c. ...... In [the] evening visited President Samuel Huntington with son Christopher [and] Paul Fooks. Some company there, but went away. Stayed in close conversation with him some time. He requested to see me again before I went home and behaved very friendly and politely. This day were brought to town from thirty to forty prisoners. A person told me that had seen them.

7. Dined at Charles's; paid for him on account of his not mustering on militia days, for which he was fined, Two hundred and fifty-five pounds, thirteen shillings and six pence, unto John Jacobson, Collector. ...... I made a present to Sally and Hannah Empsons of Two Hundred Dollars. News of the day is that the French fleet, so long expected, was arrived at St. Martin's, having twelve thousand land forces on board in good order. This comes by a vessel into Baltimore, in a short passage from St. Martin's and adds further that the French and Spanish fleets in [the] West Indies amount to fifty-five sail of the line and thirty-six hundred land forces.

8. Arose early; packed up my clothes, &c.; got shaved at Robert Fleming's, unto whom I now paid thirty Dollars. Gave Charles's three maids twenty-four Dollars; negro man, five Dollars. Sally's negro, four Dollars; Christopher's white maid, eight Dollars; his white man, boy and negro girl, twelve Dollars. ...... Great plenty of peas, beans [and] various kinds of vegetable, but high priced; rum, sugar, salt [and] coffee plenty, but rising daily....... Near eleven, took leave of my children, relations and acquaintances present. In Christopher's carriage with him in it and Charles [on] horseback left Philada. ...... Reached Thomas Reese's in good time....... Drank tea, supped and lodged there.

10. We equipped our carriage, took leave of Charles, who was for returning home, and Polly, as Joseph rode with us over Schuylkill, where we took leave of him and proceeded for [the] sign of [the] White Horse, where we arrived past three. The weather was warm; the road really bad with ruts, hills, stones, &c., yet it was beautiful to behold the blessings of kind heaven visibly

displayed in the fields of wheat, rye, oats, Indian corn, barley, flax [and] hemp. After feeding our horses with hay [and] six quarts of oats [and having] drunk [a] gill of spirits and water, for which Christopher paid seventeen Dollars, we set off near five, reached Downing's house in Downingtown, where we put up, drank [a] bowl of sangaree [and] drank coffee.

11 Arose early, got our horses, gave them six quarts of oats, fixing our sundries; paid reckoning by Christopher, one hundred and twenty dollars. Proceeded to the sign of [the] wagon, where we gave [the] horses hay [and] six quarts of oats; eat breakfast ourselves on coffee, for which Christopher paid twenty dollars. ......
Reached home past six; found my wife in good health and spirits, who received us very affectionately, for which great blessings and favors, great thanks and acknowledgments are due to our great Lord and wonderful Benefactor, both now and forever, saith my soul, Amen and Amen.

12. Just came Robert Taggert and wife in [a] chair, having left Philada. yesterday morning; brought news that "Ireland had formed a Bill of Rights and determined to support it; that the Russians and Dutch had declared a neutrality and that a prize ship was arrived in Philada. with sugar, coffee, &c."

14. Came Sam[l]. Boyd, who in conversation related that some of the English prisoners, being down at the river, talked very impertinently, so that James Wright resented it; came and informed Judge Atlee, who is Commissary of Prisoners, who sent for him, but he showing no signs of remorse, he committed him to prison, as also another who had behaved insolently so as to come and deliver up his parole; he was also committed.

15. Orders came this day from [the] War Office that all prisoners should wear their regimentals. This has also offended those gentlemen prisoners.

16. I served [the] horse and kept him in, as there are bad folks on First Day that want to be riding.

18. Reading Saturday's paper left me by L. Lauman last night; confirmation of the arrival of [the] French and Spanish fleet, with twenty-four thousand land forces at Martinico; that the French fleet was off the Capes of Virginia some days past, as an English frigate barely escaped by throwing over her guns, spars, &c., and by that means got into New York. Blessed time for getting in [the] harvest, which by accounts, there has not been such a plentiful one for twenty-four years past. Blessing and praise be rendered to the great Giver, who alone is worthy. Paid Henry Lechler, Collector [the] Continental tax for Dec., Jan., Feb., March and April, One hundred and fifty-three Pounds, fifteen shillings.

19. Visited by Wm. Henry; took a walk in the garden [and] stayed some time in conversation; said [that] three soldiers from the camp, going after deserters, related to Judge Atlee that four thousand French troops were landed on Rhode Island; that part of their fleet was off Black Point, some cruising off Long Island [and] the Narrows, and had chased in the Guard Ship; that Slough, he said, had acted very imprudently, as he heard; that he had caused the gold, before he paid it away, to be clipped very close, and thereby procured a large sum by this, his depreciation, very unjustly.

20. I'm told that this week and the [last] two hundred horses have been sent from this place, that were purchased for the use of the French army by Matthias Slough.

21. News from Philada., dated the fifteenth, says, "there arrived here with an account of the arrival of the French fleet and troops under Monsieur Ternay at Rhole Island the tenth instant in good order." From New York on Saturday says, "Admiral Greaves has fallen in with Admiral Ternay, and that Greaves had lost a seventy-four gun ship, sunk; that Admiral Ternay had arrived at Rhode Island in a shattered condition."

22. News from Freehold, New Jersey, dated July [the] seventeenth, says that "yesterday afternoon there came to, off Long Island, six ships of Admiral Greaves's fleet, I presume some of them of eighty guns, none under sixty. I observe that Arbuthnot had augmented Greaves's fleet to thirteen ships. Ten of these appear to be of sixty guns and upwards, three of them large frigates. Arbuthnot's ship and others from the west line, immediately to cover the entrance into Sandy Hook; that they were exerting themselves at New York to complete their complement of men on board their ship of war; every volunteer that will enter on board, for this exigency, is to be discharged from all duty by land or sea for three years." From L'Orient, of May the twenty-second, "By a vessel from Isle Dieu, we learn that two English privateers have cut out five Dutch vessels that were at anchor there."

24. Orders came up last week for one hundred wagons, to be sent to camp. Letter answered that as the horses were going down to the camp for [the] use of [the] French troops, they might have orders to put them in the wagons, [to] the which, as no answer was returned but to press, if no way else, it's taken for granted that the farmer is to be deprived of his horses at this busy time of ploughing for winter's grain. O wretched rulers! O monstrous directors of our State! At this time an officer confined for ill behavior, with orders to [the] jailer not to suffer him to converse or hold communication with any of his brethren here, but upon an officer's applying to converse with him and this being refused, the prisoner wrote [a] letter, threw it out of [the] window to the other who received it. Upon complaint made by [the] gaoler's wife to the magistrates, none of them would take any notice, as Judge Atlee was out of town. O glorious Whigs for magistrates! Poor Pennsylvania! It's said that the proceedings of this county, with what other news concerns the public, are collected

and sent by those officers to New York and return with newspapers [which] are duly received here by them, and no notice taken of their proceedings.

25. The horse race that was begun yesterday, but not ended, was completed this morning. The wager, it's said, was Twenty-five hundred Pounds, won by Gasper Dull's black horse. ...... A brigade of wagons left this borough to-day. More horse racing this afternoon. ...... Had our government by their officers exerted the authority that they have used with some degree of cruelty on the poor farmers by taking their horses out of their ploughs, &c., they might have collected a great number of useless yet valuable ones to-day and yesterday on the race ground. This would have been praiseworthy by showing they were true friends to government, by *first*, suppressing the breakers of the law of the state, and *secondly* by supplying our friends the French army who are [in] want of that necessary creature at so cheap and saving a rate, as they were brought to their hands on so illegal and dissolute [an] use.

27. News by a gentleman of veracity from Virginia that a number of Scotch and disaffected people in N. Carolina collected in force in order to distress the well meaning inhabitants, many of whom they pillaged and obliged to take the oath of allegiance to the tyrant George, in their march into Virginia, where they expected to perform great feats, but our people collected and were joined by [a] small part of the army. They made a stand on the borders, where a sharp engagement ensued, which turned out in our favor. It's said they killed forty, took eighty prisoners, fifteen hundred horses, many negroes, cattle, sheep and a quantity of baggage, which, by this informant, they were selling from day to day by public auction, for the benefit of the sufferers and the soldiery. Yesterday, sixty horses were sent from here, it's said, for the use of the French army. Visited by Saml. Boyd, who related the above and that

there was a handbill come to town printed by B. Town, giving an account of an engagement between the combined fleet of France and Spain and the English in the West Indies, in which, it's said, "the latter lost two seventy-four gun ships and two taken; that the fleet of nine sail of ships under Admiral Greaves with two regiments of Hessians has sailed from New York but don't say where."

AUGUST 5. Got Wm. Shuttleburgh to examine and new leather our pump box, paid him Thirty Dollars.

6. I went to Friend's Meeting, where were fifteen menkind and eight womenkind, among which were included four strange men and one woman, likewise Polly Dickinson, who with Thoˢ. Vickers, spoke for some time.

8. Called and stayed to breakfast Wm. Hardie and Patrick Martin, going from Northumberland to Philada., who gave me this relation, viz: that a person there, going under the denomination of Col.—— Montgomery, who said he left Philada., the thirtieth ult., reported that no French fleet was arrived; the report of their arrival arose from this, that on Admiral Greaves's arrival off Rhode Island, the Commander there took them to be the French fleet, and, according to signals agreed upon, hoisted his flag, which was answered by the English Admiral with the same flag agreed upon. This caused the express to be sent off for head quarters [and] from there to Philada. To this effect Patrick Martin said he heard Wm. Hamilton (clerk to one of the three Commissaries at Northumberland, don't know which), tell in his presence unto Col. Cox, Commissary at Cox's town near Harris's ferry,[1] and Wm. Hardie said he heard partly the same thing related at sundry places, and gave the said Montgomery for the author, to which they added that they perceived it to have a bad effect upon the country people, who before seemed elated with the

---
[1] Now Harrisburg, Pa.

account of the French fleet's arrival, and discouraged them from enlisting. ...... Bought one bushel of rye; cost seven shillings specie.

9. Arose early, being a warm night and some of our neighbors too free in the orchard.

10. Antony in [the] orchard to watch [the] boys. As I was doubtful, sometime, whether, if any came for apples, Antony would prevent, I took a walk to the back fence, made [a] noise [by] pounding as [if] I would break the fence, with other noise, this convinced me Antony sat in the chair. [He] took no notice until my wife, Debby and old Rachael, who were alarmed as they knew nothing of me, came to him, roused him and scolded him for neglect. His answer seemed to be that he thought it his duty to be still and not disturb them, as by so doing he should have peace in himself and a blessing would attend him, with a deal of such ignorant and trifling say so. He continued till it was proper to command him to be silent, which was very difficult for him to comply with.

11. Many new recruits for seven months, say twenty-six, left this place for camp.

13. Last evening Robt. Purdie called; stayed some time giving us a relation of the conduct at times of Daniel Whitelock, when half or quite over (in the seaman's term) and particularly with sundry dialogues that passed between him and his wife on those occasions. Purdie's relation of their behavior on the night of [the] Fourth [of] July, being the Anniversary, was really humorous, but too long to write down in this place; but the result was that he would in future pay his taxes to the state as other good people do.

15. Towards evening I caught Antony giving a quantity of our only best ripe apples in the orchard through the fence to Dr. N ...... and some of his grandchildren. This I thought exceedingly mean and below the character of a man of honor and a neighbor (and who had

about a week past collected what he had upon such a like tree and stowed them away. Upon my seeing them collected, he being at his door, I asked the reason as they were not yet ripe. He said some of them had been stolen as that night, and he did this to have some for themselves). After Antony came in, I queried how he could serve me so in giving what was not his own. He justified himself by saying the Doctor was a good man. Talked kindly to him, upon which the negro woman said, Why Antony, you did so yesterday when Master and Mistress were out. I talked to him but to no purpose, as he still justified himself in so doing and desired me not to use him ill, as looking upon himself to be the person offended by my calling him to an account; so in order to keep my temper I let him pass for this time, with a severe charge not to do the like again, as I had before reprimanded him for handing over apples at the back fence to the boys and some officers, prisoners here.

16. This morning, nigh about one hundred horses were sent from here towards our or the French camp.

19. Last evening were brought from Philada. Capts. Campbell of [the] forty-fourth regiment, Mure of the eighty-second regiment, Lyman of [the] Prince of Wales's regiment, Murray of Wentworth's Dragoons, and Wollop of Kniphausen's regiment, all prisoners, taken coming from England in the packet.

23. Came also Robt Whitehill, going down to Council; stayed and dined. He gave this account, received by a gentleman lately from New York, who called at his house, viz. This person dined at New York with Saml S...... his wife [and] an English officer. At dinner, which was homely and scarce of vegetables, Mrs. S...... with grief saith, oh the quantities that I have thrown away! how glad I should be to have some of them to eat. He answered, My dear, don't be disheartened, we shall soon have plenty again. When? she said. Why,

said he, as Charleston is in our hands, we shall soon, that is the kingly government will be established and we return to our own homes. She sighed [and] said, Ah, thou mayest return and stand the chance of being hanged, for I see no other prospect for my part. Don't despond, my dear, he said, I see better times approaching, for the Royal army must and will prevail in a short time and we shall then be happy in spite of the rebels who now rule. She opposed and requested him not to talk so vainly, as she saw no prospect of returning but under the fear of a halter. After some more altercation, the officer replied, Sir, your wife seems to have a true sense of your situation, and, believe me, I'm of her mind that you, sir, may return, if you please, and take the chance of a halter: but for my part, I've no expectation, and I'll be —— if any of our officers will go there if they can help it, or our soldiers either, nor see I any prospect of any other return you are likely to be favored with, as there appears to be no great probability at present of subduing the states.

25. It's said that sixteen prisoners in our jail broke out last night, chiefly servants to the officers confined for malpractices. Yesterday there were sundry accounts from Charleston (said to be by flag to Philadelphia with women, &c.), giving relation of the success of our troops in several skirmishes, in which the English have suffered greatly; that the Continental flag was flying at Camden and Georgetown; that Cornwallis was retreating towards Charleston, but Gen. Gates had thrown his army between him and the town, and Gen. DeKalb with his army pressed him hard in the rear; six hundred of our people who were with him had deserted to our side and that great sickness prevailed in his army and in the town.

26. Enclosed were three Dunlap's newspapers of the fifteenth, nineteenth and twenty-second, the which gave sundry accounts of the prodigious mobs that were assembled in London [in] the beginning of the month of

June and had continued for several days with great havoc and destruction.¹

29. Michael Schriner and son brought twenty-six sheaves of rye straw; paid him twenty-four paper dollars.

30. It's said that three classes of this county's militia are ordered to hold themselves in readiness to march on very short notice.

SEPTEMBER 1. A complaint in town by the men enlisted in the back parts and detained here till orders come for their marching to the camp, that the meat allotted, stinks so badly that they cannot eat it, so throw it about the streets; to which add that information was given to Judge Atlee by Christian Wertz of a report propagated by John Whitemore the elder that the second division of the French fleet was totally defeated by Admiral Greaves off Rhode Island, but that [neither] the Judge nor Michael Hubley, who was present, paid any regard to it.

13. In the newspaper enclosed is [an] account of poor Gen. DeKalb's being killed in the late engagement to the southward.

16. A great number of young men, Menonists, met at Kap's tavern, as usual, to play sling bullets, &c., early in the afternoon.

20. Paid Henry Lechler, Collector, four months' Continental tax due [the] first instant, One hundred and ten Pounds, ten shillings, and the County tax, Two Pounds, ten shillings.

24. Last evening Samuel Boyd was in the yard with us; in came Stephen Wells, shoemaker, and in a loud, boisterous manner said to me, How came you to say that you let me into the house to live for charity? I can prove it. I endeavored to pacify the man, but to no purpose, by telling him I said no such thing. He said

---

¹ These were the "No Popery" riots instigated by Lord George Gordon, a lunatic Scotchman.

he had overpaid me the rent, &c. I then told him if he could not behave himself to walk out or I would turn him out, for, said I, you have never paid me one penny of rent in your life. He said he had overpaid me. Upon my asking how, he answered, mending shoes for my man. I then let him know I had never sent him and I had nothing to do with it, upon which he declared he would send the sheriff for him to-morrow. As to that, I said he might do as he would, but if he did not know how to behave himself better I should soon teach him. Upon this S. Boyd took him away and I have not seen him since. I'm pleased that I was preserved to keep my temper so well as I did.

29. Visited in the evening by L. Lauman; brought the account, said by express to Philada., last Fourth Day, that two English officers, spies, were taken at West Point, upon which Gen. Arnold made his escape to the English at New York. Further particulars expected.

OCTOBER 3. Antony went into town and did what he pleased, but I think he is far from pleasing us; that he is never content except acting in the line of contradiction, not only in his small employment but in and about the house, a few instances will demonstrate. When we have no fresh broth, he wants some; when we have it, he can't sup it; when we have lean of bacon, he wants the fat; when the fat, he can't eat it without spreading salt over it, as, without it, it's too heavy for his stomach; if new milk, he can't eat it till it is sour, it curdles on his stomach; when sour or bonnyclabber, it gives him the belly ache; give him tea, he don't like such slop, it's not fit for workingmen; if he hasn't it when he asks for it, he is not well used; give him apple pie above once for some days, it's not suitable for his belly, it makes him sick; if the negro woman makes his bed, she don't make it right; if she don't make it, she's a black lazy jade. Thus he would, and has been exceedingly troublesome, until Mammy found out that by indulging him, he grew past bearing, and she came to this resolution and, I hope, will keep to it, that is, to give him plenty of such provisions as she judges suitable for him, and if he eats it, it's well, if not, he must leave it, as he will get no other, and by this method she has eased herself and negro of a deal of trouble which he formerly gave them. This night he could not eat exceedingly good apple pie, but after we went to bed, he boiled some crusts of bread in water and eat that, as he could not drink cider to-night; it griped him. This the negro tells, as she sat up in the kitchen till he went to bed.

6. Took a walk to Daniel Whitelock's; bought of him [a] very large cedar tub for making soap; paid him for that and cutting box with two knives Two hundred and fifty Dollars. ...... A. in his tantrums, while I was out; used Mammy very impertinently and treated me in the same manner before he went to bed, so that he was then, as he has often been before, requested to leave the house, as we cannot for pity's sake turn him out, as he has no place to go unto.

7. Engaged about sundries, as A. was the gentleman to-day.

9. Took sundry walks in the orchard; boys stealing; moonlight.

12. Smith, the cooper, hooping several casks; paid him thirty-five Dollars.

16. We have now particulars relative unto Arnold's treachery, viz: that Arnold was gone over to the enemy; that Col. André, General Clinton's principal Aide and confidant, was apprehended in disguise in our camp; that West Point, where Arnold commanded, was to be the sacrifice, in which was to be the Commander-in-chief, with the Marquis de la Fayette, who were to lodge there on Monday night the twenty-fifth [of] September, but the plot, by the hand of Providence, was timely discovered. Upon full proof, Col. André was hanged as a

spy at the camp at Tappan [on] the second instant. See *Pennsylvania Packet*, Sept. 30th and October 3d; *Pennsylvania Journal*, October 4th and 11th.

18. About two o'clock the first class of militia left this town, going towards the frontiers against the inroads of the Indians; John Hubley, Captain; Dr. Newman, Lieutenant.

21. Took a walk into town; proffered Forty Dollars for a bag of potatoes, said to be two bushels, but rejected. ...... Bought of Simon Snyder, miller, thirty pounds [of] butter; paid him one shilling per pound; gave him a guinea; he had no change; he owes me five shillings, hard money.

23. Bought twelve yards of tow linen at two shillings hard money per yard and gave two pounds [of] rice in the bargain.

25. This evening [there] was [a] bonfire at [the] Court House, firing guns, drums beating, fifes playing, &c., and continued some hours on account of some great news received from the Congress.

27. Breakfasted with us Peter Bowman, who brought [a] hind quarter of veal, twelve pounds at three pence, old price, say three shillings hard. ...... Bought of Peter Bowman twenty bushels of new wheat for which I am to pay him eight shillings per bushel, in specie, and he is to keep it until I give directions where [it is] to be taken unto.

28. Got our kitchen chimney swept, cost fifteen Dollars.

29. This afternoon Antony in his way preached at the English Presbyterian meeting in this place. It's said that most of the hearers laughed at him, but he was highly pleased.

30. Dined with us Abraham Hare to whom I gave One Thousand Continental Dollars and four half Joes in gold to purchase as many bushels of wheat as he can procure for that money and keep it at his mill to grind for us, as we shall give directions.

31. Dined with us Gaspar Singhauser....... for eight and [a] half bushels of new wheat [I] paid [a] half Joe in gold and half a dollar; two bushels of Indian corn for which I stand indebted to him ten shillings, specie.

NOVEMBER 7. Bought seven pounds of beeswax at eighteen pence specie per pound.

10. One hundred and fifty [of] Lee's troop [of] light horse and one hundred and fifty foot soldiers came to Lancaster this afternoon on their way to the southward.

11. Breakfasted Peter Bowman; brought [a] load of wood, this makes eight loads, for which I paid him in specie, Five Pounds, twelve shillings. I paid him also for twenty-four bushels of wheat, I had agreed with him for, Nine Pounds, twelve shillings, and for two bushels of Indian corn, nine shillings. ...... I paid him for three bushels of buckwheat nine shillings and for [a] quarter of veal we had received before, three shillings.

12. It's said that the Susquehanna and Conestoga rivers through the long drought [are] so low that people may walk over them by stepping from stone to stone.

14. The foot troops left Lancaster this day.

15. Bought a side of beef, hind quarter, one hundred and twenty pounds at five pence, fore [quarter] one hundred and fifteen pounds at four pence half penny, say Four Pounds, thirteen shillings in specie. ...... Bought [a] loin of mutton [which] our butcher sent, at Five Dollars (say Forty Dollars).

18. Bought [a] hind quarter of beef, weighed one hundred and forty pounds at seven pence per pound, Four Pounds, one shilling and eight pence specie. Bought [a] hind quarter of pork, weighed forty-five pounds, at Six Dollars, say Two hundred and seventy Dollars.

20. Paid Smith the cooper thirty dollars for coopering, making head for the cask of antimony to send to Philada. Many of the officers that were prisoners here went off to-day for New York, being exchanged.

23. News to-day that Gen. Cornwallis, with three

hundred horse and two hundred foot, was waylaid near Reed's bridge, defeated and he and most of his troops that escorted him taken prisoners.[1] I then went to Gaspar Shaffner's; stayed in settling the accounts till after dark. Then Gaspar Shaffner, Daniel Whitelock, Jacob Miller and self went to John Franks's [and] drank three pints [of] Madeira wine. Jacob paid for it One hundred and fifty Dollars. Both he and Daniel were pleased with the settlement.

27. By accounts from [the] West Indies, it appears that there was [a] violent hurricane that began [on] the eleventh [of] October and continued about ten days. The same destroyed about two-thirds of their principal town with three thousand of the inhabitants. The island of Nevis almost all destroyed. St. Eustatia sustained damages, it's said, to the amount of One hundred thousand Pounds sterling with great loss of vessels and [a] great number of people belonging to them, as some were seen to founder, others blown ashore, &c.

28. Bought [an] old jacket; cost seventy-five dollars.

DECEMBER 5. Near noon came Isaac Taylor; brought three fat hogs [which] weighed four hundred and ninety-two pounds; paid six pence per pound in specie, say Twelve Pounds, twelve shillings.

8. It's said that sixty light horsemen, who had served their time out, left their horses here, in order to go home to Virginia, as they could not get their pay in the army for [a] considerable time past. So they went away pennyless.

10. Went to meeting that consisted of six men and self, four boys, three women [and] two girls. At this meeting Daniel Whitelock was disowned for excessive drinking and joining with the company that celebrated the Independency of America on the fifth of last July.

14. Came Michael Gross; bought twenty-five bushels

---

[1] This was a false report.

of oats; paid three shillings per bushel in specie, (say Three Pounds fifteen shillings). Came likewise Michael Finicune [with a] load of green hickory firewood, Three Dollars specie (say twenty-two shillings and six pence).

16. Two bushels of turnips three shillings specie.

23. My wife rose early, having some things to do; made a fire in my room; called her negro woman, which affronted her so that she behaved very saucy to her mistress. Hearing the noise in the kitchen I arose, went, found Madam very impertinent. This obliged me to give her sundry stripes with a cowskin, but as she promised to behave better in future I was pacified for the present.

30. John Huber sent us five bushels [of] buckwheat ground into fine meal at three shillings specie per bushel, say fifteen shillings.

1781.

JANUARY 5. This day Major Wertz was bound over before Wm. Henry for refusing to take the state money at the value of gold and silver.

6. Report brought here that the Pennsylvania line of troops mutinied on the first instant, in which some lives were lost, had left their camp and were marching for Philada.

11. News that the Pennsylvania line halted at Princeton, where our President, with Gov. Livingston[1] and [a] Committee of Congress met them, promised them their pay, clothes, &c., on which they returned after delivering up two men, who came to them to persuade the army to go to New York with them, making them great promises which they rejected with contempt. It's farther said that the army had committed no violence of any kind, either before they set out or on the road, as was represented in the first news that was brought here.

---

[1] Of New Jersey.

14. I went to meeting that consisted of eight men and self, two women, two boys and two girls (silent). At the close Caleb Cope stood up and read a paper of excommunication against Alice Harry (maiden name) for marrying James Ramsey, who and she are constant attenders of this meeting. I thereupon got up and came home.

15. News to-day of the English under Benedict Arnold, landing in Virginia, going to Richmond and Williamsburgh.

17. A. still the same idle, saucy, impertinent old man, never seemingly contented or happy. Here is one of our daily crosses in bearing with his unpolite and proud spirit.

29. Henry Huddlestine with me being appointed; fixed the tax for providing a soldier in the fourth class, my tax being One hundred and fifty Dollars, which I paid to Wm. Burkett, the captain, who was collector of it.

FEBRUARY 5. I visited Dr. Neff, very poorly; prescribed and mixed a julep, gave him. Although he and son [are] so cried up for skill, &c.,my judgment is that they are quite Ignoramuses in preparing and administering physic with any degree of sound judgment.

6. Paid One hundred and twenty Dollars for redwood, madder, indigo, &c., for Mammy's counterpane.

10. A piece of news was sent me up from town by Joseph Hubley, viz: "General Morgan against Lieut. Colonel Tarleton. Action on the seventeenth January, 1781. Our loss twelve killed and sixty wounded. The enemy, ten commissioned officers and one hundred men killed, two hundred wounded, twenty commissioned officers and five hundred privates taken prisoners, with two standards, two pieces of artillery, eight hundred muskets, one travelling forge, thirty-five baggage wagons, seventy negroes and one hundred dragoon horses with their music; our force eight hundred against eleven

hundred of the Seventh and Seventy-First British Regiments. This happened at a place called the Cowpens, near Pacolet River, about sunrise, the seventeenth of January. The above account may be depended upon, was brought to Philada. by Gen. Morgan's Major of Brigade. P. S. The King's Speech is also [in] town. I hope this is an agreeable dish of news from your humble servant J. H."

12. At breakfast received ...... likewise the express from Gen. Morgan to Gen. Greene dated at camp near Cain Creek, January 19th, sent by express to Congress. (See above) ...... Went and attended the evolutions of the Light Horse and company of the militia in their exercises and street firing till near dark; left them at that employment, bells ringing, drums, fifes, trumpets, &c. They afterwards had bonfires, carousing at all or most of the taverns, as there was a collection made to treat the soldiery, who it's said behaved orderly, manly and pleasantly agreeable. No quarrels, as I have heard, although, as I'm informed, many drunken heads, before two o'clock in the morning.

15. It's said that one hundred and eighty prisoners were brought from Fort Frederick, going to Philada. These were part of those Scotch taken at sea a year or two ago.

17. This morning the Scotch prisoners that came [a] few days past marched towards Philadelphia. They don't appear to be those that were taken at sea, but part of those that were taken in a hospital about seven or eight months past.

20. Received the keg of five and a half gallons of wine sent by my sons in the wagon under the care of L. Lauman Jr. Freight thirty-seven and a half dollars.

21. Visited by Michael Mercer; says there's account of Paul Jones's arriving at Philada. from Europe. ...... Ball held this night at Barge's Tavern. The young woman that attended with coffee, &c., had two hundred dollars.

24. A., as commonly, saws [a] little firewood, sufficient for the present, cleans [the] stable, sits by [a] good fire, pretends to mend his breeches, stockings, clothes, &c., visits his neighbors, &c., &c. ; thus he employs himself from the time he arises between seven and eight in [the] morning to between nine and ten at night, as he never makes [a] fire in the house, cleans knives, forks, with other little occurrences that other men servants about house do and should do.

28. News that the French fleet under the Count D'Estaing met the English fleet bound to America off the Western Islands, ten men-of-war, six frigates and one hundred sail of transports. The French engaged, took seven men-of-war and three frigates with forty-five transports out of the hundred. This in Town's *Evening Packet*, it's said, just brought from Philadelphia. I waited on Edward Shippen with this news.

MARCH 1. We have an account that the Confederation was signed and ratified by the delegates of Maryland in Congress this day and announced publicly. See *Hall and Sellers's Gazette*, No. 2647.

7. Dined with us James Shields, light-horseman ; gave an account that some prisoners in the barracks, refugees, had some conversation amongst themselves on the practicability of blowing up our magazine. I went with him to Wm. Henry's, and Wm. Atlee had the person who told him sent for and examined, who related what he knew of the conversation. Atlee said he would send for the persons and send them to prison.

8. Visited by —— Shaffer. Account, he says, from Philadelphia that the English fleet has taken St. Eustatia. ...... It's said that fifteen hundred French troops are at the head of Elk, going to join our troops in Virginia.

17. Viewed near upon thirty of what's called St. Patrick's men, with effigy, drum, &c., parading the streets.

18. My wife and I went to meeting, that consisted of eight men, seven women, five boys, three girls (silent).

As we returned home C...... C...... was got home before us, where at his door which we passed, he, with three refugee officers who board there, was standing. One or more of the officers began to sing aloud out and so continued while we could hear. The others with C—— highly delighted. O wretched Toryism!

21. After [we] breakfasted, [visited] by Wm Henry, who said that account was just brought from Philada., that the English had taken St. Eustatia, Curacoa with all the shipping and had declared war against the Dutch and taken —— vessels in the Texel; particular and farther accounts expected.

23. Called at Henry's store; a large number there on the news brought of the defeat and surrender of Lord Cornwallis and his troops after a bloody engagement on the ninth instant, in which it's said several thousands were slain on both sides. Confirmation hourly expected.

28. News from C...... C...... that Gen. Greene was defeated by Cornwallis with the loss of three hundred of his men killed upon the spot.

30. News that Gen. Greene and Lord Cornwallis had an engagement; that Greene retreated one mile and [a] half, with [the] loss of three hundred men, but intended to attack Cornwallis [the] next morning but [a] heavy rain in the night prevented. It's observable that Cornwallis did not attempt to pursue Gen. Greene. An engagement, it's said, happened off the capes of Virginia between the English fleet and [the] French, the former thirteen ships, the latter nine, and not such heavy ships and metal, but were forced to run and got all safe into Rhode Island, but the English did not pursue them but put into Chesapeake Bay. Great trophies of victory! ...... Bought of Christy Snyder, nine pounds of butter at nine pence (say six shillings and nine pence, specie).

31. After breakfast took a walk to Wm. Burkett; paid him forty Continental dollars for fixing [a] small glass case for Ed. Milne of Philada. to send him.

April 4. Visited by Mrs. Cunningham; tells me there's news of a second engagement between [the] English and French fleets; that two seventy-four gun ships of the former were towed into the Bay.

5. Received a letter from sons of the third instant ...... also acquainted [me] with the death of Paul Fooks last sixth Day; buried next day.

10. News from Gen. Greene of [the] seventeenth [of] March says, he waited three days at the Ironworks, expecting Lord Cornwallis would have followed him in order to renew the action, but, by accounts, Lord [Cornwallis] was so galled in the former [of] the fifteenth, though he kept the ground and we lost our artillery, yet they of a sudden took their departure, leaving behind them evident marks of distress. All our wounded at Guilford who had fallen into their hands and seventy of their own, too bad to move, were left at New Garden. There is not one of the officers of the Guards, that formed the column of his army, but is either killed or wounded. Among the latter is Gen. O'Hara, mortally.[1] [Among the] killed is Lord Bute's son, Col. Stewart, &c., &c.

12. I am retired to my front room, going no where from home this week. ...... Indeed the behavior and conversation of most here on the nature of the times gives me pain. Men in words assuming to be hearty Whigs, but in their behavior rank Tories and enemies to Independency, there being but a small number of the true, sincere hearted Whigs left here at present to mourn for the abomination of the times, and of such there is great need, as so great a number are engaged in monopolizing, gaming, drinking, dancing, swearing, idleness, &c.

18. Yesterday, it's said, came to town on his journey to head quarters, Gen. Gates, with two Aides de camp

---

[1] He survived this wound and was one of those who surrendered at Yorktown.

and two baggage wagons. There came last week one hundred prisoners from Winchester, &c.

20. Near six, returned from [the] barracks, where I went to see, it's said, between five and six hundred prisoners, just brought from Virginia, among whom may be one hundred refugees or tories, whose appearance was the picture of human poverty and want, both in clothes, flesh and meager looks.

21. A. and Diana had had a scuffle, but as she made no complaint to me of his striking her in the face, I took no notice to her of it, though she complained to her mistress of her head's aching where she said he struck her; but in order to make up with her, he said, Diana, I will do anything for thee, but why does thee wear that handkerchief yesterday and now about thy head? thou shouldst wear a pretty cap and then I would love thee, &c. ...... Paid eighty dollars for mending sundry pewter tea-pots, &c.

25. A. got into his airs with the negro woman, and as I could not venture out, he triumphed for the space of near two hours, I think, without interruption, with vile ribaldry, papist swearing, cursing, &c., incoherent, scurrilous language that imperious pride, vanity and folly could invent or express.

26. Mrs. Cunningham at breakfast, who is very intelligent, says, News in town is that twenty sail of armed merchant ships in [a] few days had arrived in Philada. from [the] French West Indies; that Portugal had acceded to the neutrality [and] had joined the combined fleets; that on the fourth of January the important post San Juan was retaken by the Spaniards; that twenty-five English merchant ships are arrived at St. Lucia and that a fleet of French and Spanish had invested Pensacola. . .... Four hundred prisoners came, it's said, to-day.

30. Some time now about, three or four (as called) refugee officers being exchanged, there accompanied

them, from C...... C......'s, where they lodged, several of our light-horse officers, who, with C......, escorted them in grand order some miles out of town.

MAY 1. Received [a] letter from Samuel Wetherill, Jun[r]., with an address to the disowned of the People called Quakers where [ever] dispersed, dated [the] twenty-fourth [of] Fourth Month, signed by Sam[l]. Wetherill, Jr., Clerk.

6. Received [a] letter of the fourth, with two newspapers [and the] resolve of Council fixing exchange this month at one hundred and seventy-five per cent.

7. After breakfast went down to Wm. Henry's store; great debates there as the collector by Henry's order refused to receive the tax as [it] was laid by [the] Commissioners, which gives great uneasiness. ...... Went down town on public concerns; spent some time with Judge Atlee and sundry others, but to little purpose. [The] train of Artillery of [the] Pennsylvania line, under Major Eustace arrived here yesterday on their route to the Southward.

8. Mammy went to the potter's; bought eight hundred dollars' worth of earthenware. ...... The train of Artillery marched away this morning towards Wright's ferry.[1]

9. News just brought by Capt. Carson [who] left Philadelphia yesterday that a packet arrived in [a] short passage to New York with orders to Gen. Clinton to proceed to England with all the forces he can master, as rebellion had broken out in Scotland; upon which all our American prisoners there were discharged on their parole to the amount of three hundred, as they kept fifty sailors to help to navigate their vessels to England, and that many of the refugees in New York were determined to throw themselves on the mercies of the States from which they had run away, in consequence of which, it's said, many were arrived in the Jerseys, &c. It's further

---

[1] Now Columbia, Lancaster county.

said that [there has been] an engagement between the combined fleets and the English, in which the latter were defeated. Confirmation looked for.

12. Counting Continental money to know my stock. ...... Paid John Jones's tax, forty-five dollars. Paid Peter Shaffner my Continental two months' tax and county tax, Two Hundred and Eight Pounds.

15. Gen. Wayne with his suite came to town last evening, on his route to the southward. Near nine, attended [the] Grand Jury, where bills were found against Abraham Behm, Jacob Barkman [and] John Thompson for [a] high misdemeanor against the State, in aiding, abetting and encouraging the enemies of the state.

17. Went down to [the] Court House, where [the] Grand Jury found a bill against Josiah Brown for giving money, say three silver dollars, to Francis Steel and Peter Dill, two evidences against Abraham Behm, John Thompson and Jacob Barkman, in order to evade[1] their evidences. ...... Lent John Jones yesterday three hundred Continental dollars to pay Jacob —— for four State dollars at seventy-five for one.

18. Gen. Wayne with his suite left here yesterday

19. About noon George Robinson, light horseman, went to the barracks in order to rescue his comrade, a prisoner for abusing one of the militia. The sentry, one ——, refusing, he cocked his pistol, which the sentry observing, fired and killed him on the spot.

20. After breakfast came to town a number, say three hundred, of the Pennsylvania Line, on their route to the southward.

21. Account that last night, some of [the] light horse intended to assault the militia upon guard, on account of revenge, they said, for the murder of their comrade upon Seventh Day, but by the vigilance of the guards and

---

[1] Get rid of.

the careful intervention of the officers of [the] light horse, [it] was timely prevented without any hurt to either side. ...... In the afternoon a small shock of an earthquake.

    27. Arose early ; breakfasted, set off with Christopher in his carriage ; baited at Samuel Hopkins's ; proceeded to Thomas Downing's ; reached it near sundown; roads extremely muddy ; supped and lodged there in Downing Town.

    28. Arose early ; breakfasted ; fine pleasant morning; set off with Hambright ; the roads so bad, by his advice left [the] Great Road ; crossed John Baldwin's place into the Boot Road ; baited at [the] sign of [the] Boot ; thence to the Square ; dined there ; set off, went through Derby, got to Philada. by sundown. The roads were good this way.

    29. Viewed the City Militia under arms in Market street.

    31. Paid tax to Robert Cather, Eighty-two pounds, eleven shillings, class tax for High Street Ward. ...... Paid tax to Christopher Barthing, One Hundred and fifty-two Pounds, class and county for Mulberry Ward.

    JUNE 3. Account that the Holker, with three other vessels, arrived here and that the French fleet was arrived in the West Indies, had engaged the English fleet, &c.

    4. To monthly meeting of Friends held at Sam[l] Wetherill's house ; very solid and weighty ; adjourned near one to four o'clock ; dined at Christopher's ; returned to the meeting, that broke up near seven o'clock, at which several weighty rules were adopted in the same line on the same principles that Friends first established.[1]

    5. With John Hopson, engaged in preparing Bills regular for the Loan Office. Last Seventh day [the] Committee of the whole House of Assembly [met] to

---

    [1] From these meetings sprang the society of Free Quakers, formerly worshiping in the building still standing at the S. W. corner of Fifth and Arch streets. The Whigs of Philadelphia contributed to its erection.

consider the repeal of the Tender Act ; adjourned to yesterday.

9. News of the day is that the Spaniards had taken Pensacola [on] the twenty-fifth [of] last month ; that all the conquests made by the English on the French at the time when they took Pondicherry are now retaken by Hyder Aly Kan, an Indian King, and offered by him to the French nation ; that the English were beaten in the country of Arcot ; their armament in India inferior to that of the French there under the command of Mons. D'Orvis.

12. Three vessels arrived this afternoon from the Havannah.

14. Spent some time at Francis Bailey's with Sr James Jay, a writer in Bailey's paper under the signature of the Independent Whig, Plain Truth, &c.

22. Visited by Col. Bayard and S^r. James Jay ; spent some time in conversation on the publications going to the press respecting the conduct of [James] Duane, &c.

24. To Friends' Meeting at [the] Academy, where Saml. Wetherill and Jehu Eldridge spoke. After dinner to meeting [at the] said place, when the aforesaid persons spoke. After worship over, a few of us had a conference relating to future proceedings.

30. I went in chair to my old pasture house, where associated twenty-two men, women and children. Drank tea there, came back in the evening.

JULY 2. Went to the monthly meeting held at Saml. Wetherill's ; consisted of sixteen men, who very amicably adjusted sundry weighty matters. Adjourned to this day week; James Howell, Tim. Matlack and self appointed to draw up a paper to Friends of this city against that time for their approbation.

4. This being the anniversary of [the] sixth year [of] Independency, bells rung, guns fired, a cold collation at the State House. I went not to partake of it, but went in the evening to see some fireworks played off. There

was a great number of people but no accident happened, as I've heard.

6. Went to Tim. Matlack by appointment in order to frame an address to the Friends of the three monthly meetings in Philada. in order to communicate our sentiments respecting our right to the use of the meetinghouses of this city in common with them, and also to their burial ground. Adjourned to six this evening to meet at the house of Sam¹. Wetherill, where we accordingly met. The address [was] read, with some small alterations agreed to, [a] copy of which is to be presented at the three next monthly meetings in this city.

8. Yesterday arrived a flag [ship]; brought a number of the distressed, virtuous inhabitants of Carolina. This is, I think, the third vessel come from there, in a few days, on that account.

9. I went to Friends' monthly meeting at Sam¹ Wetherill's house, where the sundry affairs relating to the good and orderly conversation of Friends was amicably settled in brotherly love and condescension, the three copies for the three monthly meetings to be signed by the clerk, and Moses Bartram, Peter Thompson and Timothy Matlack appointed to attend and deliver one of them at each meeting-house, after meeting of worship is finished and the proceeding to business.

11. Butter in market [is] said to sell from eighteen pence to two shillings and six pence per pound. ......
Bought one pound of green tea; cost forty shillings, hard.

14. President Huntington came, took his leave of me very politely, as he with his family was leaving this state for his own home.

20. A flag [ship] from Carolina with many of the virtuous, unfortunate inhabitants, few men, but many women and children.

22. Set off in Christopher's carriage with son Charles and grandson Charles about six; stopped and baited

about fourteen miles from town; thence to the widow of John Jacobs; dined there; in the evening went to Thomas Downing's, tavern keeper, Downing Town; supped and stayed all night.

23. Breakfasted, set off; baited at the sign of the wagon, from thence to Wm. Bispham's; dined there; thence home.

24. Visited by Dr. Neff, Dr. Houston, Ed. Shippen and sundry neighbors. I returned the visit to Dr. Neff's, as his daughter Esther was married while I was from home.

25. Within two days the prisoners encamped here on the commons, being part of Burgoyne's [army], to the number of five hundred men and near the same of women and children, marched from here to their encampment near Little York.

29. I was obliged to rise soon, as our A. had his humor, so that he did not so much as turn the cow out. He was up, up stairs; seeing me about, came down. I said, A. why did you not turn the cow, &c., out? thou deservest to be turned out as well as she. He turns about in his usual manner, says, What! are you beginning again to trouble me? I stopped or I should have had a set down. He went up stairs again.

31. Paid George Burkett thirty shillings, hard, fourth class tax.

August 6. [A] countryman brought two pecks of potatoes; paid him eighteen pence, hard.

9. A. has been so much indulged that he can't cut [a] bit of grass for [the] cow without great uneasiness, yet eats and drinks quite hearty; can clean himself and go abroad, and stay from after dinner till late in the afternoon, and must be asked no questions. ...... Indeed we have the most lazy, impertinent, talkative, lying fellow that, I think, ever any family was troubled with. ...... News for some days past of the English's landing at [the] head of Elk, in order to pay Lancaster

a visit. Some people, I understand, talked of moving their goods and families. The militia were ordered to hold themselves in readiness upon call, &c.

11. A. gone into town for a considerable space of time. No account to be received from him for his proceedings, for, as he says, he is a righteous, good man; every thing he does is right.

14. A. went out, I was told, to preach to some people that asked him.

16. Last night my wife had some trouble with A. to get him to bed (as I was gone to bed); she got [him] up at last; whether he came down again don't know. For at these times he sets a talking such monstrous, foolish ribaldry to the negro woman that she has been afraid to go to sleep for fear, as he tells her, that the devil will come and fetch her away, &c. How that may be last night, I can't say whether he had frightened her or not, but this morning she is not to be found. I have hunted round about the place and neighborhood, but to no purpose; her clothes are all left except an old petticoat and jacket over her shift. By all our enquiry no news as yet of her. A. says she went out about day break, but there is no dependence upon any thing he says. He adds that she told him some dreams some time past and he had told her the interpretation, right, true, &c. ...... In the afternoon account brought [that] our negro woman was about two or three miles from town. Got Jeremiah Mosher and John Jones who brought her home.

17. When I arose, had the prospect of Antony cutting my carrots; had cut up one bed and would soon have served our whole little stock so. I was really put out of humor, as but a few days before he had stripped a parcel of my fine colderoe cabbage and destroyed great part of our potatoes under the notion of making them grow better.

26. Went to meeting; consisted of six men and self;

five women, three boys [and] one girl. Two of the women spoke by way of exhortation. The recruiting party here on Seventh day [had] possession of the meeting place, but left it during the meeting and behaved civilly. The Friends had moved all their chairs in the part locked up, but left our large chair that held four of the women, to take its fate. I remark this to show the little esteem and regard they have for our family, as this large garden chair was taken there for the use of the women Friends.

31. Engaged about sundry occurrences, as A. is still the sick, religious, wise and goodnatured, obliging man, &c.

SEPTEMBER 1. Visited to-day by Joseph Montgomery; stayed some time in conversation; he had got leave from Congress on account of his health. Received [a] letter from sons of the thirtieth (with some newspapers) giving an account that Gen. Washington and Count Rochambeau had arrived that [day] in Philadelphia, on their way to Virginia; that from five to seven thousand troops were on the road after them, and most of the small craft was gone to Trenton to forward them down to the head of Elk, &c., as it's not doubted that the French fleet are in Chesapeake Bay.

2. A. still in his wicked humors. ...... A. after dinner, though so poorly, he said, as not able to pull [a] few weeds for [the] cow, yet after eating a hearty dinner went abroad; returned by evening, but, as it was First Day, said it would not suit to pull weeds for [the] cow or cut grass for [the] horse, so I served them with hay. He was really very provoking this day, but as I had purposed, I said but little unto him, except requesting him to pack up his clothes to-morrow morning and be gone from here.

3. Afterwards came into the orchard, Antony; addressed himself to me by saying, Mr. Marshall, I am very sorry that I should give thee any trouble. It

troubles myself, and if thee will pass it by, I shall grow better and that every day. I answered him to this effect, Antony, thou hast so often misbehaved thyself, I can't tell what to say, but remember thee that long ago I would have turned thee away upon account of thy behavior: then thou desired me to pass all by, that thou didst not desire I should give thee any wages but such clothes as I thought convenient and thou wouldst strive to behave well for [the] time to come. [To] this he consented and said [it] was true, and desired that I would try him once more, in the same way, as he knew of no dlace to go to and would be contented with such necessaries as we thought suitable for him, upon which I took him again into favor.

5. My wife arose early; went to market. Loin of mutton, six and a half pounds at four pence; two shillings and two pence.

7. Various pieces of news but none I find to depend upon, as what is reported as yesterday [is] contradicted to-day.

8. Last night a feu de joie in Lancaster, firing guns, bonfire, &c., on account of the news.

10. A. little or nothing to do, yet still grumbling. He could not [eat] bread and butter with his tea this morning; he must and would have toast, and, as we had none ourselves, my wife thought he might do without, which offended him, so that he left it very much affronted.

11. A. little to do, but don't seem to be pleased; in [the] evening, gave me a set down by saying we fed every body else well but him, and he could be hearty and well if we gave him better victuals, &c., with a deal of such stuff that was becoming a man that had lost his reason.

15. Attending on A., who is now got into a fit of stillness which is very desirable.

19. News just verbal by Capt. Simmons [who] said [he] left Philadelphia yesterday at eleven A.M. Ex-

presses just arrived with accounts of [an] engagement between the English and French fleets near [the] Chesapeake; that the latter had taken from the former three [ships of] seventy-four guns and two smaller and were in possession of the bay, as the English returned to New York. By deserter from Lord Cornwallis (come, I think, yesterday) that Lord Cornwallis had put his garrison upon half allowance, and the negroes obliged to eat horseflesh, &c. From Pittsburg it's said the English and Indians from Detroit, on the eighteenth [of] last month, took possession of the Moravian settlement between North Carolina and Virginia on the Muskingum River, took all the whites and Indians prisoners, carried them bound to Detroit, say two or three hundred.

21. The artillery recruits marched for Philadelphia. News just come by Richards's son for the Lieutenant to call the militia, as it's said that Clinton has embarked five thousand troops to invade Philadelphia. ...... In the evening came Christopher Gadsden; stayed some time in conversation. I went with him to the tavern; stayed some time with him and his companions.

22. Past eight, came Christopher Gadsden, his son, Thomas Ferguson, ——— Hutson, ——— Cattill, ——— Beresford, ——— Roberts, Wilson and Phillips; breakfasted with us. These were on their journey towards Charleston. I afterwards accompanied them to the tavern; waited till they departed in high spirits. Received [a] letter from my sons of the twentieth, with some newspapers. Their letter informed [that] all our families were well, but there was a rumor of the English's embarking five thousand men at New York to destroy their city. This to some gave great uneasiness. This day the light-horse here marched for Philad^a. and orders came for calling the militia. Passed through this afternoon, one hundred and fifty-three recruits from York, but raised at Reading, for Philad^a.

24. A. the most pleasant and obliging of any time I

can recollect for these two years past. ...... Bought [a] loin of mutton, weight eight and a half pounds, cost two shillings and eleven pence hard. ...... No person, that I know of, had affronted A., as he eat his dinner just at dark, yet he took an opportunity, something passed in the stable, that he really paid me most severely with his tongue. I desired him to be quiet and behave himself. I had not asked where he had been spending his time, so that he might be quiet, as I was. This rather encouraged him to talk the more. Susanna heard him, came to the stable to quiet him. All to no purpose. He said he was [a] quiet, still, good man and he loved to be quiet. I at last told him A. it is quite uncivil and unmannerly to serve me so. I will, thou mayest depend upon it, give thee a good whipping if thou goest on in this manner. I can not nor will not put up with it and I desire thou mayest in the morning pick up thy things and go somewhere else, for I cannot bear it. So I left him, and I went, served and put up the creatures. Afterwards in [the] kitchen he got to preaching in a strange manner to the negro woman, so that my wife was obliged to interfere upon his saying he would strive to please no man, for he acted as the Lord bid him.

APPENDIX.

(A)

At the close of the First Volume of Mr. Marshall's Remembrancer are the accounts of the Overseers of the Poor (Christopher Marshall, James Eddy, George Morrison and Hugh Forbes) for the year commencing in March, 1758. Many of the entries are curious as throwing light upon the manners of the time; others, as furnishing us with the prices of that day. A few are subjoined. The accounts are in Pennsylvania currency.

City of Philadelphia for the Poor, Dr.

1758			£.	s.	d.
May	7.	To two negroes, wheeling Cath. Shannon to Alms House		1	6
	8.	To turning an old beggar out of town, 1s. His coffee, 1s. 6d.		2	6
	15.	To Saml. Crispin for Margt. Grant's child's coffin		5	0
	18.	To Granny Ganderwit for laying Mary Mackinary	1	0	0
	19.	To Mary Mackinary, lying in		5	0
July	7.	To John Wallace's bill for wood, being twelve cords	6	10	3
	14.	To amount of Pension Book [1] from March 30 to June 25	67	14	0
Oct.	3.	To amount of Pension Book from June 30 to Sept. 22	63	13	6

[1] For the out-door poor.

1758
Oct.	23.	To cash, quart of rum for tailor		1	1
	31.	To Hannah Pearson, for *part* curing Mary Carter's scald head	1	10	0
Nov.	18.	To Capt. Campbell for *freight* for Rachael Maguire and children to Carolina	1	7	0
	25.	To William Young *earthenware for a horse*	1	3	10
Dec.	16.	To poor woman to pay for lodging	0	0	4
	29.	To amount of Pension Book to the 15th inst.	57	13	11
	"	To cash to Granny Pawling for laying Peg Neal		10	0
	30.	To cash to taking man to workhouse and conveying him thence to Charleston		3	6

1759
Jan.	4.	To two pairs of breeches		6	8
	27.	To cash gave John Burden, his family very sick		5	0
Feb.	15.	To cash for four yards Osnabrigs for a shift for Rachael Glover		5	4
	27.	To cash for ferriage of Alice Holland to the Jerseys		0	4

Cr.

1758   £   s.   a.

Apr.	10.	By cash, of Robert Strettle fining a woman for swearing		5	0
July	22.	" " of Capt. Mitchell for expenses in burying of John Lindsey	1	0	1
	"	" " " of Capt. Mitchell,			

1758	his fine for swearing three oaths	15	0
Aug. 2.	" " of Widow Woman for restoring a little black pig, taken to the Alms House	10	0
8.	" " of Ed. Shippen, for five fines, viz. Aquila Jones, Geo. Bryan, Thomas Smith, John Jones, and John Jennings, for refusing to serve as Constables, at £5 each	25 0	0
28.	" " of the Mayor, for a fine, received of Mary Zebulum, for entertaining negroes	1 0	0
Oct. 7.	" " of Mary Chesnell, for entertaining a strange woman	10	0
Nov. 1.	" " of the Mayor, a fine he received of Capt. Gash, for refusing to entertain the officers billeted on him	3 0	0
9.	" " of James Coultass, late Sheriff, being a fine paid by Laughlane McClain for kissing of Osborn's wife (after his commissions and writing bond were deducted)	24 5	0
1759 Jan. 6.	" " for a poor sailor, of Capt. Farris	10	0

The totals for the period embraced in these accounts (from March 29, 1758, to March 26, 1759) are

				Receipts	£1189	s.	d.
Expenditures	£1103	4	10½			0	1
Commissions at 3¾ per c. on £1189		44	11	9			

$$£1147 \quad 16 \quad 7½$$

$$£41 \quad 4 \quad 2½$$

To which add for sum short in one of the duplicates

$$9 \quad 1 \quad 11$$

$$£50 \quad 6 \quad 1½$$

There appear in these accounts no receipts of taxes for the support of the poor. There is no mention of any money spent for segars, wines, liquors, &c., for the overseers, the charges for which, swell up Alms House accounts in these more modern times; nor does the word "sundries" once occur.

On the 20th of August, 1759, Thomas Lawrence, the Mayor of Philadelphia, directed the overseers to pay the above balance to their successors (Robert Towers, William Faulkener, James Stevenson, and James James). The receipt of Mr. Stevenson is endorsed upon the order.

(B)

Dr. Chovet's Lectures were on Anatomy. The following was his Advertisement.
"At the Anatomical Museum in Videl's Alley, Second Street, on Wednesday, the Seventh of December at six in the evening
DR. CHOVET
will begin his course of Anatomical and Physiological Lectures, in which the several parts of the human body will be demonstrated, with their mechanism and actions, together with the doctrines of life, health and the several effects resulting from the actions of the parts; on his curious collection of Anatomical wax-works, and other

natural preparations; to be continued the whole winter until the course is completed.

As this course cannot be attended with the disagreeable sight or smell of recent diseased and putrid carcases, which often disgust even the students in Physick, as well as the curious, otherwise inclined to this useful and sublime part of natural philosophy, it is hoped this undertaking will meet with suitable encouragement.

Tickets to be had for the whole course at Dr. Chovet's house in Second Street, Philadelphia."

A writer in the *New York Gazette* in 1828, over the signature of "An Old Philadelphian," speaks of Dr. Chovet as follows:

"Dr. Chovet, a most eccentric man, full of anecdote and noted for his propensity for what is now termed quizzing, resided in Race above Third Street. The Doctor was what was termed a Tory; was licensed to say and do what he pleased, at which no one took umbrage. He one day entered the Old Coffee House, corner of Market and Front Streets, with an open letter in his hand. It was twelve o'clock, change hour; the merchants all assembled. On seeing the Doctor they all surrounded him, enquiring what news he had in that letter, which he stated he had just received by a king's ship, arrived in New York. In reply to this inquiry, he said that the letter contained information of the death of an old cobbler in London, who had his stall in one of the by-streets, and asked the gentlemen what they supposed the cobbler had died worth. One said £5,000, another £10,000, and another £20,000, sterling. No, gentlemen, no; You are all mistaken; not one farthing, gentlemen; running out, laughing at the joke at the expense of the collected mercantile wisdom of the City.

"Another time, having been sent for to the Spanish Minister, Don Juan (I forget his name) who resided in old Mr. Chew's house in Third Street, between Walnut and Spruce Streets, the weather being rather unpleasant, the Minister ordered his carriage to the door to convey the Doctor home. The Doctor, full of fun and joke, directed the coachman to drive by the Coffee House, which, as he approached, was perceived by the merchants, who immediately drew up in order, hats off, to pay their respects to Don, as minister from a friendly power. The Doctor kept himself close back in the carriage until directly opposite the Coffee House, the gentlemen all bowing and scraping, when he pops out his head — good morning, gentlemen, good morning; I hope you are all well; thank you in the name of his Majesty King George; and drove off, laughing heartily at having again joked with the Philadelphia Whigs.

(C)

ETYMOLOGY OF THE WORD YANKEE.
(From the *Evening Post*, No. 53.)

When the New England colonies were first settled, the inhabitants were obliged to fight their way against many nations of Indians. They found but little difficulty in subduing them all, except one tribe, who were known by the name of Yankoos, which signifies *invincible*. After the waste of much blood and treasure, the Yankoos were at last subdued by the New Englanders. The remains of this nation (agreeably to the Indian custom) transferred their name to the conquerors. For a while they were called Yankoos, but from a corruption common to names in all languages, they got through time to the name of Yankees, a name which, we hope, will soon be equal to that of a Roman or an *ancient* Englishman.

(D)

LETTER OF THE HON. THOMAS M'KEAN, RESPECTING THE DECLARATION OF INDEPENDENCE.

PHILADELPHIA, *June* 16, 1817.

Messrs. William McKorkle and Son.

GENTLEMEN: Several applications having been recently made to me, to state the errors which I had observed and often mentioned in the publication of the names of the members of the Continental Congress, who declared in favor of the Independence of the United States on the 4th day of July, 1776 — I have not at present sufficient health and leisure to reply severally to each application. There can be but one correct statement of facts; one public statement, therefore, through the press, will serve the purpose of the gentlemen who have made the request, and may also give satisfaction to the minds of others, who have turned their thoughts upon the subject. If I am correct in my statement, it may be of use for future historians; if not, my errors can be readily corrected. I wish, therefore, by means of your paper, to make the following statement of the facts within my knowledge, relative to the subject of enquiry.

On Monday, the First Day of July, 1776, the arguments in Congress for and against the Declaration of Independence having been exhausted, and the measure fully considered, the Congress resolved itself into a Committee of the Whole; the question was put by the Chairman, and all the *States* voted in the affirmative, except Pennsylvania, which was in the negative, and Delaware, which was equally divided. Pennsylvania at that time had seven members, viz., John Morton, Benjamin Franklin, James Wilson, John Dickinson, Robert Morris, Thomas Willing, and Charles Humphreys. All were present on the First of July, and the three first named voted for the Declaration of Independence, the remaining four against it. The

State of Delaware had three members, Cæsar Rodney, George Read, and myself. George Read and I were present. I voted for it; George Read against it. When the President resumed the chair, the chairman of the committee of the whole made his report, which was not acted upon, until Thursday, the Fourth of July. In the mean time, I had written to press the attendance of Cæsar Rodney, the third delegate from Delaware, who appeared early on that day at the State House in his place. When the Congress assembled, the question was put on the report of the Committee of the Whole and approved by every *State.* Of the members from Pennsylvania, the three first as above, voted in the affirmative, and the two last in the negative. John Dickinson and Robert Morris were present and did not take their seats on that day. Cæsar Rodney, for the State of Delaware, voted with me in the affirmative, and George Read in the negative.

Some months after this, I saw printed publications of the names of those gentlemen, who had, as it was said, voted for the Declaration of Independence, and observed that my own name was omitted. I was not a little surprised at, nor could I account for the omission; because I knew that on the 24th of June preceding, the deputies from the Committees of Pennsylvania, assembled in Provincial Conference, held at the Carpenters' Hall, Philadelphia, which had met on the 18th and chosen me their President, had unanimously declared their willingness to concur in a vote of the Congress, declaring the United colonies, Free and Independent States, and had ordered their Declaration to be signed, and their President to deliver it into Congress, which accordingly, I did, the day following; I knew also that a regiment of associators, of which I was Colonel, had at the end of May before, unanimously made the same declaration. These circumstances were mentioned at the time to the gentlemen of my acquaintance. The error remained uncorrected until the year 1781, when I was appointed to publish the laws of Pennsylvania, to which I prefixed the Declaration of Independence and inserted my own name with the names of my colleagues. Afterwards, in 1797, when the late A. J. Dallas, Esqr., then Secretary of the Commonwealth, was appointed to publish an edition of the laws, on comparing the names published as subscribed to the Declaration of Independence, he observed a variance: and the omission in some publications of the name of Thomas McKean; having procured a certificate from the Secretary of State that the name of Thomas McKean was affixed in his own hand writing to the original Declaration of Independence, though omitted in the Journal of Congress, Mr. Dallas then requested an explanation of this circumstance from me, and from my answer to this application, the following extracts were taken and published by Mr. Dallas in the Appendix to the first volume of his edition to the laws.

"For several years past I have been taught to think less unfavorably of skepticism than formerly. So many things have been misrepresented, misstated and erroneously printed (with seeming authenticity) under my own eye, as in my opinion to render those who doubt of every thing not altogether inexcusable. The publication of the Declaration of Independence on the 4th day of July, 1776, as printed in the *Journals of Congress*, vol. 2, page 242, &c., and also in the acts of most public bodies since, so far as respects the names of the delegates or deputies who made that declaration, has led to the above reflection. By the printed publications referred to, it would appear as if the fifty-five gentlemen, whose names are there printed, and none other, were on that day, personally present in Congress and assenting to the declaration; whereas the truth is otherwise. The following gentlemen were not members on the 4th of July, 1776, namely, Matthew Thornton, Benjamin Rush, George Clymer, James Smith, George Taylor, and George Ross, Esquires. The five last named were not chosen delegates until the 20th of that month; the first not until the 12th day of September, following, nor did he take his seat in Congress until the 4th of November, which was four months after. The *Journal of Congress* vol. 2d, pages 277 and 442, as well as those of the Assembly of the State of Pennsylvania, page 53, and of the General Assembly of New Hampshire establish these facts. Although the six gentlemen named had been very active in the American cause, and some of them, to my own knowledge, warmly in favor of its independence previous to the day on which it was declared, yet I personally know that none of them were in Congress on that day.

"Modesty should not rob a man of his just honor, when by that honor his modesty cannot be offended. My name is not in printed journals of Congress, as a party to the Declaration of Independence, and this, like an error in the first correction, has vitiated most of the subsequent publications, and yet the fact is that I was then a member of Congress for the State of Delaware, was personally present in Congress, and voted in favor of Independence on the 4th of July, 1776, and signed the Declaration after it had been engrossed on parchment, where my name in my own hand writing still appears. Henry Wisner, of the State of New York, was also in Congress and voted for Independence.

"I do not know how the misstatement in the printed journals has happened. The manuscript *public* journal has no names annexed to the Declaration of Independence, nor has the *secret* journal; but it appears by the latter that on the 19th day of July, 1776, the Congress directed that it should be engrossed on parchment and signed by *every member*, and that it was so produced on the 2d of August and signed. This is interlined in the secret journal in the hand writing of Charles Thomson, Esq., the Secretary. The present Secretary of State of the United States and myself have lately inspected the journals, and seen this. The journal was first printed by Mr. John Dunlap, in 1778, and probably copies, with the names they signed to it, were printed in August 1776, and that Mr. Dunlap printed the names from one of them."

Your most obedient servant,
Thos. McKean.

(E)

The following Proclamations and General Orders were issued shortly after General Putnam's assuming the command in Philadelphia.

Philadelphia, *December* 12, 1776.

All officers of the Continental army who are now in this City by furlough or order (those only excepted who are in the recruiting service or who may have leave of absence in writing from the Commander in Chief) are hereby required to join their respective corps before tomorrow evening.

Officers who have the charge of sick soldiers in or near the City, and who are included in the foregoing order, are directed to make returns to Dr. Jonathan Potts, at Mr. John Biddle's in Market Street, of the numbers and places of residence of their sick, that proper care may be taken of them.

The late advances of the enemy towards this place oblige the General to request the inhabitants of this City not to appear in the streets after ten o'clock at night, as he has given orders to the picket guard to arrest and confine all persons who may be found in the streets after that hour. Physicians and others, having essential business abroad after the hour, are directed to call at Head Quarters for passes.

Israel Putnam.

HEAD QUARTERS, PHILA., *December* 13, 1776.

The General has been informed that some weak or wicked men have maliciously reported that it is the design and wish of the officers and men in the Continental army to burn and destroy the city of Philadelphia. To counteract such a false and scandalous report, he thinks it necessary to inform the inhabitants who propose to remain in the City, that he has received positive orders from the Honorable Continental Congress and from his Excellency General WASHINGTON, to secure and protect the city of Philadelphia against all invaders and enemies. The General will consider every attempt to burn the city of Philadelphia as a crime of the blackest dye, and will, without ceremony, punish capitally, any incendiary who shall have the hardness and cruelty to attempt it.

The General commands all able bodied men in the city of Philadelphia who are not conscientiously scrupulous against bearing arms, and who have not been known heretofore to entertain such scruples, to appear in the State House Yard to-morrow morning, at ten o'clock, with their arms and accoutrements. This order must be complied with; the General being resolutely determined that no person shall remain in this City an idle spectator of the present contest who has it in his power to injure the American cause or who may refuse to lend his aid to the support of it, persons under conscientious scruples before mentioned, only excepted.

All persons who have arms or accoutrements which they cannot or do not mean to employ in defence of America, are hereby ordered to deliver them to Mr. Robert Towers, who will pay for the same. Those who are convicted of secreting any arms or accoutrements will be severely punished.

ISRAEL PUTNAM, *Major General.*

GENERAL ORDERS.

Head Quarters, Phila., *Dec.* 14, 1776.

Col. Griffin is appointed Adjutant General to the troops in and about this City. All orders from the General through him, either written or verbal, are to be strictly attended to and punctually obeyed.

The General, to his great astonishment, has been informed that several of the inhabitants of this city have refused to take the Continental Currency in payment for goods. In future, should any of the inhabitants be so lost to public virtue and the welfare of their country as to presume to refuse the currency of the American States in payment for any commodities they may have for sale, the goods shall be forfeited, and the person or persons so refusing committed to close confinement.

In case of an alarm of fire, the city guards and patrols are to suffer the inhabitants to pass unmolested at any hour of the night, and the good people of Philadelphia are earnestly requested and desired to give every assistance in their power with engines and buckets to extinguish the fire. And as the Congress have ordered the City to be defended to the last extremity, the General hopes that no person will refuse to give every assistance possible to complete the fortifications that are to be erected in and about the city.

Israel Putnam, *Major General.*

(F)

From *McFingal*, lines 1274-1301.

Hath not Heaven warned you what must ensue
And Providence declared against you ;
Hung forth its dire portents of war

By signs[1] and beacons in the air;
Alarmed old women all around,
By fearful noises under ground,
While earth for many dozen leagues
Groaned with her dismal load of whigs?
Was there a meteor far or wide
But mustered on the Tory side?
A star malign that has not bent
Its aspects for the parliament,
Forboding your defeat and misery,
As once they warred against old Sisera?
Was there a cloud that spread the skies
But bore our armies of allies?
While dreadful hosts of fire stood forth
Mid baleful glimm'rings from the north;
Which plainly shows which part they joined,
For North's the minister, ye mind,
Whence oft your quibblers in gazettes
On northern blasts have strained their wits;
And think ye not the clouds know how
To make the pun as well as you?
Did there arise an apparition
But grinned forth ruin to sedition?
A death-watch but has joined our leagues
And clicked destruction to the Whigs?
Heard ye not when the wind was fair
At night, our or'tors in the air,
That loud as admiralty libel
Read awful chapters from the Bible,
And death and deviltry denounced
And told you how you'd soon be trounced?
I see to join our conquering side
Heaven, earth and hell at once ally'd.

---

[1] Such stories of prodigies were at that time industriously propagated by the tory party in various parts of New England, to terrify and intimidate the superstitious.

(G)

Abstract from the return of the number of houses and inhabitants in the city of Philadelphia, Northern Liberties and the district of Southwark, delivered to Lord Cornwallis by persons appointed for that purpose soon after the British troops took possession of the City.

	Occupied Dwellings.	Empty Dwellings.
City,	3,480	383
Northern Liberties,	1,151	135
Southwark,	764	72
	5,395	590

Total number of dwellings, 5,985.

	Occupied Stores.	Empty Stores.
City,	116	199
Northern Liberties,	.....	35
Southwark,	.....	6
	116	240

Total number of Stores, 356.

	Males under 18.	Males over 18 & under 60.	Females.
City,	3,411	3,359	9,077
Northern Liberties,	1,254	1,034	2,727
Southwark,	670	603	1,599
	5,335	4,996	13,403

Total number of Males under 60, 10,331

Total, 23,734

(H)

PRICES IN CONTINENTAL MONEY.

At Lancaster.

1779

Aug.	11.	A quarter of lamb, per pound, ...	$0.80
"	"	A pint of yeast, ...	0.50
Oct.	19.	Butter, per pound, ...	4.00
	27.	Two pence worth of yeast, ...	0.50
Nov.	11.	Rye, per bushel, ...	37.33½
"	"	Potatoes, per bushel, ...	32⅔
"	"	Turnips, per bushel	2.00
"	"	A load of wood, ...	35.00
"	18.	Butter, per pound, ...	5.00
Dec.	8.	Milk, per quart, ...	0.66⅔
"	"	Oak wood, per cord, ...	44.00
"	10.	Hogs, per pound, ...	2.00

1780

Mar.	24.	Shingle nails, per pound, ...	45.33⅓
Apr.	13.	Butter, per pound, ...	6.00
"	27.	Pine boards, per foot, ...	1.00
"	"	A pound of large nails.	12.00
May	26.	Butter, per pound, ...	8.00

At Philadelphia.

June	3.	A peck of green peas	38.00
"	"	Butter, per pound, ... 7.00 to	10.00
"	10.	Green peas, per peck, ... 10.00 to	15.00
"	"	Veal, per pound, ... 5.00 to	7.00
"	17.	Coffee, per pound, ...	8.00
"	22.	A piece of bobbin, ...	22.00
"	"	Teneriffe wine, per gallon, ...	85.33
"	23.	A pair of shoes, ...	120.00⅓
"	"	An iron bound painted barrel, ...	120.00
"	"	A pound of thread, ...	87.75
"	24.	A pair of razors (at auction), ...	29.00

1780.

JUNE	24.	Currants per pound (at auction),	$16.00
"	"	Tamarinds per pound (ditto),.........	20.00
"	"	White lump sugar, per pound (ditto),	20.00
"	27.	Figs, per pound,.......................	20.00
"	"	Bohea tea, per pound,................	80.00
JULY	5.	Butter per pound,........... 12.00 to	18.00
"	6.	Coarse tape, per yard, ...	1.11
"	7.	A pair of shoes,........................	120.00
"	8.	Butter, per pound,.. .... 12.00 to	16.00
"	"	A quarter of lamb,.....................	50.00

At Lancaster.

JULY	11.	A Bushel of oats,......................	21.00
"	15.	Hind quarter of mutton, per pound,	4.00
"	20.	Whortleberries, per quart, ...	3.75
"	21.	Butter, per pound,.....................	7.00
"	26.	A dough trough, ...	55.00
"	28.	Butter, per pound,.....................	10.00
"	31.	Fore quarter mutton, per pound,..	3.00
AUG.	1.	Sixpenny nails, per pound,...........	14.00
"	"	Hoops for barrels, hogsheads, &c., each,.............	2.00
"	12.	Oats, per bushel,......................	18.00
SEPT.	1.	Butter, per pound,.....................	12.00
"	18.	A hickory broom, ...	4.00
"	23.	Loin of mutton, per pound, ...	4.50
"	25.	Tenpenny nails, per pound,.........	11.00
OCT.	6.	Loin of mutton, per pound, ...	4.00
"	7.	A broad ax, ...	20.00
"	12.	A skein of thread,.....................	2.00
"	13.	Butter, per pound,.....................	15.00
"	14.	A loaf of bread,..	4.00
"	31.	Hind quarter of beef, per pound,	4.50
NOV.	3.	A dozen of horn jacket buttons,	10.00
"	8.	Chestnuts, per quart,.................	3.00
"	14.	Loin of mutton, per pound, ...	5.00

1780.
"   18.   Hind quarter of pork, per pound, $3.00
"   21.   Eightpenny nails, per pound,........   20.00
"   23.   Madeira wine, per pint,.............. 50.00
1781.
Feb. 2. Butter, per pound,.................... 12.00
"   17. A straw bread basket,...............   8.00
"   28. A peck of white beans, ... 23.00
Mar. 2. Butter, per pound, ... 12.00
"   "   Eggs, per dozen,......................   6.00
"   20. Butter, per pound,.................... 12.00
"   21. Tow linen, per yard,... ....   20.00
Apr. 28. Butter, per pound,.................... 12.00

(I)

DEATH OF MRS. MARSHALL.

From the *Pennsylvania Freeman's Journal*, September 4, 1782.

On Monday, the 26th ultimo, died at Lancaster, in the 61st year of her age, Mrs. Abigail Marshall, the late admirable consort of Christopher Marshall, Esq., and on Wednesday, the 28th, her corpse was interred in the Friends' burying ground, attended by a numerous and respectable concourse of people both from town and country. The character of this truly virtuous woman is beyond all panegyric; to enumerate the various instances of her benevolent and charitable actions would far exceed the bounds usually allotted for this purpose in a newspaper; sufficient be it to say that in her was united the amiable manner, the heart of tenderness and sensibility, and every Christian and social virtue. Her surviving partner has lost in her a most prudent and affectionate wife; the necessitous and the stranger by he rdeath are deprived of a most humane, hospitable and generous benefactress, and her relations and acquaintances of a religious, faithful and steady friend.

> Onward she moved to meet her latter end,
> Angels around befriending virtue's friend;
> Sunk to the grave with unperceived decay,
> While resignation gently sloped the way;
> Saw all her prospects bright'ning to the last.
> And heaven commencing ere the world was past.

INDEX.

A., 241, 263, 268, 270, 273, 279, 280, 281, 283, 284.
A........, Wm., 244.
Abington, 167.
Active, sloop, 239.
Adams, John, 9, 25, 30, 31, 43, 49, 61, 63, 83, 91, 228.
Adams, Mr., 22.
Adams, Samuel, 9, 25, 30, 31, 43, 49, 52, 53, 59, 61, 63.
Address, an, 228.
Adgar, James, 184.
Advertiser, Dunlap's, 229.
Agnew, General, 134.
Albany, 47.
Alexander, ship, 9.
Alfrund, Benj., 212.
Allegiance, oath of, 120.
Allen, Andrew, 68; lieut. gov., 133.
Allen family, 68.
Allen, John, 168.
Allen, William Jr., 91.
Allison, Dr., 108.
Allison, F., 6.
Alms house, 28.
Alsop, John, 26.
Ambassador from the Free and Independent States of America, 175.
Amboy, 10, 113; troops for the army at, 87.
Amherst, Gen., 178.
America, 153; friends of, 57; French, Spanish, Prussian and Polish courts declared for the independency of, 175; Great Britain would mortgage, 63;
America. Independent states of, 214; invectives against the liberties of, 45; troops expected to be sent into, 69.
American, 169; army, baker to, 184; congress, 15; Crisis, 108, 113; magazines, 228; manufactory, 36; of wool, etc., subscribers to, meet, 54.
Americans, 153, 179, 213.
Amurath, sieges of, 209.
Anatomical museum, 288.
Anatomy, Dr. Chovet's lectures on, 288.
Anderson, 212.
Anderson, Captain, 118.
Anderson, James, 135.
André, Col., 263; hung, 263.
Andrew Doria, brig, 108.
Andrews, Mr., 159.
Annals of Ephrata, 153, 154, 158; of the Brethren at Ephrata, 122.
Antigua, 98; vessel fitted out at, 180.
Antis, Col., 153.
Antis, Frederick, 83, 102.
Antony, 222, 225, 230, 233, 235, 237, 258, 259, 262, 264, 281, 282.
Appendix, 285–303.
Apollo, the, 139.
Arbuthnot, 255.
Arcot, English beaten in the country of, 277.
Armitage, B., 83.
Armstrong, Gen., 151.
Arnold, 263.

Arnold, Benedict, 268.
Arnold, Col., 55.
Arnold, General, 94, 190, 211, 212, 262.
Arnold's treachery, particulars of, 263.
Arrall, Mrs., 86, 87.
Articles of confederation, etc., read in council, 146.
Ascension day, 240.
Ash, Captain, 48.
Ashley river, 221.
Ashton's ferry, 48.
Asia, the, 56, 79.
Assembly, the, 6, 7, 8, 10, 47, 48, 50, 78, 199.
Assembly, act of, 214.
Assembly, petition to, 174, 182, 240.
Associators, return of the, 89.
Atkinson, Wilton, 227.
Atlee, 242.
Atlee, Col., 240.
Atlee, Judge, 202, 232, 253, 254, 255, 261, 274.
Atlee, Mrs., 155.
Atlee, William, 124, 155, 175, 270.
Atlee, Wm. Augustus, 176.
August, the, 139.
Aurora, ship, 44.

B......, 129, 224, 225.
Bache, 162.
Bache, Richard, 56.
Badcock, Mr., 60.
Bailey, Francis, 167, 206, 277.
Baker, Jacob, 165.
Baldwin, Capt., 96.
Baldwin, John, 101, 276.
Bales, William, executed for street robbery, 69.
Ball, Col., 235.
Ball, William, 113.
Balls, Widow, 80.
Balm tea, 28.
Baltimore, 87, 125, 185, 209, 218, 244, 251; French ships arrived at, 219; ship arrived at, 196; sugars fallen at, 180.

Bambay Hook, 80.
Bannister, Col., 212.
Baptist meeting house, 64.
Barbadoes, 104; sugar, 159.
Barge, 269.
Barge, J., 78.
Barge's tavern, ball at, 269.
Barker, P., 213.
Barkman, Jacob, 275.
Barley, 253.
Barns, Cornelius, 248.
Barry, Capt., 172, 175.
Barthing, Christopher, 276.
Bartholomew, Benjamin, 86.
Bartholomew, Edward, 83.
Barton, Captain, 24.
Barton, Parson, 184, 200.
Barton, Thos., 182, 185.
Bartram, Job, 19.
Bartram, Moses, 278.
Basseterre, St. Kitts, fire at, 94.
Bath, Pa., mineral waters at, 31.
Battle of the kegs, 157, 186.
Bayard, Col., 98, 114, 134, 146, 277.
Bayard, Col. John, 91.
Bayard, John, 56, 58, 78, 92, 102, 139.
Bayard, Major, 42, 55, 57.
Bayonets, 63.
Bears, Isaac, 21.
Bedford, 227.
Bedford Co., 147.
Behm, Abraham, 275.
Belfast, 29; ship arrived from, 5, 8.
Belisarius, 232.
Bell, 57, 98.
Bell, William, 159.
Benezet, Anthony, 98.
Benezet, John, 44, 160.
Bengal, 235.
Benjamin, 119, 132, 137, 141, 165, 173; death of, 165.
Benny, grave of, 190.
Beresford, 283.
Berks Co., Pa., 8, 130.
Bermudas, vessel from, 95.
Bern, Lieut. Col., 123.
Berry, 214.

Bethlehem, 131; Moravian minister from, 183.
Bettering House, 28, 106, 130, 190.
Betterton, Benjamin, 39, 251.
Beulah, ship, 15.
Betsey, 248.
Betty, 203.
Bible, 167.
Biddle, Edward, 8.
Biddle, John, 295.
Biddle, Owen, 67, 68, 83, 86.
Billingsport, 81, 169.
Bill of rights, 253.
Bills of credit, 116; of Exchange, Cunningham's book on, 200.
Bispham, William, 236, 243, 279.
Bissel, Trail, 18.
Black Horse, the, 189.
Black Point, 254.
Blackwell, Thomas, 167.
Blair, 6.
Bland, Col., 205.
Bland, Richard, 25.
Bland Papers, 212.
Blewer, J., 78.
Blewer, Joseph, 83, 86.
Blue Ball, the, 199.
Blue mountains, 148.
Board of War, 164.
Boehm, 82.
Boehm, Philip, 86.
Bohea tea, 174.
Bond, Joseph, 212.
Bonham, 117.
Bonham, Mrs., 193.
Bonham, William, 193, 202.
Boot, sign of the, 276.
Bordentown, 108.
Bordge, Drewry, 212.
Boston, Thomas, 231.
Boston, 5, 6, 7, 8, 15, 16, 17, 18, 19, 21, 22, 26, 29, 30, 33, 34, 35, 37, 38, 43, 44, 46, 49, 57, 73, 159, 200, 243; committee, 226; delegates from, 30; frigate arrived at, 216; harbor, 32; Light house at entrance, burnt, 34; letter from, 205;

Boston, transports bound for, vessels arrived at, 182.
Bostonians, 5, 15, 23.
Boudinot, Mr., 186.
Bowers, Captain, 113.
Bowman, Peter, 264, 265.
Boyd, Sam'l, 253, 256, 261, 262.
Boyds, 177.
Bradford, Captain, 26, 27.
Bradford, William, 61, 91.
Bradford, W. and T., 19, 21.
Brandford, 18.
Brandywine, the, 138; shoals, 67.
Brant, 229.
Brattle, James, 56.
Brewer, 246.
Brewer, Wm., 245.
Brewster, Captain, 113.
Brewster, S., 78.
Brigantine beach, ship stranded at, 48, 49.
Bright, 62.
Bristol, 153; ship from, 14; Pa., 31.
Britain, 185, 187.
British, America, 8; army, 227; fleet returned to Sandy Hook, 200; Parliament, proceedings of, 6; story, 212.
Brookline, 18.
Brooks, J., 46.
Brooks, James, 45, 48, 131, 152.
Brown, Capt., 44, 242.
Brown, Dr., 32.
Brown, John, 144, 147, 164.
Brown, Josiah, 275.
Brown, Major, 51.
Brown, Mary, 142.
Brown, Mr., 60.
Brown, Wm., 135.
Bruce and Co., 65.
Brunswick, 114; news of Howe's army at, 105, 107, 108; heights of, 113.
Bryan, 242.
Bryan, George, 79, 144, 159, 186. 287.
Buck, sign of the, 243.
Bucks county, Pa., 8, 31, 88, 157; election in, 94; militia, 247.,

Buckwheat destroyed, 134.
Bull, Col., 116, 133, 153.
Bull, John, 44, 83, 86.
Bullock, 181.
Bullock, Archibald, 37.
Bunker's hill, 31, 38.
Burden, John, 286.
Burgesses, candidates for, 66.
Burgoyne, Gen., 35, 95, 130, 134, 135, 136, 137, 138, 139, 140, 145, 160, 188, 206, 207, 211, 220, 238, 279.
Burgoyne's army, 135, 206, 207; defeat, 137, 138; Light horse, 95.
Burkett, George, 279.
Burkett, Wm., 271, 268.
Burlington, 26; minister of, in the Jerseys, 46.
Burnell, Capt., 99.
Burnet, Bishop, 236.
Burnside, 70.
Burnside's school room, 70.
Burr, Thaddius, 19.
Bush, 208.
Bustleton, 181.
Bute, Lord, 272.
Butters, 229.
Byrne, James, 85.
Byron, Commodore, 205.
Byron, George, 206.

C...., C....., 271, 274.
Cadiz, 249.
Cadwalader, General, 132.
Cadwalader, John, 102.
Cain creek, 269.
Calais, 249.
Calbreth, Col., 126.
Caldwell, Charles, 177.
Cales, vessel from, 247.
Calleson, Mrs., 187.
Calvinist church, 60.
Cambridge, 18, 51: Lady Washington goes to camp at, 53.
Camden, continental flag flying at, 260.
Campbell, Capt., 259, 286.
Camphill, Gen., 136.

Campingtown, 99, 198.
Camptown, 86.
Canada, 58, 59, 103; gov. of, 35.
Canadians, 44, 122.
Cannon, 63.
Cannon, J., 66.
Cannon, James, 14, 16, 21, 32, 48, 62, 64, 65, 67, 68, 69, 70, 73, 74, 81, 83, 86, 88, 98, 122, 139, 197, 209, 233, 238, 742.
Cannon, Jane, 187.
Canterbury, 19.
Cape May, 55.
Carlisle, 124, 128, 143.
Carlisle, Abraham, 201, 204.
Carlton, Guy, 103.
Carolina, 25, 162, 231, 244, 249, 286; flag ship from, 278; province of, 5.
Carpenter's Hall, 79; election at, 14; funeral at, 49; meeting at, 7, 8.
Carryle, John, 187.
Carson, 62.
Carson, Capt., 274.
Carstins, William, 88.
Carter, 238.
Carter, Christopher, 45, 46.
Carter, Mary, 286.
Caruthers, John, 87.
Caruthers, Mr., 88.
Casco bay, 36, 178.
Cassandra, essays of, 62.
Castle, William, 38.
Caswell, Richard, 10, 25.
Cather, Robert, 276.
Cattill, 283.
Catty, 203.
Cecil county, Md., 225.
Chad's ford, 126, 127.
Chalkley, ship, 14.
Chambers, Lieutenant, 73.
Chamblee, fort, surrender of, 51.
Champlain, Lake, 94.
Chance, privateer, 75, 95.
Chandler, John, 163.
Charity, 150.

Charles, 119, 135, 147, 148, 159, 173, 179, 189, 190, 191, 194, 195, 196, 197, 198, 202, 203, 208, 209, 217, 218, 220, 226, 229, 230, 231, 245, 246, 248, 250, 252, 278; letter from, 226, 230, 231.
Charles, Chevalier, 80.
Charleston, 9, 17, 197, 218, 220, 227, 232, 244, 283, 286; attack on, 221; Cornwallis retreating towards, 260; dispute about, 247; flags of truce from, 248; Packet, brig, 24.
Charming Polly, schooner, arrives at Chester, 55.
Chase, Samuel, 25.
Chatham, 113.
Chatham, Lord, 164, 175.
Chemung, 229.
Chesapeake bay, 232, 271; engagement near the, 283; French fleet in, 281.
Chesnell, Mary, 287.
Chester, 45, 55, 84, 85; flags of truce at, 248.
Chester Co., Pa., 8, 126, 136, 138, 162, 170, 177; election in, 94; militia, 247.
Chestnut hill, 133, 182; Washington's army at, 148, 149.
Chevalier, Peter, 102.
Chevers, Capt., 9.
Chew, Mr., 289.
Chocolate, 62.
Chovet, Dr., 197, 198, 288, 289; lecture, 113.
Christ Church, 30, 32, 49, 153; bells muffled, 6; yard, 112.
Christian, the true, 225.
Christiana, 125.
Christianity, badge of, 150.
Christopher, 120, 128, 140, 147, 150, 191, 192, 195, 234, 247, 248, 251, 252, 253, 276, 278.
Church, 68; burial ground, 49; of England, 194; minister of the, 182.
Churchill, 212, 232.

City militia, 1st battalion, sermon preached to, 30.
City Tavern, 112.
Civil society, the, 120.
Clark, Col., 213.
Clark, Nancy, 217.
Clarke, Col., 174.
Clay, Captain, 41.
Cleamuns, Mrs., 46, 47.
Clementine, ship, 44.
Clifton, William, 61.
Cling, John, 251.
Clinton, 246, 283.
Clinton, Arnold, 135.
Clinton, Gen., 17, 60, 85, 135, 143, 186, 188, 263, 274; defeat of, 85.
Clymer, 49.
Clymer, George, 34, 37, 48, 50, 58, 67, 68, 83, 102, 117, 293.
Clynn, 86.
Coates, 250.
Coates, Col., 116.
Coates, William, 78, 83, 109, 167.
Cocoa, 62.
Cæcil county, Maryland, committee of, 86; court house, 125.
Coffee, 62; House, the, 29, 37, 39, 40, 41, 42, 43, 44, 48, 49, 50, 53, 56, 61, 62, 67, 69, 72, 75, 76, 77, 80, 86, 91, 98, 100, 105, 189, 198, 217, 245, 249.
Colden, Governo, 27.
College, part of the, used as barracks, 84; yard, 31.
Collins, Captain, 24, 217.
Collins, Stephen, 35, 189, 190, 202.
Colonial Records, 164, 198; of Pa., 201.
Columbia, Lancaster co., 274.
Combs, Thomas, 51.
Comet, sloop, 247.
Commissary of prisoners, 253.
Commissioner from the U. S., 228.
Committee, 19; called to meet, 45; of inspection, 83, 89, 99; of privates, 66; of Safety, 31, 33, 45, 46, 55, 75, 83, 90, 91, 93, 112, 147, 166,

Committee's store, saltpetre lodged in, 72.
Common Sense, 57, 113.
Concord, 18, 19, 26, 331; meeting, 127; road, the, 126; Court House, burnt, 19; ship, 5.
Conestoga creek, 143; river, 265.
Confession of faith, 121.
Congress, 9, 14, 26, 27, 29, 39, 44, 46, 47, 52, 54, 58, 59, 60, 66, 67, 72, 79, 91, 93, 108, 147, 148; committee of, 82, 267; handbills published by order of, 103; letters to, from Gen Lee, 85; money, 163; of deputies, 8; petition to the king, 37, 47; privateer, 75, 88; resolve of, 95, 110, 164; sloop, 95; vessel, takes a prize, 71.
Connecticut, 9, 18, 21, 58, 227; colony of, 25.
Connestoga creek, 207, 223.
Considerations on the mode and terms of a Treaty of Peace with America, 213.
Constitutional, Letter, 215; Post, account by, 35; arrived, 36; society, 15, 215, 217.
Continent, fast to be kept through this, 71.
Continental, army, 115, 121; bills, counterfeit, 177; of credit, refusal to receive, 101; of exchange, 150; congress, 13, 24, 29, 33, 35, 37, 80, 291; flag, at Camden and Yorktown, 260; fleet burnt, 180; money, prices in, 200; refusal to take, 59, 63, 65, 95; stables, 133, 164; tax, 275; collector of the, 200; paid, 261; troops; 192.
Convention of Pa., 78.
Conway, 159.
Conway, Gen., 151, 164.
Cooks, Major, 43.
Cooper, Dr., 238.
Cooper river, 221.
Cooper, Wm., 114.

Cooper's ferry, 127, 139, 157.
Cope, Caleb, 268.
Corbyn, Thomas, 45.
Corinthians, 194.
Cork, 26; ship from, arrived, 11.
Cornwallis, 248, 260, 265.
Cornwallis, Gen., 130, 142, 145, 250.
Cornwallis, Lord, 188, 271, 272, 283, 299; surrender of, 271.
Corryel's ferry, 143.
Corunna, 228.
Coultass, James, 287.
Council of safety, 103, 106, 108, 109, 110, 112, 113, 147, 165, 176; transcript from order of, 101.
County court, 122; memorial to, 75.
Court House, bonfire at, 264.
Court martial, held, 172; spy condemned by, to be hanged, 170.
Cowpens, action at, 269.
Cowperthwaite, Captain, 43.
Cox, Colonel, 84, 118, 183, 184, 188, 257.
Cox, John, 78, 92.
Cox, Major, 48, 56.
Cox, William, 186.
Craig, Capt., 75, 88.
Craig, Com., 188.
Creighton, the, 98.
Crisis, 16, 24, 173; the Present with respect to America, 16.
Crispin, Saml., 285.
Crooked Billet, the, 180, 181.
Crosswick's, 114.
Crown Point, 80, 99, 103; gov. of, 29.
Cruse, Capt., 54.
Cumberland Co., 84, 87, 167, 174, 210; militia, 143.
Cunningham, 200.
Cunningham, Mrs., 272, 273.
Curacoa, 271.
Cushing, Thomas, 9, 25, 30, 49.
Cuthbert, Thomas, 180, 238, 242, 247.

D......, 21.
Dallas, A. J., 293.
Danish officer, 104.
Darby, Captain, 34.
Darby, retreat of Gen. Howe's army from, 153
Darragh, Charles, 177.
Darragh, John, 199.
Darragh, Lydia, 179.
Davidson, 173.
Davidson, Jane, 63, 67, 77, 88, 144, 151, 160, 170, 187, 197, 233, 238, 244.
Davis, Captain, 84.
Davis, Colonel, 182.
Day, Capt., 239.
Dean, 218.
Dean, Capt., 16.
Deane, J., 78.
Deane, Silas, 25, 31, 49, 56, 58, 60, 178.
Deane, Simeon, 178, 179.
Death or Glory, motto, 16.
Debby, 230, 258.
Declaration of independence, 82, 83; letter respecting, 291–295; of rights, the, 103.
Dehaff, Henry, 127.
Deitrick, Jacob, 191.
DeKalb, Gen., 135, 159, 178, 247, 251, 260, 261.
DeKermorvan, Baraset, 150.
Delaware, 9, 94, 105, 116, 292, 240; the, 25, 88, 107, 127, 164; Indians, 216, 232; river, 120, 172; vessels in the, 201.
Delaney, 49.
Delany, S., 77.
Delany, Sharp, 52.
De Meralles, Don Juan, 197.
D'Estaing, 227.
D'Estaing, Admiral, 194.
D'Estaing, Count, 206, 230, 231, 232, 270.
Detroit, 125, 214, 283; fort, 151; garrison of, 192.
Deuteronomy, 194.
Dewees, William, 44.
De Weldke, General Baron, 63.

Diana, 273.
Dickenson, John, 7, 8, 10, 13, 44, 102, 105, 291, 292.
Dickinson, Col., 98.
Dickinson, Polly, 257.
Dill, Peter, 275.
Dinah, 42, 179; died, 179.
Dingee, 162.
Dobbs's ferry, 103.
Dominica, 98.
Dorsey, Capt., 58.
D'Orvis, Mons., 277.
Downing, Thomas, 276, 279.
Downing's, 253.
Downingstown, 197, 243, 253, 276, 279.
Douglass, Capt., 216.
Dover, 77; tea ship arrived, 5.
Doyle, Capt., 238.
Drinker, John, 59.
Drinker, Thomas, 59.
Duane, James, 26, 56, 277.
Dublin, 37, 38.
Duché, Jacob, 26, 27, 30, 49, 132, 142.
Duché, Parson, 198.
Duck Creek, 21.
Duffield, 6.
Duffield, William, 174, 199.
Dull, Gasper, 256.
Dunks, 143.
Dunks's ferry, 143.
Dunlap, 159, 206, 225, 238, 280.
Dunlap, John, 164, 188, 295.
Dunlap's Advertiser, 229; Gen. Advertiser, 54, 94, 95; newspaper, 159, 201, 206, 225, 260.
Dunmore, Governor, 24, 27.
Dunmore, Lord, 34.
Dunn, Robert, 194.
Dunop, Count, 139.
Dutch, 208, 209, 213, 253; and Spanish, ship arrived at Baltimore, 196; butcher, 31; disturbance among, 68; fashion, houses built in the, 199; holiday, 240; Presbyterian meeting house, 194; prisoners, 201; vessels, 255; war declared against, 271.

Dutchman, a, 131.
Dyer, Colonel, 31, 32, 53.
Dyer, Eliphalet, 25, 49.

E......, Saml., 244.
Eagle Point, 124.
Eagle, the ship, 141.
Eastburn, Robert, 168.
Easton, 115.
East Haven, 227.
East India tea, 14, 15.
East Indies, 228, 235.
East Jerseys, 114.
East river, 93.
Ecclesiastes, 194.
Eddy, James, 285.
Eden, William, 187.
Egg harbor, 48, 55, 88, 193, 201; French vessel puts into, 69.
E. Guilford, 18.
Eldridge, Jehu, 277.
Election day, 135.
Elizabethtown, 10, 15, 87, 211, 245; letter from, 205; point, 96.
Elk, head of, 270, 279, 281; Howe getting his men on shore at, 125.
Elliot, Christopher, 101.
Embden, port of, 145.
Empsons, Sally and Hannah, 252.
England, 14, 15, 34, 38, 92, 160, 229, 274; advices from, 73; commissioners from, arrived at Phila., 186; ministry in, changed, 175; war declared by, against France, 181.
English, 115, 196, 218, 232, 257, 277, 283; ambassador, 145; and French fleets, engagement between, 270, 271, 272, 183; arms, 80; army, 163; bondage, anniversary of freedom from, 251; church, 183; deserters, 177; engagement with militia, 180; fleet, 120; beaten, 227; frigates, 238; sunk, 161; guinea, 203; light horse, 182; magazine ship blown up, 196; English, men-of-war, 205; horses, 114; officer, 259; entertainment for, 237; visited by, 229; Presbyterian meeting, 264; prisoners, 111, 123, 200, 201, 249, 253; sent into Va., 281; routed, 234; shilling, 203; soldiers, 94; troops, 175, 234; cutting down wood in the Jerseys, 179; tyrants, 201; vessels, seized by Count D'Estaing, 231.
Englishman, 169; ancient, 290; the, 176.
Ephrata, 240; hospital at, 153.
Epsey, Daniel, 86.
Ereson, Benja., Jr., 121
Erskine, General, 134.
Erwine, Robt., 140.
Essays of Cassandra, 62.
Europe, arrival of Paul Jones from 269.
Eustace, Major, 274.
Eustatia, 54.
Evans, John, 176.
Evening Packet, Town's, 270.
Evening Post, 26, 27, 28, 29, 31, 40, 47, 54, 55, 64, 65, 69, 71, 72, 75, 76, 82, 85, 89, 90, 93, 94, 290.
Everlasting Gospel, the, 25, 215.
Ewing, Brig. Gen. James, 87.
Ewing, Rev. Dr., 233.
Executive Council, 150, 154, 171; of Pa., 186; pass from, 178; proclamation by, 126.
Expenditures, 288.
Experiment, 230, 232.
Eyre, Messrs., 65; building frigate, 65.

F...., Jabez, 21.
F., John, 198.
F...., Joshua, 72; and sons, 74.
F...., Tench, 54.
F...., Thomas, 74.
Fair American, the, 245.
Fair hill, 146.
Fairfield, 21, 51, 227.

Index. 313

Falconer, Nathaniel, 86.
Falmouth, town of, burned, 50.
Farey, Captain, 54.
Farmoah, Gen. 116.
Farran, James, 193, 208, 209, 210, 211.
Farris, Capt., 287.
Father Paul, 195.
Faulkener, William, 288.
Ferguson, Thomas, 283.
Finicune, Michael, 267.
Fire, cry of, 64.
Fisher, 59.
Fisher, Harry, 77.
Fisher, Henry, 67.
Fisher, Joshua and Sons, 91.
Fisher's island, 37.
Fishkill, 134.
Fitz, Capt., 196.
Flax, 253.
Fleming, Col., 111.
Fleming, R., 244.
Fleming's, Robert, 252.
Floyer, Col., 58.
Flying camp, 79, 82.
Fooks, 171, 173.
Fooks, Paul, 53, 56, 60, 63, 70, 75, 80, 83, 92, 95, 96, 106, 116, 117, 118, 142, 161, 169, 175, 176, 177, 181, 185, 195, 197, 200, 207, 209, 216, 218, 226, 228, 232, 233, 244, 245, 251, 272.
Forbes, Hugh, 285.
Ford, 198.
Forestalling act, 175.
Foster, Col., 18.
Fort, Chamblee, 51; Lee, 100, 104; Mifflin, 131, 144, 198; Montgomery, 134, 136; Pitt, 125; Washington, 114; taken by Gen. Howe, 104.
Foster, 117.
Fountain Tavern, 57
Fowey, man-of-war, 24, 57.
Fox, 219.
Fox, Joseph, 13, 95.
France, 118, 153, 162, 179, 201, 213, 243; court of, 178; fleet France, of, 257; goods from, 173; war declared against by England, 181.
Franklin, B., 61, 77, 85, 226.
Franklin, Benjamin, 44, 83, 91, 291.
Franklin, Dr., 15, 34, 116, 167, 175.
Franklin, Dr. Benjamin, 23, 26.
Franklin, Gov., 80; sent prisoner to Hartford, Ct., 80.
Franklin, privateer, 73; ship, 242.
Fredericksburgh, 194, 247.
Frederick, fort, prisoners brought from, 269.
Frederickstown, 194.
Freehold, N. J., 255.
Free Quakers, 276.
Free states of America, 132.
French, Major, 37.
French, 227, 228, 231, 277; admiral, surrender of Rhode Island to the, 196; ambassador, 197, 228; and English fleets, engagement between, 270, 271, 272, 283; army, 254; horses for, 254; brandy, 53; certificates, 248; court, 175; creek, 199; fleet, 182, 205, 206; at St. Martins, 252; off Cape Hatteras, 249; off Sandy Hook, 193, 194; gone to R. I., 194; reported defeated off Rhode Island, 261; frigate, 216; king, 226; ships, arrived, 245; spy, 171; West Indies, ships from, 273.
Friends, from Va., 177; meeting, 55, 123, 276, 277, 278; sent out of town, 127.
Friendship, ship, 11, 88.
Frog's point, 98.
Fulson, Col. Nathaniel, 9.
Furniture destroyed, 134.

G....., 215, 224.
G....., Samuel, 90, 93.
G....., Wm., 244.
Gadsden, Christopher, 9, 24, 32, 43, 57, 283.

Index.

Gafney, Capt., 7.
Gage, General, 26, 27, 33, 35, 38.
Galbraith, Col. Bartram, 87.
Gallaher, William, 126.
Galloway, Joseph, 8, 149.
Ganderwit, Granny, 285.
Gardiner, ——, 21.
Gardiner, Col., 20, 21.
Gardiner, Joseph, 139.
Gardiner's island, 37.
Garrigues, John Jr., 227.
Garrigues, Polly, 219.
Garrigues, Sam. Sr., 143.
Gartley, John, 87.
Gasp, Capt., 287.
Gates, 159.
Gates, General, 74, 75, 108, 137, 143, 145, 160, 161, 176, 179, 232, 260, 272.
Gates, Major General, 73.
Gazette, the, 12.
General Advertiser, 24.
General Assembly, act of, 208; committee, 7; Congress, 11; Orders, 295, 296, 297.
Gentleman's Calling, etc., 209.
George, 256; III, king, 6; king, 290; the third, 126, 149, 183; the third's fleet, 81; the tyrant, 256.
Georgetown, continental flag at, 260.
Georgia, 33, 38, 230, 231; Packet, 37; regiment, 124.
Georgians, 33.
Gerard, M., 197.
German men and women, 242; redemptioner, 188; riflemen, 93; papers, 221; printer, 184;
Germans, second division of, 208; first division of, 208.
Germantown, 79, 122, 131, 132, 133, 138, 142, 148, 184; part of burnt by British, 173; wheat seized near, 218.
Gerry, Elbridge, 147.
Gibraltar, Spaniards beseiging, 24.
Glasgow, 232.
Glentworth, D., 247.

Gloucester, 157.
Gloucester, Duke of, 24.
Glover, Rachael, 286.
Glotz, Col., 225, 227.
Glotz, Col. Jacob, 222, 223.
Gondolas, captains of, 75.
Goodwin, G., 78.
Gordon, Lord George, 261.
Governor's island, arrival of Gen. Clinton at, 60.
Govett, William, 31.
Gov. of Canada, 35.
Graeff, Mathias, 149.
Graff, Sebastian, 205.
Graham, R., 11.
Granada, 88, 158.
Grant, General, 134.
Grant, Major, 136.
Grant, Margaret, 285.
Gray, G., 10.
Gray, George, 44, 86, 102.
Gray, Isaac, 14, 73.
Gray, James, 244.
Great Britain, 8, 38, 63, 66; king of, 70; opposition to tyranny of, 81.
Greaves, Admiral, 35, 254, 255, 257, 261.
Greene, Gen., 145, 169, 176, 269, 271, 272.
Grenada, 227.
Grieb, Curtis, 187.
Griffin, Col., 297.
Gross, Michael, 266.
Guadaloupe, 243.
Guest, Col., 236.
Guilford, 18.
Guinea ship, 97.
Gunpowder, 63; landed near New York, 55.
Guns, 63.
Gurney, Col., 179.
Gurney, F., 78.
Gurney, Francis, 92.

H......, 224.
H... .., B., 218.
H. J., 269.
H......, Joshua, 244.

Index. 315

H... .., Levi, 218.
Haddonfield, 139.
Hale, 88.
Hale, Thomas, 209.
Halifax, 57, 200, 249; commissioners and Hessians arrive at, 72; taken by French fleet, 206; transports from, 81.
Hall, 56.
Hall, Charles, 215, 234, 239.
Hall, John, 25, 149, 168.
Hall and Sellers, 213; Gazette, 62, 270.
Halloway, Betsey, 219.
Hambright, 276.
Hambright, Councillor, 243.
Hamilton, 238.
Hamilton, Captain, 95.
Hamilton, Wm., 257.
Hammond, Capt., 177.
Hancock, brig, 99, 100.
Hancock, Col., 51, 52, 60, 61, 66, 92, 104.
Hancock, John, 25, 28, 35, 49.
Hancock, Mr., 22.
Hancock, Mrs., 52.
Hancock, President, 130.
Hand, Gen., 122.
Hannah, 190, 219; ship, 9.
Hanoverians, battalion of, 208.
Harbeson, Benj., 70, 73, 83, 84, 123, 153, 174, 188, 195, 217.
Hardie, William, 257.
Hardy, Sir Charles, 232.
Hare, Abraham, 264.
Hare, Robert, new house burnt, 64.
Harp and crown, sign of the, 78.
Harlem. 93.
Harris, 212.
Harris, Mary, 28.
Harris's ferry, 257.
Harrison, 206.
Harrison, Benjamin, 25, 44.
Harrison, Col., 53.
Harrisburg, 78, 257.
Harry, Alice, 268.
Hart, Joseph, 78.
Hart, sign of the, 196.
Hartford, 20, 80.

Hartley, Col., 161, 188, 193, 215.
Hartley on the Millenium, 187.
Haselet, Col. John, 115.
Hastings, 177.
Hastings, Captain, 49.
Hastings, Grace, 30, 177, 178, 207, 219, 245.
Hat, sign of the, 189, 220.
Hatteras, French fleet off cape, 249.
Hazard's Register, 219.
Hazlehurst, 93.
Head of Elk, 124, 125.
Hemp, 253.
Hemphill, William, 87.
Henderson, Archibald, 177.
Henry, Mr., 221.
Henry, Patrick, 25, 247.
Henry, Samuel, 124.
Henry, William, 139, 163, 175, 190, 194, 205, 208, 225, 226, 232, 236, 239, 254, 267, 270, 271, 274.
Hermione, ship, 244.
Hervey, Capt., 130, 194.
Hessian band of music, 170; chasseurs, 103; grenadiers, cross the Delaware, 139; prisoners, 109, 110, 123, 124, 200; soldiers, 94; troops, 108, 249; defeated, 112.
Hessians, 108, 168, 257.
Hewes, Joseph, 10, 25.
Hewey, 124.
Highlanders, taken by Col. Scott, 111; defeated, 112.
High treason, Molesworth, hung for, 201; John Roberts tried for, 201; Abraham Carlisle tried for, 201.
Hill, Henry, 83.
Hillegas, Michael, 10, 34, 44.
Hills, Richard, 49.
Hispaniola, 75; vessel from, 33.
Historical Society of Pa., 80.
History, Bishop Burnet's, of his own time, 236; of Chester county, Lewis's, 196; of Ephrata, 151; of Sumatra, 209; of the Brethren at Ephrata, 123.

Hoar, 61.
Hodge, 96.
Hodge's Wharf, 96.
Hoffs, Col., 222.
Hoffs, George, 222.
Hofnager, Peter, 237, 238.
Hogg, Esquire, 206.
Holker, John, 234.
Holland, Alice, 286.
Holland, 11; states of, 214; vessel from, 11.
Holliday, Robert, 21, 26.
Hollingshead, John, 123.
Holtzendorff, Baron De, 147.
Hope, ship, 9.
Hopking, 191, 216.
Hopkins, Governor, 60.
Hopkins, Samuel, 276.
Hopkins's Tavern, 191.
Hopson, John, 222, 276.
Horse racing, 256.
House, of Assembly, still sitting, 134; of commons, debates in, 5; of Employment, 112.
Houston, Dr., 240, 279.
Houston, Hon. John, 37.
Howe, 105, 121, 123, 124, 125, 126, 130, 134, 136, 137, 141, 144, 154, 162, 167, 168, 172, 173, 179.
Howe, Gen., 17, 35, 80, 82, 91, 97, 98, 100, 103, 104, 106, 107, 110, 113, 116, 120, 131, 132, 140, 143, 148, 149, 150, 152, 153, 156, 160, 163, 164, 169, 170, 183, 184, 186.
Howe, Lord, 91, 93, 136, 188.
Howe's light horse, 126.
Howell, Isaac, 14.
Howell, James, 277.
Howell, Samuel, 68, 86, 102.
Huber, John, 267.
Hubley, John, 86, 157, 264.
Hubley, Joseph, 268.
Hubley, Michael, 124, 261.
Huddlestine, Henry, 268.
Hughes, Hugh, 163.
Hughes, Isaac, 102.
Humphreys, 161.

Humphreys, Charles, 8, 291.
Humphrey's, J., Ledger, 13.
Humphreys's newspapers, 161.
Humphries, Capt., 22.
Hunt, Isaac, 38, 39, 40, 41.
Hunter, 136.
Hunter, Daniel, 86.
Huntington, 278.
Huntington, Samuel, 246, 251.
Husbands, Hermon, 171, 172.
Hutson, 283.
Hysham, Capt., 88.

Independence, celebration of the anniversary of, 222, 223; continental sloop, 104.
Independency, sixth year of, 277.
India, 277.
Indian, 68; corn, 253; destroyed 134; country, 214; custom, 290; king, 277; Queen, the, 79, 197.
Indians, 115, 122, 125, 147, 189, 192, 215, 283, 290; inroads of, 264; news of a defeat, 229; pretty still, 160.
Ingles, George, 239.
Ireland, 11, 23, 38, 57, 228, 253; Royal regiment of, 10; vessels arrived from, 11.
Iris, ship, 244.
Irish, 238; prisoners, 123, 201.
Irishman, 169.
Ironworks, the, 272.
Irvin, Gen., 148.
Irving, Gen., 111.
Isle Dieu, 255.

J...., 21.
Jack, ship, 242.
Jackson, Capt., 181.
Jacob, 275.
Jacob, John, 191.
Jacob, Israel, 10.
Jacobs, 105.
Jacobs, Ed., 197.
Jacobs, John, 189, 220, 243, 279.
Jacobson, John, 252.
Jagers, or German riflemen, 93.

Index.

Jamaica, 76, 95, 97, 200, 216, 239; ship, 11, 75.
Jann, Capt., 11.
James island, 222.
James, James, 288.
Jay, James, 277.
Jay, John, 26, 31.
Jennings, John, 287.
Jeremiah, 167.
Jersey, militia, 175; people, 157; shore, 155.
Jerseys, 26, 48, 49, 80, 82, 84, 85, 89, 106, 107, 108, 111, 112, 114, 170, 183, 186, 244, 274; English troops cutting down wood in, 179; ferriage to the, 286; minister of Burlington in the, 46; news from the, 247, 249; salt works in, 144.
Jewell, Robert, 44, 102.
John, 192, 225, 230.
Johnson, Caleb, 131, 239.
Johnson, Col. Obadiah, 19.
Johnson, Thomas, 25.
Johnston, Caleb, 152.
Johnstone, Capt., 187.
Jones, 49, 80, 147, 199.
Jones, Aquila, 287.
Jones, Capt., 9.
Jones, James, 69, 187; executed for street robbery, 69.
Jones, John, 214, 226, 230, 275, 280, 287.
Jones, Owen, Jr., 149, 245.
Jones, Paul, 226, 243, 269.
Jones, Robert Strettle, 14, 37.
Jorden, 137, 164.
Joseph, 250, 252.
Journal of congress, 293, 294.
Joy, Capt., 214.
Juan, Don, 289.
Judas, 156.
Junto, a, 121.
Juno, ship, condemned, 80.

K......, Dr., 210.
K......n, Peter, 218.
Kan, Hyder Aly, 277.
Kap, 261.

Keassler, Leonard, 106.
Kearsley, Dr., 41, 45, 46, 48, 76, 131, 143.
Keith, Capt., 8.
Killingworth, 18.
Kennedy, Dr., 120, 196, 197.
Kensington, 65, 67, 84, 86, 157; ships of war launched at, 101.
Kent Co., Delaware, 13, 25, 26.
Kepler, Henry, Jr., 167.
Keppele, Henry, Jr., 86.
Keppele, Major, 96, 99.
Kerchland, 88.
King, of Britain's speech, 116; congress's petition to, 37, 47; of Prussia, 145; ship, 44; of Spain's declaration, 229.
King William's county, 27.
King's. Arms, to be taken down, 80, 82; taken down, 83; sign of the, 80; proclamation, 50; ships, 69; speech, 55, 88; in town, 269; stores, burnt, 196.
Kitty, 119, 191, 199, 216, 219, 220, 230.
Kitty's horse, 191.
Kniphausen, 259; regiment, 259.
Knyphausen, Gen., 245.
Know, Robert, 102.
Knox, Col., 248.
Kuhl, 82.
Kuhl, Frederick, 14, 16, 67, 68, 83, 86, 104.

Lacey, General, 180.
La Fayette, Marquis de, 164, 166, 182, 242, 243, 263.
Lancaster, 86, 118, 119, 126, 128, 159, 167, 168, 171, 178, 179, 180, 181, 191, 195, 198, 199, 203, 204, 207, 220, 235, 265, 279, 282, 300, 302; ball in, 170, 174; borough of, 224; clothier general's store in, 152; com. of, 225, 227; county, 8, 87, 172; Court House, 174; friends, 11, 20; jail of, 123; letter read from com. of, 74; road, 149, 150; soldiers removed from, 193.

Lancastrians, 194, 236.
Land, Cornelius, 237.
Landiss, B., 203.
Lang, Capt., 171, 174, 175, 179, 188, 211.
Lang, James, 212.
Langdon, John, 23, 49.
Laughman, Ludwick, 226.
Lauman, L., 240, 254, 262.
Lauman, L. Jr., 269.
Launian, Ludwick, 135, 231, 234, 238, 239.
Laurel Hill Cemetry, 112.
Laurens, Henry, 186.
Laurens, President, 251.
Law of Assembly, 116.
Law, Wm., 221.
Lawrence, Thomas, 60, 288.
Leach, Thomas, 113.
Leamington, 82.
Leamington, John, 88.
Lebanon, 123, 124.
Le Bonhomme, Richard, 226.
Lechler, Henry, 254, 261.
Lecond, Joseph, 67.
Ledger, J. Humphrey's, 13, 31.
Lee, 159, 265.
Lee, fort, 100; taken by enemy, 104.
Lee, General, 29, 60, 85, 95, 105, 107, 113, 134, 176, 178, 215; letters to congress from, 85.
Lee, Major, 229, 244.
Lee, Richard Henry, 25, 247.
Leech, 241.
Legislature, representatives in the, 11.
Lehman, George, 99.
Leidiel, Wm., 174.
Leipels, Capt. Ephraim, 212.
Leverings, 198, 219.
Levy, Sampson, 51.
Levy, Simon, 225.
Lewis, Col., 60.
Lewis, Francis, 26.
Lewis, Mr., 196.
Lewis's History of Chester Co., 196.
Lewistown, 67, 118.
Lewsley, Thomas, 132.
Lexington, 18, 19, 26, 34; brig, 69.
Life of Gen. Joseph Reed, 118, 201.

Lightfoot, Susannah, 171.
Lightfoot, Thomas, 79.
Light Horse, Howe's, 107.
Lime House, 16.
Lincoln, Gen., 231, 246, 247, 248, 250.
Lindsey, Captain, 7.
Lindsey, John, 286.
Little York, encampment near, 279.
Liverpool, 69, 97, 104, 153, 232; ship from, 11.
Livezey's mill, 132.
Livezey, Thomas, 132.
Livingston, 91.
Livingston, Gov., 267.
Livingston, Philip, 26, 51.
Lockart, Josiah, 225.
Lockwood, James, 20.
Lollar, Major, 116.
Loller, Robert, 38.
London, 5, 13, 14, 16, 23, 27, 29, 33, 44, 45, 47, 76, 88, 153, 164, 216, 242, 245; bridge, 16.
Londonderry, 9; ship from, 15.
Long Island, 32, 57, 90, 103, 184, 254, 255.
L'Orient, 255.
Loosly, Thomas, 22.
Lord of the Household, 171.
Lords and Commons, address of the, 15.
Loring, Col., 186.
Lottery Office, 175, 185; tickets, 175.
Louis 16th, 223.
Love, 150; Almighty hand of, 156.
Low, Isaac, 19.
Lowery, Alexander, 135.
Lowman, William, 78.
Lowry, Col., 240.
Loxley, B., 78.
Loxley, Major, 198.
Loyd, Peter, 37.
Ludwick, Christopher, 14, 174, 184.
Ludwig, C., 78.
Lukens, Jesse, 54.
Lutheran church, 183.
Luzerne, Chevalier de, 228.

Index. 319

Lyman, Capt., 259.
Lyme, 18.
Lynch, Thomas, 9, 25, 44, 51.
Lynn. John, 49, 81, 83, 99, 189.
Lynn, sister, 43.
Lyon, William, 86.
Lyons, Lieutenant, 148.

M......, 218.
M......, John, 55.
MacKay, Gen., 17.
Mackinary, Mary, 285.
Macksfield, Gen., 249.
McCalla, Mrs., 45.
McClain, Laughlane, 287.
McClenahan, Capt., 9.
McClenachan, Blair, 175, 197.
McClenagan, Blair, 38, 39.
McCoy, Captain, 88.
McCullough, Capt., 123.
McCullock, Captain, 5, 29.
McCutcheon, Capt., 79.
McDougall, Gen., 114.
McFingal, 297.
McFarlan, Mr., 19.
McIntosh, Gen., 215.
McKean, 49, 242.
McKean, Col., 71, 75, 77, 98, 131.
McKean, Mr., 50.
McKean, Thomas, 37, 77, 78, 176, 291, 293, 295.
McKinsey, Captain, 8.
M'Kinley, Hon. John, 116.
McKorble and Son, 291.
McLane, Capt., 251.
McLane, Capt. Allen, 188.
McLane, Capt. John, 188.
McLean, James, 144, 174, 207.
McLean, John, 171, 199.
McLean, Mr., 155.
McMullen, John, 135.
Madeira, brig arrived from, 14; wine, 51, 266, 302.
Magdalen, schooner, 24.
Maguire, Rachael, 286.
Maidenhead, 110.
Malsbary, Jonathan, 40.
Malt house burnt, 64.
Manheim, 164.

Markoe, Capt., 123, 124, 127, 157, 160, 174, 188.
Markom, Capt., 238.
Marks, Levy, 204.
Marrow of Divinity, the, 231.
Marseilles, France, 88.
Marshall, Benjamin, 23, 49, 59.
Marshall, Betsey, 31.
Marshall, C. Sr., 78.
Marshall, Charles, 31, 60, 95.
Marshall, Christopher, 14, 27, 30, 32, 68, 105, 118, 285, 302.
Marshall, Humphrey, 74.
Marshall, Mr., 86, 114, 281, 285.
Marshall, Mrs., 185; death of, 302.
Marshall, Sally, 175.
Marson, Henry, 172.
Marston, Capt. Samuel, 76.
Martin, Patrick, 257.
Martinico, 180, 184.
Martinique, advice from, 232.
Maryland, 9, 25, 113, 114, 116; province of, 5; troops, 84, 81.
Massachusetts Bay, 15, 25, 27; delegates from province of, 9; forces, 32.
Masterlett, Squire, 215.
Masters, William, 102.
Mastiler, Philip, 135.
Mason, Capt., 60.
Matlack, 49, 61.
Matlack, Col., 77.
Matlack, T., 78.
Matlack, Timothy, 63, 64, 70, 73, 81, 83, 86, 98, 102, 137, 180, 184, 187, 188, 189, 197, 277, 278.
Matthew, 156.
Maurice river, 193, 201.
Maxwell, Gen., 42, 127.
May, Capt., 95.
Mead, 61.
Mease, John, 152.
Melchor, Captain, 26.
Meloy, Mr., 20.
Memorial to the county court, 75.
Memoir of Richard Henry Lee, 247.
Men-of-war, French, 238; and Spanish, 232.

Menonists, 187, 195; preacher, 21.
Mercer, 236, 239.
Mercer, Gen., 112, 113.
Mercer, John, 149, 232, 245.
Mercer, Michael, 269.
Merchants' Coffee House, 10.
Mercury, sunk, 161.
Meredith, Samuel, 37.
Mermaid, 235.
Messencope, John, 226.
Middle ferry, 149, 172.
Middleton, Henry, 9, 24.
Middletown, 214; Point, ship lost off, 235.
Mifflin, Captain, 39.
Mifflin, Col. Thomas, 70.
Mifflin, fort, 198.
Mifflin, General, 74, 75, 94, 105, 114, 141, 165, 176, 179, 211.
Mifflin, Jonathan, 145.
Mifflin, Samuel, 86.
Mifflin, Thomas, 8, 10, 44, 58, 59.
Miles, William, 73.
Millenium, Hartley on the, 187.
Miller, Jacob, 266.
Miller, Major, 131.
Miller, Peter, 122, 151.
Miller, Tobias, 171.
Miller, Widow, 197.
Milligan, James, 78.
Mills, Samuel, 44.
Milne, Ed., 125, 195, 271.
Minerva, ship, 7.
Ministers, 167.
Missionary, Thomas Barton, 185.
Mitchell, Capt., 9, 286.
Moderates, 68.
Moebale, Capt., 104.
Molasses, 62.
Molesworth, 118; hung, 118; body of, taken up by Friends, 201.
Molesworth, James, 201.
Monmouth Court House, 190.
Montford, Major, Count, 209.
Montgomery, Col., 84, 85, 257.
Montgomery, Gen., 55, 57, 60; sermon on the death of, 60.
Montgomery, Joseph, 281.

Montgomery, county, 73; privateer, 104.
Montreal, 44, 53.
Moor Hall, 187.
Moor, John, 229.
Moore, Capt, 9.
Moore, Col., 46.
Moore, John, 86.
Moore, William, 116, 117.
Moorestown, 108.
Moralez, Mr., 216.
Moravian minister, 182, 183; settlement, 283.
Morgan, Col., 139, 143, 161, 186.
Morgan, Dr., 234, 240.
Morgan, General, 268, 269.
Morgan, Major, 54.
Morgan, Samuel, 212.
Morris, 139.
Morris, Cad. Samuel, 92.
Morris, Ensign Antony, Jr., 115.
Morris, Lewis, 26.
Morris river, 193, 201.
Morris, Robert, 44, 85, 102, 116, 144, 146, 147, 211, 291, 292.
Morris, Samuel, 92, 229.
Morris, Samuel, Cadwalader, 78.
Morris, Samuel Jr., 86, 91, 102.
Morris, Samuel, Sen., 86.
Morris, ship from France, 118.
Morris's mill, 139.
Morrison, George, 285.
Morristown, 113, 114.
Morton, John, 8, 85, 94, 291.
Moses, 219.
Mosher, Jeremiah, 280.
Motchs, 131.
Moulder, Joseph, 78, 81.
Moulder, William, 44.
Moultrie, Gen., 221, 227.
Mount Holly, 108.
Moyamensing, 217.
Moyer, John, 163.
Mugford, Captain, 75.
Muhlenburgh, Rev. Henry, Jr., 87.
Mulberry wharf, 84.
Mure, Capt., 259.
Murray, Messrs. Robert and John, 15.

Muscovado sugar, 135.
Museum, anatomical, 288.
Muskingum river, 283.
Muselman, Chrisley, 184.
Myer, Wendal, 172.
Myng, 79.
Myner, 236.

N......, Dr., 258.
Nantz, letter from, 96.
Narrows, the, 60, 79, 254.
Nazareth, Gen. Gates at, 160.
Neal, 56.
Neal, Peg, 286.
Neale, Capt. James, 62.
Needham, 9; letter of marque ship, 239.
Neff, Chrisley, 242.
Neff, Dr., 121, 122, 184, 230, 268, 279.
Neff, John, 184.
Negro, 68; woman, 123.
Nelson, Alexander, 174.
Nesbit and Co., 112.
Nevil, Col., 235, 236.
Nevis, brig from, 88; island almost destroyed, 266.
New Brunswick, 249.
Newburyport, 59.
New Castle, 69, 70; ship arrived at, 7, 8, 9; county, 25.
Newcomb, Silas, 15.
New England, 22, 23, 30, 31, 298; colonies, 290; troops, 174.
New Englanders, 290.
New Englandmen, 114.
Newfoundland, 21.
New Garden, 126, 272.
New Hampshire, 9, 23.
New Haven, 18, 19, 21; ship arrived, 175.
New Holland, 199.
New Jersey, 21, 31, 94, 155, 193, 267.
New London, 18; arrival of fleet at, 65.
Newman, Capt., 80, 99.
Newman Dr., 160, 214, 264.
Newry, ship from, 7, 9.

New Tavern, the, 10, 29, 52.
Newtown, 109, 169, 229.
New York, 5, 7, 9, 16, 19, 20, 21, 22, 24, 26, 27, 44, 49, 73, 81, 82, 84, 87, 93, 94, 97, 99, 106, 113, 115, 158, 184, 232, 234, 239, 242, 245, 257, 267, 283, 294; arrival of Washington at, 65; brig from, driven ashore, 155; fire at, 195; Gazette, 289; Gen. Clinton sails from, 60; part of, burnt, 178; Post, 57; provisions at, scarce, 194; refugees in, 274.
Niagara, 192.
Nicola, Col. Lewis, 244.
Nixon, John, 7, 83, 99.
Noy, Mr., 20.
No Popery riots, 261.
Norrington, 73.
Norris, Isaac, 145.
Norris, Widow, 131.
Northampton Co., Pa., 8.
North Carolina, 10, 25, 143, 283; troops, 234.
North, Lord, 175, 178.
North river, 84, 135.
Northumberland co., 58, 227.
Northumberland, duke of, 17.
Norwich, 18.
Nottingham meeting house, 127.
Nottingham, Samuel, 103.
Nulling, Lieut. Col., 207.

Oats, 253.
Obed, 122.
Ogden's ferry, 140.
O'Hara, Gen., 272.
Old France, 96.
Oley Hills, 130.
Ordale, 46.
Osborn, 287.
Osborne, Capt., 11, 23.
Osnabrigs, 286.
Otis, Mr., 159.
Overseers of the poor, accounts of, 285.
Owen, Mrs., 142.

P...., 224, 244.
P...., J...., 23, 30, 110.
P...., James, 245.
P...., John, 245.
Pacolet river, 269.
Paine, 65.
Paine, Robert Treat, 9, 25, 30, 51.
Paine, T., 108.
Paine, Thomas, 64, 68, 70.
Paine, Treat, 49.
Palasky, Pame, 213.
Palmer, J., 18.
Paoli massacre, 129.
Papists, 68.
Parish, John, 164.
Parker, Joseph, 10, 44, 48, 102.
Parker, Peter, 232.
Parliament, Lord North's proposal to, 178.
Parrish, Nancy, 190.
Passyunk road, 84.
Patience, 175, 177, 248; pass for, 175.
Patrick, St., 270.
Patriotic society, the, 66.
Paul, Father, 195.
Paulus Hook, garrison at, surprised, 229.
Pawling, Granny, 286.
Pawling, Henry, 10.
Payne, 171.
Payne, John, 75, 85.
Peace and Plenty, ship, 8.
Peale, Wilson, 217.
Pearson, Hannah, 286.
Pedree, Captain, 232.
Pedro, Capt., 206.
Peel Hall, burnt by the enemy, 145.
Pendleton, Edmund, 25.
Penn, Governor, 232.
Penn, John, 6, 133; appointed governor, 133.
Penn, Richard, 47, 234.
Pennsylvania, 156, 163, 291; Archives, 164, 198, 201; convention of, 78; Weistling's, 79; currency, 285; Farmer, sign of the, 80; Freeman's Journal, 302; Gazette, 92, 93, 95, 227, 238;

Penn., Hist. Soc., 80; Journal, 5, 15, 28, 33, 36, 37, 41, 64, 73, 83, 86, 91, 93, 94, 99, 102, 103, 104, 105, 264; and Gazette, 17; Ledger, 21, 34, 54; Packet, 27, 29, 164, 172, 235, 238, 264; ship, 11, 23; plan of government for, 92; troops mutinied, 267.
Pennsylvanians and Connecticut people, skirmish between, 54.
Pennytown, 111.
Penrose, L. Colonel, 94.
Pensacola, 234; invested by fleet of French and Spanish, 273; taken by Spaniards, 277.
Pension book, amount of, 285, 286.
Pepper, 62.
Pequea, account of a fray at, 168; church, 126.
Percy, Lord, 17, 20.
Permel, Mons., 96.
Peters, Capt., 85.
Philadelphia, 19, 26, 51, 86, 105, 119, 121, 122, 124, 126, 127, 140, 141, 142, 148, 149, 150, 153, 154, 159, 160, 161, 163, 164, 168, 169, 172, 174, 178, 181, 185, 186, 203, 204, 205, 206, 211, 214, 215, 220, 221, 233, 234, 249, 253, 257, 260, 262, 267, 269, 274, 277, 281, 282, 283, 285, 292; almshouse, 28; assembly of, broke up, 199; committee of, 225, 226, 227; city, 83; county, 73, 74, 83, 177; La Fayette arrived at, 243; college, commencement at, 251; friends, 119; number of houses and inhabitants in, 229; Rattlesnake, 180; militia, 89.
Philadelphian, 167; an old, 289.
Philadelphians, 119.
Philosophical Hall, 78; committee at, 49, 50, 52; meeting at, 7.
Phillips, 283.
Phillips, Gen., 211.
Phipp's farm, 18.

Phyle, Dr., 118, 131, 137, 140, 145, 151, 158, 159, 188, 189, 190, 218, 219, 247.
Pickering, Tim., 198, 244.
Pitt, fort, 239.
Pittsburgh, 214, 283; Dr. Newman arrived from, 160; news from, 122.
Place, the, 28, 32, 61.
Plainfield, 19.
Plan of government, 97.
Pliarne, Monsieur, 165.
Plumstead's wharf, 67.
Plymouth, burial ground, 190.
Polish court, 175.
Poll, 42, 43, 84, 88, 108, 116, 121, 123, 182, 185, 186, 194, 195, 200, 202, 203, 204, 207, 209, 210, 217, 229, 230.
Polly, 12, 199, 252.
Polly and Peggy, ship, 13.
Pondicherry, 228, 277.
Pool's Bridge, 96.
Poonah, 235.
Poor Richard, 226; almanac, 226.
Popham, James, 14.
Popish dialect, 238.
Port au Prince, 244.
Port Orient, French vessel from, 69.
Porto Rico, 229.
Port Royal, Jamaica, 184.
Portland, Me., 50.
Portugal, 200, 273.
Post master general of the United Colonies of North America, 34.
Potter, Gen., 136, 151.
Potts, 140, 199.
Potts, Capt., 44.
Potts, Dr., 139, 211, 295.
Potts, T., 102.
Potts, Thomas, 44, 83.
Pottses, 127.
Pottsgrove, 127, 178.
Powder, arrival of, 56.
Powell, Samuel, 44.
Practice of Physick, Brooks's, 120.
Preachers, 167.

Presbyterian burial ground, 115; meeting house, 191.
Prescott, 134.
Prescott, Gen., 178; Gen. Lee exchanged for, 134.
President and council, letter to, 147.
Price, 62, 80.
Price, Capt., 174.
Priests, 167.
Princeton, 86, 107, 111.
Prisoners, England Scotch and Irish, 123.
Prison Society, 60.
Proclamation, 295; Gov. Dunmore's 27; President Reed's, 211; published, 139.
Procter, Col., 145.
Proctor, 105.
Proctor, Capt., 109.
Proctor, Col., 150, 151, 217.
Prophets, 167.
Proprietary party, 68.
Prosperity, ship, 5, 29.
Providence, 19, 99.
Province ship launched, 64.
Provincial conference, 78, 79, 292; congress, 32; convention, 24.
P. Journal, 26, 235.
Provincials, loss of, 51.
Proverbs, 158.
Provost, Gen., 221.
Prussia, king of, 145.
Prussian, the, 63; court, 175.
Pryor, Captain, 26.
Pryor, Norton, 148.
Public Ledger, 161.
Pulaski, Gen., 221.
Pulasky, 213.
Pultney, Thomas, 250.
Purdie, Robt., 258.
Purdies, 239.
Putnam, General, 34, 106, 108, 109, 111, 127, 134, 143, 295.
Putnam, Israel, 295, 296, 297.

Quaker, monthly meeting, 12; preacher, 28; visited meeting houses, 28; prisoners, 149.

Quakers, 68, 274; in England, 180; interest, petition by, 14; memorial presented by, 49; meeting of, 30; testimony of the people called, 13; yearly meeting, 10; serious address to, 202.
Quebec, 57, 58; letter from camp before, 55; lower town, 71.
Quiberon bay, 179.

R., G., 236.
Rachael, 258.
Rachel and Francis, ship, stranded, 40.
Ramsay, 173.
Ramsey, James, 268.
Randolph, Peyton, 10, 25, 26, 27, 49.
Ranger, schooner, 54.
Rankin, Col. William, 87.
Rankin, James, 128.
Rapelja, 103.
Raritan, the, 114.
Rattlesnake, privateer, 116, 180.
Read, Col. Charles, 114.
Read, General, 132, 175.
Read, George, 25, 292.
Reading, 127, 128, 132, 134, 138, 139, 283.
Rebecca, schooner, 54.
Receipts, 288.
Redbank, 23, 139, 140, 141, 142; fort, 145; spies hanged in, 143.
Red creek, 125.
Red Lion, 128.
Reed, 266.
Reed, Capt., 44.
Reed, Col., 133.
Reed, Gen., 210, 211.
Reed, James, 182.
Reed, Joseph, 7, 37, 56, 58, 59, 206, 217.
Reed's bridge, 266.
Reedy island, 121, 172, 175.
Rees, Thomas, 140, 141, 190.
Reese, Capt., 199.
Reese, Thomas, 161, 252.
Reeves, Pau, 143.
Regulars, 122.

Reigart, Adam, 240.
Reigart's, 224.
Reprisal, the, 88.
Remembrancer, Mr. Marshall's, 285.
Remonstrance, 73; to congress, 66; signed, 60; to the assembly, 63.
Renown, ship, 9.
Reynolds, John, 95.
Rhoad, Peter, 86.
Rhoads, Samuel, 8, 10, 42, 44.
Rhode Island, 55, 115, 141, 194, 271; assembly of, 70; colony of, 26; forces, 32; French troops landed on, 254; report of surrender of, 196; that French fleet defeated off, 261.
Richard, 283.
Richardson, Samuel, 104.
Riché, Robert, 149.
Richmond, 35, 268.
Richmondtown, Henrico Co., Va., 196.
Right of instruction, the, 103.
Rising Sun, the, 131.
Rittenhouse, David, 61, 83, 86, 102, 139, 189, 191, 197.
Rivington, 245.
Rivington's Paper, 13, 245.
Roberdeau, 218.
Roberdeau, Col., 64, 67, 84, 147.
Roberdeau, Daniel, 68, 217.
Roberdeau, Gen., 84, 85, 116, 151
Roberts, 283.
Roberts, John, 201, 204.
Roberts, Jonathan, 10, 44.
Robins, Joseph, 161.
Robinson, 28.
Robinson, Captain, 23.
Robinson, George, 275.
Robinson, William, 78.
Robison, Capt., 47.
Rochambeau, Count, 281.
Rodney, Admiral, 245.
Rodney, Cæsar, 25, 292.
Roebuck, the, man-of-war, 67, 69, 118, 235; lieut. of the, 176.
Rogers, Major, 100.
Roman, 290.
Rose, Wm., 174.

Ross, 167.
Ross, Capt., 98.
Ross, Col., 129.
Ross, George, 8, 85, 127, 293.
Ross, John, 7.
Ross, William, 165; ball at house of, 165.
Ross's, ball at, 167.
Rotterdam, 44; sign of, 67.
Rowland, Andrew, 19.
Roxborough township, 132, 190.
Roxbury, 32; camp, 32.
Royal Scotch Fusileers, colors of, brought to congress, 51.
Rum, 62; poisoned, 98.
Rush, Benjamin, 85, 293.
Rush, Dr., 70, 78, 159.
Rush, William, 41, 84, 198.
Russians, 253.
Ruth, 84.
Rutledge, Gov., 251.
Rutledge, Edward, 9, 24, 91.
Rutledge, John, 9, 24.
Rye, 253.

S......, 215, 224.
S......, Major, 117.
S......, Mrs., 259.
S......, Samuel, 22, 259.
S........y, Thomas, 218.
Saint Eustatia, 76, 108, 244, 246, 251, 270; account that English had taken, 271; damaged, 266.
St. John's, 44; fort, 55; news of the taking of, 51; prisoners from 84.
St. Lawrence river, 57.
St. Lucia, English merchant ships at, 273.
St. Martin's, 75, 246; French fleet at, 252.
St. Patrick, 238; men, 270.
St. Peter's church yard, 113.
Salem, ship arrived at, 242; creek, 175.
Sally, 173, 190, 191, 248, 252; letter from, 213; tea from, 248; ship, 29; sloop, 76.
Salmon's Collection, etc., 54.

Salt, 62.
Salter, Thomas, 116.
Saltpetre, arrival of at Chester, 56.
Samuel, 229.
Sandy Hook, 80, 103; fleet sailed from, 234; French fleet off, 193, 194, 230; news that English fleet left, 200.
Sandy Puxton, Va., 72.
San Juan, retaken by the Spaniards, 273.
Santa Cruz, 246; flag of truce from, 218.
Satan, 203.
Saul, 11.
Savannah, 230.
Saybrook, 18.
Scarborough, man-of-war, 57.
Schema Sacra, 167.
Schlosser, C., 39.
Schlosser, G., 38, 39, 78, 83, 120, 123, 181, 182, 185, 189, 243.
Schriner, Jacob, 67, 78, 82, 86, 102.
Schriner, Michael, 261.
Schuykill, 140, 145, 146, 149, 150, 170, 191, 199, 216, 252; ferry, 51.
Scotch prisoners, 125, 200; marched to Philadelphia, 269; soldiers, 94; stove, 197.
Scotchmen, 169; a lunatic, 261.
Scotland, 44; rebellion in, 274.
Scott, Col., 111.
Scotten, John, 174.
Seabrook, Capt., 196, 197.
Seachrist, Jacob Jr., 231.
Sea Nymph, brig., 9.
Searles, James, 61, 185.
Sergeant, Jonathan, 139, 198.
Shaff, Henry, 87.
Shaffer, 202, 270.
Shaffer, Frederick, 207.
Shaffner, Capt., 238.
Shaffner, Gaspar, 266.
Shaffner, Peter, 275.
Shamokin, 215.
Shannon, Cath., 285.
Sharpless, Benjamin, 63.

Sherburne, brig, 99.
Sherlock, Dr., 209.
Sherman, Roger, 25, 32.
Shewell, Messrs., 89, 91.
Shields, James, 270.
Shipley, Elizabeth, dying words of, 144.
Ship, sign of the, 191, 216.
Shippen, 235.
Shippen, Capt. Wm., 115.
Shippen, Dr., 141, 186, 187, 240.
Shippen, Dr. Jr., 112.
Shippen, Dr. William, 113.
Shippen, Dr. Wm., Jr., 234.
Shippen, Ed., 194, 221, 230, 239, 270, 279, 287.
Shirt battalion, 75.
Shoemaker, Saml., 134, 143.
Shrewsbury, 235.
Shubart, Michael, 102.
Shuldam, admiral, 57.
Shuttleburgh, Wm., 257.
Sigevolk, Paul, 25.
Simmons, Capt., 282.
Simpson, Capt., 88.
Singér, Gasper, 236.
Singhauser, Gaspar, 263.
Skene, Major, 29.
Skippack road, 139.
Skyles, 177.
Slough, 238, 254.
Slough, Matthias, 149.
Small, 228.
Small Pox, society of inoculating for the, 5.
Smallwood, Col., 155.
Smallwood, Gen., 127, 136, 183.
Smith, 49, 55, 263, 265.
Smith, Col., 98, 111, 177.
Smith, Col. James, 85.
Smith, Dr., 60, 62.
Smith, James, 293.
Smith, John, 242.
Smith, J. B., 37, 66, 78, 86, 102, 116, 139.
Smith, Parson, 54.
Smith, Thomas, 106, 183, 184, 188, 193, 287.
Smith, William, 14.

Snow, Charlotte, 9; Sir William Johnson, 16.
Snowden, Jedediah, 163.
Snowden, Leonard, 45, 46.
Snyder, Christy, 271.
Snyder, Jacob, 206.
Snyder, Simon, 225, 264.
Society Hall, committee at, 49.
Solomon, Simon, 208.
Somerset, man-of-war, 205.
Sorrel Horse, the, 149.
Souchong tea, 248.
South Carolina, 9, 24, 25, 57, 85, 158, 187.
Southwork, district of, 299.
Sower, Christopher, 184.
Spain, Capt., 14.
Spain, 153, 183, 200, 228; fleet of, 257; king of, 178.
Spaniards, 213, 231.
Spanish ambassador, 197; court, 175; envoy, 216; fleet, arrival at Martinico, 254; minister, 289.
Spankstown, 112.
Speaker of assembly, 105.
Spear, John, 87.
Spechts, regiment of, 208.
Spiegel, 88, 89.
Spikeman, 45.
Spikeman, Townsend, 65.
Spring Garden, destroyed by the enemy, 146.
Spring mill, 146.
Springer, Gabriel, 87.
Springfield, 244; skirmish at, 249.
Sprout, 6.
Stage wagon, the, 121.
Stark, Gen., 123.
State House, congress at the, 26; meeting at, 7, 10; attempt to spike the guns in, 33.
Staten Island, 96, 97, 98.
States of America, friends of, 1200.
Staunton, Augusta co., 149.
Steel, Francis, 275.
Sterling, 212.
Sterling, General, 127, 141.
Sterling, Lord, 90.

Index. 327

Stevens, Capt. Walter, 54.
Stevenson, James, 288.
Steward, Andrew, 28.
Steward, Capt., 136.
Steward, James, 79.
Stewart, Col., 272.
Stonehouse, George, 5, 63.
Stony Point, 227.
Story, William, 238.
Stott, Mrs., 188.
Stout, Capt., 98.
Stow, John, 87.
Stileman, Samuel, 64.
Stiles, Capt., 14.
Stiles, Joseph, 14.
Stillé, Major, 136.
Strettle, Amos, 229.
Strettle, Robert, 286.
Stricker, Daniel, 200.
Stringer, Parson, 28.
Sturgis, Jonathan, 19.
Sugar, 62, 121.
Sukey, ship, 23.
Sullivan, Brigadier General, 29.
Sullivan, General, 90, 91, 108, 113, 127, 146, 153, 229.
Sullivan, Major John, 9, 23.
Sunbury, 216, 227.
Surinam, vessel from, 95.
Susanna, 284.
Susquehannah, 126; flour lying on the banks of, 152; low, 265.
Sussex Co., 25, 77.
Swart, Peter, 187.
Swedes' church, 104.
Swift, Joseph, 68.
Switzerland, 37.
Swope, Michael, 86.
Sykes, 104.

Taborro, Antony, 214.
Taggert, Mrs., 130.
Taggert, R., 137, 174, 193, 194, 195, 202, 212, 228, 230, 231, 252.
Tappan, André hanged at camp at, 264.
Tarleton, Lieut. Col., 268.
Taylor, 98.

Taylor, George, 85, 293.
Taylor, Isaac, 266.
Taylor, Robert, 31, 200.
Tea, East India, 14; green, 88, 177.
Temple, 136.
Temple's Farm, 21.
Teneriffe wine, 300.
Tennant, Lieut. Col., 247.
Ternay, Monsieur, 254.
Test, Act, 174; of allegiance, etc., 182.
Texel, vessels taken in the, 271.
Thanksgiving sermon, 209.
The Everlasting Gospel, 215.
The Marrow of Divinity, 231.
Thetis, prize ship from Jamaica, 95.
Thomas, Arthur, 76, 88.
Thomas, Joseph, 191.
Thomas, Philip, 215.
Thompson, 133.
Thompson, John, 275.
Thompson, Peter, 275.
Thompson, Rosanna, 56.
Thomson, Charles, 10, 26, 88, 294.
Thornberry, Sus., 239.
Thornburgh, Robert, 231.
Thorn, 117.
Thorn, William, 66, 67.
Thorne, 81, 171, 173, 176.
Thorne, Squire, 215.
Thornton, Matthew, 293.
Ticonderoga, 43; fort, 27; governor of, 29.
Tillbury, Mr., 43.
Tillbury, Thomas, 14, 40.
Timmons, Capt., 189.
Tinicum island, 143.
Toasts, 223.
Todd, William, 172.
Topham, the potter, 184.
Torbay, English fleet blockaded in, 231.
Tories, 68, 196; chosen to patrol the streets, 33; confined in new jail, 117; lodged in jail, 98; plundered, 103.
Tory prisoners, 111.
Towers, Robert, 288, 296.

Town, B., 257.
Trap, the, 119, 128.
Treaty of commerce, 175.
Trenton, 34, 84, 85, 90, 105, 107, 108, 111, 117, 180, 281; Col. Knox at, 248; news of an engagement at, 110.
Trial, sloop, 56.
Trumbellon, privateer, 244.
Troops, English and foreign, 69.
Tryon, Governor, 56.
Tucker, Major, 36.
Tybout, Andrew, 87.

Union, the, 189.
United American States, 92; Colonies of North America, postmaster general of, 34.
United States declared free and independent, 81.
Universal Restitution, etc., 63.
Urie, Thos., 167, 170.

Valans, Captain, 5.
Valentine, 171.
Valley Forge, 154.
Valley hills, the, 199.
Vanchamp, 155.
Vanzening, Crugillus, 40.
Vessels, taken by the British, 104.
Vickers, Thos., 257.
Virginia, 24, 27, 34, 57, 112, 114, 128, 142, 143, 147, 159, 193, 201, 214, 233, 249, 266, 268, 270, 283; Col. Nevil's regiment leave for, 236; continental troops, 160; engagement off the capes of, 271; Friends from, 177; light horse, 113, 115; letter from gov. of, 247; news from, 256; prisoners from, 273; province of, 5; troops from, 176, 180, 183, 234, 236.
Virginian, killed, 168.
Virginians, 235; came into town, 164.

W....., James, Sr., 129.
W......, Jer., 244.
W......, Richard, 218.

Wagon, sign of the, 189, 191, 196, 202, 220, 243, 253, 279.
Waldeckers, 112.
Wales, Prince of, 259.
Walker, Col. Edward, 212.
Walker, Joseph, 123.
Walker, Robert, 13.
Wallace, Capt., 177.
Wallace, George, 249.
Wallace, John, 285.
Wallace, Sir James, 230.
Wallingford, 21.
War, declared, between French and English, 210; against Great Britain, at Martinique, 200.
Ward, Governor, 43, 60, 63, 64; funeral of, 64.
Ward, Hon. Samuel, 26.
Warner, Joseph, 250.
Washington, 134, 150, 153, 216.
Washington, Col., 248.
Washington, fort, taken by Gen. Howe, 104.
Washington, Gen., 28, 31, 57, 65, 73, 74, 75, 81, 98, 107, 108, 109, 110, 112, 113, 115, 117, 121, 122, 124, 125, 128, 129, 132, 137, 141, 142, 143, 146, 147, 148, 149, 155, 159, 161, 162, 170, 175, 183, 188, 190, 191, 211, 214, 223, 234, 245, 249, 281, 296.
Washington, George, 25.
Washington, Lady, 51, 53, 221, 248, 250.
Washington, Mrs., 52.
Wasp, continental schooner, 96, 97.
Waterford, 9.
Watertown, 32.
Wayne, Gen., 129, 169, 170, 227, 275.
Webb, James, 122, 214.
Weed, Capt., 197.
Weistling, John S., 78.
Weitzel, John, 86.
Wells, Richard, 14.
Wells, Stephen, 261.
Weltze, Anthony, 206.
Wentworth, 259; dragoons, 259.

Index. 329

Wertz, 202.
Wertz, Christian, 261.
Wertz, Major, 126, 137, 140, 169, 225, 227, 229, 267.
West Indies, 200, 215, 232, 257; French fleet arrived at, 276; hurricane in, 266.
Western islands, 270.
West Point, 250, 263; spies taken at, 262.
Wetherill, Saml., 276, 277, 278.
Wetherill, Samuel Jr., 14, 274.
Wharton, Thomas, 7, 144, 170, 183, 186; death of, 183; burial of, 183.
Wharton, Thos. Jun., 86, 102, 116.
Wheat, 253.
Whigs, plundered, 103.
White, Alexander, 166.
White, Col., 124, 125, 208, 212, 213, 214.
White Horse, sign of the, 187, 197, 252.
Whitehill, 117, 173.
Whitehill, John, 118.
Whitehill, Robert, 75, 105, 131, 139, 144, 145, 147, 168, 171, 187, 199, 210, 233, 238, 259.
Whitelock, Daniel, 258, 263, 266.
Whitemarsh, 148.
Whitemore, John, 205, 261.
Wigdon, James, 64.
Wigdon, John, 174.
Wilcox, 49.
Wilcox, Alexander, 68.
Wild, William, 92, 93.
Williams, Eb., 19.
Williams, Major, 94.
Williamsburgh, 24, 27, 28, 268.
Williamson, Charles, 212.
Williamson, Horvlet, 212..
Welling, Richard, 106.
Willing, Thomas, 7, 26, 68, 144, 162, 291.
Wilmington, 183; brig run ashore near, 159; creek, 155; evacuated by the enemy, 136; Gen. Washington at, 125; goods landed at, 155; New Castle co., 87.

Wilson, 198, 283.
Wilson, James, 26, 85, 117, 177, 298.
Wilson, John, 198.
Winchester, 273.
Winey, Jacob, 14, 63.
Winterhill, 20, 21.
Wisdom Infinite, 192.
Wisner, Henry, 294.
Wissabicon creek, 132.
Wissahicken road, 250.
Wistar, Daniel, 189; 245.
Wold, Conrad, 140.
Wollop, Capt., 259.
Wood, 124.
Wood, G., 147.
Woodbridge, 84.
Woodbury, burnt, 145.
Woodford, Thomas, 222.
Woodrow, Henry, 87.
Woodward, Gen., 236.
Woodward, John, 69; executed for murder of his wife, 69.
Woodworth, Col., 20.
Woodstock, 18.
Wooster, General, 79.
Worcester, com. of correspondence of, 18.
World Unmasked, the, 25.
Worrall, 170.
Wright, 274.
Wright, Capt., 9.
Wright, Henry, 212.
Wright, James, 253.
Wynkoop, Henry, 86.
Wyoming, 55; country, the, 54.

Yankee, 28; etymology of the word, 290.
Yankee Doodle, 28, 33.
Yankoos, 290.
Yager infantry, 213.
Yeardwell, Dr., 153.
York, 141, 128, 129; county, 8, 86, 87, 98, 172, 210.
York island, 103.
York river, 24.
Yorktown, 74, 128, 130, 150, 151, 161, 171, 178, 179, 188, 229;

Yorktown, letters read from com. of, 74; paper, received, 181; Poll living in, 194.
Young, 161.
Young, Capt., 104.
Young, Dr., 46, 54, 62, 64, 65, 74, 81, 83, 98, 120.
Young, James, 146.
Young, Widow, 122.
Young, William, 140, 286.

Z......, 224.
Zane, Isaac, 165.
Zantzinger, Adam, 135, 195.
Zebulum, Mary, 287.
Zubly, Dr., 37.

www.ingramcontent.com/pod-product-compliance
Lightning Source LLC
Chambersburg PA
CBHW021206230426
43667CB00006B/575